OWEIN

INSTITIÚID ÁRD-LÉINN
BHAILE ÁTHA CLIATH

MEDIAEVAL AND MODERN WELSH SERIES

Published

I. PWYLL PENDEUIC DYUET, ed. R. L. Thomson. 8s. 6d.
II. BRANWEN UERCH LYR, ed. Derick S. Thomson. 8s. 6d.
III. THE POEMS OF TALIESIN, ed. Sir Ifor Williams and J. E. Caerwyn Williams. 12s. 6d.
IV. OWEIN, ed. R. L. Thomson. 12s. 6d.
    A GRAMMAR OF MIDDLE WELSH, ed. D. Simon Evans. 17s. 6d. (Supplementary Volume)

At the Press

Brut Y Brenhinedd, ed. Brynley Roberts.

In preparation

KULHWCH AC OLWEN, ed. Idris Ll. Foster
MATH FAB MATHONWY, ed. B. Rees
MANAWYDAN FAB LLYR, ed. A. O. H. Jarman
DAFYDD AP GWILYM (selection), ed. Thomas Parry
POEMS OF THE GOGYNFEIRDD, ed. J. E. Caerwyn Williams
HANES GRUFFYDD AP CYNAN, ed. G. Melville Richards
LIFE OF S. DAVID, ed. D. Simon Evans
POEMS OF THE CYWYDDWYR, ed. E. I. Rowlands
YSTORI ALEXANDER A LODWIG, ed. Thomas Jones
Armes Prydein, ed. R. Bromwich.

MEDIAEVAL AND MODERN WELSH SERIES
Volume IV

OWEIN

or

Chwedyl Iarlles y Ffynnawn

EDITED BY

R. L. THOMSON

*Senior Lecturer in English
and Supervisor of Celtic Studies
in the University of Leeds*

THE DUBLIN INSTITUTE FOR
ADVANCED STUDIES
1968

PRINTED IN GREAT BRITAIN

PREFACE

In some remarks addressed to a colloquium on the Grail, and published in 1956, Professor K. H. Jackson advised limiting speculation on the Arthurian problems to those properly qualified to deal with the matter of origins, in effect to the sort of person 'qui connaisse les langues et les littératures celtiques de première main, et qui les connaisse bien; qui entreprenne le travail sans idée préconçue d'aucune sorte, qui ait un peu de sens critique et une idée de ce qui constitue l'essence de la preuve', and urged such a person, 'qu'il évite de compromettre son entreprise en abandonnant le vraisemblable pour des constructions aventureuses; qu'il évite de jeter, en accumulant les spéculations hasardeuses, le discrédit sur toute son œuvre'. Fortunately for me, I did not notice these words until after I had set my hand to the plough and it was too late to turn back: otherwise, I should have been too conscious of falling short on all counts to have attempted the present edition.

The fact that this is the first annotated edition of *Owein* has seemed to make appropriate some changes in editorial policy from that adopted in dealing with *Pwyll*. In that case there already existed an excellent edition in Welsh, and it seemed proper to assume that my edition would be used only by those who could not make use of Sir Ifor Williams's, and that therefore all reference to works written in Modern Welsh might as well be excluded from it. This limitation seems not to apply in the present instance, and I have, therefore, referred the reader to books and articles in Welsh wherever it seemed helpful to do so. The former edition was prepared with the beginner in Medieval Welsh in mind, but in this one I have assumed a slightly more advanced knowledge and have therefore commented less freely on elementary grammatical points and have not usually translated passages quoted as parallels from other medieval texts. The glossary, however, as before, is intended to be complete and fully cross-referenced.

In the hope that the publication of this edition may encourage students of the Arthurian legend to study the Welsh version in the original language, I have in the introduction written rather more fully than might otherwise have seemed necessary on its relationship to other versions, as well as on its date and remoter origins. This tour of an ancient battlefield endeavours to be reasonable and to avoid extravagant claims, but it does not pretend to be impartial.

My thanks and acknowledgements are due to the Librarians of the National Library of Wales and of the Bodleian Library for providing photographs of the manuscripts, and to the former for the opportunity of reading some parts of Mr. R. M. Jones's M.A. thesis on *Owein* (though I have used only material from his subsequently printed articles); to Mr. R. J. Thomas, editor of *Geiriadur Prifysgol Cymru*, who kindly allowed me to examine the slips collected for that work in respect of certain words not yet dealt with in the published parts of the dictionary; to the Dublin Institute for Advanced Studies for commissioning this edition and to Professor Myles Dillon for spurring on its dilatory author; and to Dr. Proinsias Mac Cana for his careful scrutiny of the typescript and for a number of useful comments and suggestions.

R.L.T.

August, 1964.

CONTENTS

INTRODUCTION   ix
The Manuscripts, ix; The Title, xi; Relationship of the Manuscripts, xii; Date of Composition, xvi; Other versions, xxii; Comparison of the versions, xxiv; Analysis of the versions, xxix; The 'common source' theory lvii; Remoter sources, lxxxiv; Literary qualities, xcviii.

ABBREVIATIONS   ciii

OWEIN (*Chwedyl Iarlles y Ffynnawn*)   1

NOTES   31

VOCABULARY   63

INTRODUCTION

1. *The Manuscripts*

THE romance of *Owein* is preserved in whole or in part in three old Welsh manuscripts as well as in a number of copies of later date. These older manuscripts are, first, the White Book (of Rhydderch), MS. Peniarth 4, in the National Library of Wales, dated by J. G. Evans in his *Report on Manuscripts in the Welsh Language* (Historical Manuscripts Commission, 1899–1905) i 305–6 as written at 'the end of the XIIIth century'; second, the Red Book (of Hergest), Jesus College Oxford MS. CXI, this part of which Evans dated (ibid. ii 1–6) as belonging to 'the last quarter of the XIVth and the first quarter of the XVth centuries'; and third, Jesus College Oxford MS. XX, dated by Evans (ibid. ii 31–34) as 'first half of the XVth century'; this last dating, however, as was pointed out by R. M. Jones in *Bulletin* 15. 110 note 2, is misleading, for 'XVth' is a misprint for 'XIVth', and Jesus XX is entitled to rank second in antiquity among the manuscripts of this text.

Of these three only the Red Book (henceforth R), reproduced in *The Red Book of Hergest*, ed. Rhŷs and Evans (Oxford, 1887) i 162–92, presents a complete text (cols. 627–55), while the White Book (henceforth W) has lost the beginning, a portion in the middle, and the end; its text is reproduced in *The White Book Mabinogion*, ed. Evans (Pwllheli, 1907) 112–31, cols. 223–61, with the gaps filled from R. In addition to the fully preserved columns 225–32 and 249–56, the last two of which are no longer easily legible, parts of cols. 233 and 236, 245 and 248, are preserved, though the larger part of the folios concerned has been cut away. Jesus XX (henceforth J) provides a text only for the first 148 lines of our edition, and has been reproduced by R. M.

Jones in *Bulletin* 15. 114-16. The text printed below is based on W as far as possible, and on R where W fails.

This romance is also preserved in seven later medieval or early modern manuscripts, which, in view of the absence of any earlier evidence than that of R for a substantial part of the text, may be regarded as of greater interest and value than is usually accorded to such copies. Two of these, Peniarth 120 and Llanstephan 148, may be discounted as being copies of J and R respectively, while a third, Panton 68, pp. 75-78, is a copy of a portion of Llanstephan 171, corresponding to our lines 107-335. Llanstephan 171, written in 1574, has our text on pp. 11-56, but with four lacunae, which correspond to our lines 22-49, 325-52, 453-95, and 583-606. Llanover B 17, written 1585-90, contains on ff. 8a-15b the second half of our text, beginning at our line 320. Cwrtmawr 20, dated about 1750, has the whole text on pp. 71-106, but with three lacunae, corresponding to our lines 210-43, 380-417, and 447-80. There is also the early seventeenth-century Llanstephan 58, pp. 37-62, but this, especially at the beginning, is a very free retelling of the story, with relatively little value for textual purposes. It is notable that three of these later manuscripts do not contain any of those episodes of the story in which the lion plays a part (661-779), except for that of the Du Traws. It is perhaps possible that just as in *Peredur* MS. Peniarth 7 ends earlier than W and R, omitting their last section, so in *Owein* there may once have existed an older manuscript, now represented only by these three later ones, in which the lion episodes were not present (cf. M. Rh. Williams, *Essai sur la composition du roman gallois de Peredur* (Paris, 1910) 18, 34). The exception is Llanstephan 58, which, however different verbally, in this respect follows the tradition recorded in W and R. All the later manuscripts agree in ending at our line 819, omitting any reference to Owein's ever leaving Arthur's court again. Variants from these manuscripts, when of special interest, or

INTRODUCTION

where they may be of assistance in interpreting obscurities in W and R, are mentioned in the Notes.

11. *The Title*

There is no title written at the beginning of the romance in J or R, and W has lost the opening columns. Neither J nor W preserves the end of the text, so that only R has a colophon incorporating the title. It is in the form *Ar chwedyl hwn a elwir chwedyl iarlles y ffynnawn*; this, then, clearly seems to be the proper title of the story. The later manuscripts have various titles: Llanstephan 171 has 'llyma ystori owain ab urien', Cwrtmawr 20 'Lyma Ystori Owain ap Urien Reged', while Llanstephan 58 has the descriptive heading 'Yn ol hyn y canlyn Ystori: ymmha vn y dangosir trafaelion rhai o Filwyr a marchogion Bwrdd gron Arthur ag yn benna gwroldeb Owain ab Eirien, Jarll y Kawg'. At the end of Llanstephan 171 'Ag felly v terfyna ystori owain ab irien', Cwrtmawr 20 'Ac velly y tervyna Ystori Owain ar Iarlles y ffynon yn lle gwir', in Llanover B 17 simply 'Ag velly i terfynna', while Llanstephan 58 repeats the title it assigned to Owain at the beginning 'Terfyn o drafaelion Owain ap Eirien Jarll y Kawg'. The later manuscripts thus prefer a title equivalent to 'The Story of Owain', and make little or no reference to his wife.

Since *Chwedyl Iarlles y Ffynnawn* is the only title with any ancient authority some excuse must be offered for calling it *Owein* in what follows. The first excuse must be the convenient brevity of *Owein*; a second that it makes a neater parallelism with the other two romances, if the names of the heroes are used, as *Gereint* and *Peredur* usually are, as titles. The liberty may perhaps also be excused by reference to the nomenclature of the three corresponding French romances, where editors refer for brevity's sake to *Yvain*, though Crestien himself authorized only the title *li chevaliers au lyon*. There is no authority for Rhŷs and Evans's *Owein and Lunet*.

The romance has not previously been edited, though the opening section (our lines 1–230) is included in Professor Jarman's *Chwedlau Cymraeg Canol* (Cardiff, 1957) 48–56. It has been translated by the same series of writers as the rest of the Mabinogion, viz. Lady Charlotte Guest (1849), J. Loth (2 vols., Paris, 1889, second edition 1913), T. P. Ellis and J. Lloyd (2 vols., Oxford, 1929), and Professors Gwyn Jones and Thomas Jones (London, 1949).

III. *Relationship of the Manuscripts*

The relationship of W, R, and J, with reference to the romances as a group, is discussed by R. M. Jones in *Bulletin* 15. 110–14 of which pages 110–11 refer particularly to *Owein*. Before turning to his examples and conclusions it may be useful to consider briefly the subject of evidence for textual dependence.

The variations between any two of the manuscripts at any point may be classified under one of six categories. The first two of these, (1) spelling, and (2) mutation, are not usually of any value as evidence for the relationship of the manuscripts concerned unless, for example, some gross error in the older is repeated in the copy. Generally, then, these two types of variation can be ignored, for within the same manuscript there is ample evidence for divergent spellings of the same word, and for a quite capricious indication and non-indication of the mutations. With regard to mutation the most that might be said is that since the general drift of the orthography is toward a more consistent indication of mutation, an unmutated form in the later manuscript is not likely to be written in place of a mutated one in the older manuscript, and so where this correspondence is at all frequent we may have some doubt whether the later manuscript derives from the earlier; but even this is subject to such exceptions as that R's expression of the nasal mutation is more old fashioned and less phonetic than W's sometimes is. There is some evidence of mutation in W versus non-mutation in R (16 examples), and a little for W versus J (9 examples) on the same grounds. As these are not given in the footnote variants, I add them here: W mutated = R radical in *bali* 11, *debic* 60, *drannoeth* 117, *dal* 144, *debygy* 151, *val* 166, *ben* (*penn*) 169, *gerd gystal* 182, *drigywys* 562, *dwyllwr* 569, 691, *dyuawd* 577, *dorwennu* (*toruenneu*) 620, *varch* 634; W mutated = J radical in *bali* 11, *draet* (*traeit*) 54, *gnap* (*coap*) 54, *vot* 60, *degach* 60, *bali* 71, *a thweleu o wliant* (*a tweleu o bliant*) 77, *thebyccwn* (*tybygwn*) 98.

The third category may be called 'rearrangement'. In such cases the actual words remain the same (apart from any changes that are a necessary consequence of reshuffling) but they are not in the same order. A more extreme case occurs when a phrase or sentence suffers no internal change but is moved entire to a different position in relation to other phrases or sentences. In some of these the difference seems to reflect an unconscious rewording by the copyist during the time between his first reading the phrase and his finishing writing it down: an example is 77, *a thweleu o wliant gwyn a rei gwyrd* W, *a thyweleu o vliant gwyrd a rei gwynnyon* R, where there is no means of determining which is the original reading. In other instances the later manuscript gives the impression of conscious editing aimed at improving and polishing the style, and here there is a natural presumption that the more polished version is the later. But once this editing process is admitted to have taken place, and factors other than simple misreadings are allowed for, the tradition of the text may be said to have been sophisticated, and, as it is then unreliable as a witness to its own source, the form of that source, and therefore its relationship to other manuscripts, becomes impossible to determine with any degree of certainty.

A fourth type of difference between two manuscripts may be ascribed to 'alteration', where two different readings occur at the same point. In many cases the two are virtually equivalent, as when synonyms are used, e.g. 84, *ny welwn yno y gyfryw* W, . . . *y gyffelyp* R, or two terms with equivalent value in the particular context, e.g. 40, *yn diben y maes y gwelwn kaer vawr* W, *yn nibenn y maes yd oed kaer uawr* R. These, like the rearrangements discussed above, imply a process of conscious or unconscious editing. Others of the same type and origin include possible variations in idiom, e.g. 36, *teccaf or byt* W, *teckaf yn y byt* R, or differences in number where the context will allow either, e.g. *ydanaf ac ym kylch* W, *ydanam ac yn kylch* R (but see below on this passage). It is not impossible, of course, for the later manuscript to retain what may be the older reading, e.g. *Peredur*, RB 194. 5 *ry weleis*, WBM 118. 4 *a weleis*.

The fifth type may be called 'omission', where something present in the older manuscript is lacking in the later one. There are two main types of omission, neither of any evidential value. In the first we have a purely mechanical error in which the same word or group of letters occurs twice in a short space and the scribe simply omits what lies between the two occurrences: such omissions need not leave any perceptible gap in the text, though they often do, e.g. 89–90, *amofyn a oruc a mi pa ryw wr oedwn* R, *amowyn a oruc a mi pa ryw gerdet a oed arnaf, a ffa ryw wr oedwn* W. The second and most frequent type concerns words whose presence is largely optional, e.g. the supporting pronouns (*rhagenwau ategol*) with verbs and pronominal prepositions, relative *a* before *oed* or *oedynt*, *a oruc* or *a wnaeth* with a verbnoun, and the like.

The reverse of the fifth class forms a sixth type, 'addition', where something is present in the later manuscript without anything corresponding in the earlier one. In so far as these additions are of optional words they are not evidence: they

INTRODUCTION

may also be dismissed from consideration when they are the result of editing designed to improve the clarity of the narrative, e.g. 138, *a dywedut wrthyf i* W (where the subject, *y gwr du*, has not been mentioned for some time), *ac yna y dywawt y gwr du wrthyf* R; or where they represent differences of idiom, a preference for the presence of the copula, or the like. They are evidence, however, when something appears in a later manuscript that was not present in an earlier one, provided it could not be extracted from the context or from a parallel passage. Thus in 71, *orffreis lydan o eurllin* J, where the words *o eurllin* do not appear in W (or in R, which suggests they are not accidentally omitted by W), they are clearly an echo of the same phrase earlier (53), parallel to *ac ysnoden o eurllin* R. Cases which strongly suggest R had a source different from W are the two additions (in which context plays no part) *llynn a oed yn* 583, *ar gyfeir y gallon ac or byd eneit yndaw* 591. In 666, *oe vrathu* is doubtful, as being in the nature of snakes and a possible editorial addition, and the same is true in varying degrees of 669, *a sychu y gledyf*, an automatic action, and 687, *y uynnu y iarlles yn priawt*, which is factually inaccurate, but in any case is part of the story as already narrated.

Several of Mr. Jones's examples have been mentioned in the preceding paragraphs. Of those that remain, the best indications of R's independence of W seem to be the presence of 48, *ac eu carneu* in R and J with nothing corresponding in W, and the agreement of R and J on *yn nodeu udunt* 49, against *ym pob vn or deu not* in W.

Among a number of agreements between W and R against J, which would show that R is not dependent on J either, the two most convincing are 38, *a cherdet y fford a wneuthum hyt* RW, *y ford a gerdeys i hed* J, and 49, *ac wynteu yn saethu eu kylleill* RW, *yw saethu* J. It is unfortunate that because of the limited amount of J available for comparison so much should depend on lines 48–50, a passage where the true reading is uncertain (cf. Notes).

It is, however, reasonably certain that R is not directly dependent on W or on J, and similarly that J is not directly dependent on W. The conclusion remains open that all three separately descend from a common original, possibly at several removes in some cases. The variations between them are so slight and the serious differences so few as to give little support to Mr. Jones's alternative explanation that all three were taken separately (but not necessarily or even probably immediately) from a not entirely uniform oral tradition. What a period of oral transmission can do to the text can perhaps best be seen from the version in Llanstephan 58. In his M.A. thesis (pp. 11 ff.) Mr. Jones also concluded that none of the later manuscripts (except Peniarth 120, Llanstephan 148, and Panton 68, on which see section I, above) was derived from another or from one of the three old manuscripts. If these conclusions are well founded the total number of lost copies of the text must be considerable, as we should have seven independent survivors to provide an ancestry for.

Mr. Jones's suggestion (*Bulletin* 15. 115, note 1) that J is copied by a scribe in the process of learning Welsh seems rather unlikely, for such a copyist could hardly be expected to carry out the routine modernization expected of him, and furthermore one would expect a more accurate copy, for what he did not understand one would think he would not meddle with. More probably the exemplar of J was in a difficult hand, perhaps also in an unfamiliar orthography, and not in a very good state of preservation.

iv. *Date of Composition*

The date of composition of this text, like that of so much medieval literature, is, strictly speaking, irrecoverable, for the author is unknown, and this is not the kind of story to contain contemporary references, or, at least, not such as we should now be likely to recognize. We have to fall back, then, on trying to fix the earliest date at which the story attained written form. Following the technique that Sir Ifor Williams applied to the dating of the Four Branches (PKM xiii–xx, cf. *Pwyll* xii–xiii), we may look first to the orthography for clues to the antiquity of the written text.

Sir Ifor noted that in general the orthography of W preserves sporadic instances of a spelling-system akin to that of the Black Book of Carmarthen, which is usually dated about 1200. Examples in *Owein* are:

(*a*) *w* for [v], usually *u*, *v*, *f*: medially in *morwil* 47, *Gwenhwywar* 63, *amowyn* 89, *aniweileit* 121, *gowyn* 128, 703, *awwyneu* 193, *rywed* 199, *gwerthwawr* 589, *dorwennu* 620; initially, as a mutation of *b* or *m*: *waryf* 52, *wliant* 77, *wedyant* 129, *wawr* 148, 682, *wwy* 170, *wyw* 173, *wwg* 176, *warchawc* 185; (*w* for *u* in *biewed* 581).

(*b*) *v* for *w* (= [u] or [w]): initially in *vrth* 603, and as the mutation of *gw-* in *vayw* 190, *vatwar* 200, *vyrda* 559, *vreic* 626; (*u* for *w* in *dyuedut* 631, and similarly in *gwedu* 443 R).

(*c*) *t* for [ð], usually *d*: *bwrt* 81, 82, 564, *trydet* 662.

(*d*) the cases of *e* for *y* [ə] are for the most part indecisive: *emyl* 641, 665, and *emhyl* 148, 166, 168, are the regular spelling in W; *e hun* 214, 656, is also the norm; *fenitwyd* 147, *kewilyd* 597, *kedymdyeith* 689, and *lleuassei* 715, may be examples of retained *e*, though in the prefix *ked-* this variant is very common; in *kynllysc*, *kynllyskyn* 153, 173, we may have *y* wrongly modernized for *e*.

The text preserved in J shows a similar set of examples of an older orthographic tradition:

(*a*) *w* for [v]: *writh* 43, *morwyl* 49, *owyt* 98, *dyrchawel* 130; (*w* for *u* in *dynessaw* 55).

(b) *v* for *w*: *vrth* 4, *vr* 19, *vypom* 21, *vypech* 29, *vrthyf* 98, 101, 128; (*u* for *w* in *deured* 52, *deu* 64, *chaugeu* 76, *vadus* 90).

(c) *t* for [ð]: *oet* 62, *orset* 108.

(d) *d* for [d], usually -*t*: *diwarnawd* 2, *bod* 5, 32, *nyd* 5, 58, *vened* 8, *mwyd* 14, *wlad* 34, *byd* 35, *hed* 38, *gerded* 89.

(e) *e* for *y*: *vened* 8, *vypech* 29, *hed* 38, *venegleu* 44, *deu* 64, *pwe* 94; (*y* for *e* by hypercorrection: *Kynyr* 3, *lys* 102, *kyffych* 116, *gynnyf* 121, perhaps *syr* 133).

(f) *i* for *y*: *Clidno* 17, *drithyll* 31, *pengrich* 51, *gyffelip* 84, *riw* 89, *edrich* 97, *delich* 107, *gilch* 114; (*y* for *i* in *morwyl* 49, *ymdydan* 91).

(g) isolated items are *wydwn* for *oedwn* 31, which suggests the misinterpretation of an archaic spelling, and *dybot* for *dyuot* 76.

Taking W and J together there is sufficient evidence here to establish that a written text of the romance once existed in an orthography that was current about 1200.

For the word *maccwyf* Sir Ifor was able to show from the evidence of rhyme that the -*f* had already disappeared some time before 1150. For *Owein* W presents the anomalous position that -*f* remains in the one example of the singular (639), but is lost in the plural (642, 651). Assuming that the scribe of W would be more likely to omit a silent letter than to insert one not in his original and which he no longer pronounced—and we do not know how large an assumption this is—the spelling *maccwyf* would suggest that W descends from a mid-twelfth-century written version of the text. Professor Watkin, however, in YBH lix, has reservations about this interpretation, and as *macwyf* occurs there (2564), these may be justified. If the three romances do form a group (for some hint that they may not, see below, pp. xxv ff.), the evidence of *Peredur* is relevant. According to M. Rh. Williams, *Essai* . . ., p. 31, there are in manuscript Peniarth 7 seven examples without -*f* or -*u*-, and seventeen with.

INTRODUCTION xix

There may be some confirmation of this early date to be obtained from the occurrence of *l-* for *ll-* in *or lannerch* 114 W, *hyt y lanerch* 120 J, and *lwyth* 124 J, as well as from the reverse, *ll-* for *l-*, in *kaer vawr llywychedic* 40 W, all suggesting that the scribes of W and J were copying from a manuscript whose orthography antedated the adoption of *ll-* for unlenited *l*. Such an orthography is attested in the mid-twelfth-century Liber Landavensis. A slightly different case is the disagreement between *y danaf* W, *adanaf* J, and *ydanam* R; both forms are possible, though the singular seems preferable. This contrast may reflect the earlier use of *m* both for the unlenited [m] and the lenited [v] sounds, another feature common in the Liber Landavensis. A parallel instance is adduced from *Kulhwch* by Loth (*Les Mabinogion* i. 22), viz. *genhym* (WBM 457. 24) as an early spelling for *genhyf*, whereas in the parallel passage (WBM 487. 2) the expected *genhyf* is found. In this case R goes back to an unmodernized tradition, a possibility which would be virtually excluded in view of R's usual tendency to modernization were it not for the fact that both readings make acceptable sense.

The reading *a chysnoden* 53 W, *ac ysnoden* R, may imply a manuscript source in which the aspiration of *c/k* was not always indicated, and which in this case W misinterpreted; parallel examples in *Peredur* are WBM 157. 17 *a phren hir a welei*, where the *h* is correct but is dotted for deletion presumably because it did not occur in the scribe's exemplar, and 626. 23 (Peniarth 7) *a tranoeth* (cf. M. Rh. Williams, *Essai* . . ., p. 29). Such spellings also occur in the Liber Landavensis.

Somewhat similar in seeming to imply a carry-over from a much older orthography are the spellings *gwnaethaf* 90 J for *gwneuthum*, which again suggests a misinterpretation of an older *m*, and *ysgwein* 75 W beside *yswein* JR, which suggests an original with -*gu*- for medial [w], though an association with *ysgwier* may be responsible; *yswein* is a loan-form from ON *sveinn*, so that it could certainly have entered the language early enough to appear as *isguein* or the like (cf. LHEB 387).

The most striking instances of an older spelling occur in J, *yn y stauell* 2, *yr stauell* 9, and *llawyr yr stauell* 10; the first might be explained, against R, as *yn ystauell*, but the others seem certain, and the third even has the article *yr*, like Old Welsh *ir*, before a consonant. This failure to express prosthetic *y*- before *s*+consonant was noted by Sir Ifor Williams, PKM xv–xvii, as a feature of the orthography of the fragments of *Branwen* in manuscript Peniarth 6, and in view of the evidence from metre he regarded it as showing that the original of that manuscript might have been written before 1100 (cf. LHEB 527–8). Similar words in J, however, have the expected *y*-, e.g. *ysteneit* 15, 22, *ystlys* 37.

Two other lines of argument have been suggested. In their account of the copula constructions in early Welsh (*Bulletin* 18. 1–25) Mr. A. Watkins and Professor P. Mac Cana drew attention to the differing degrees of popularity of different constructions at different periods (pp. 16–17). Of the orders which can contrast freely, their orders A (copula+complement+subject) and A zero (complement+subject), and order B (complement+copula+subject), occur in the following proportions in the texts named: *Canu Aneirin*, A and A zero 104: B 19; *Canu Llywarch Hen*, A and A zero 250: B 20; *Kulhwch*, A and A zero 32: B 83; *Pedeir Keinc*, A and A zero 12: B 172. If I have rightly interpreted their categories the corresponding figures for *Owein* are A and A zero 11: B 67 (taken from W as far as it goes, otherwise from R). Watkins and Mac Cana remark that the difference between *Kulhwch* and the *Pedeir Keinc* emphasizes the difference in age between the two texts. If this argument is well founded it would follow that the age of *Owein* lies between that of *Kulhwch* and the *Pedeir Keinc*, and nearer the former (the proportions are 2·5:1 in *Kulhwch*, 6:1 in *Owein*, and 14:1 in the *Pedeir*

INTRODUCTION

Keinc in favour of B order). However, while the contrast between the early poetry and the medieval prose is certainly very marked, only a number of studies on other medieval prose and verse texts will show whether time is the only factor, or whether the differences may not be more significantly associated (as Watkins and Mac Cana recognize, ibid. 7) with the contrast between prose and verse, or with matters of style or subject. This line of argument, then, while not adding any appreciable weight of confirmation to the early date suggested on other grounds, does not conflict with it.

The second line of argument is suggested by Dr. Melville Richards in the introduction to his edition of *Breudwyt Ronabwy*, pp. xix–xxiii. He noted the increased use of rhetorical groups of compound adjectives as a feature of the style of *Breudwyt Ronabwy* and the three romances. Of the four, *Owein* shows the least trace of this device, and he very tentatively suggested an order of composition *Owein*, *Peredur*, *Gereint*, *Breudwyt Ronabwy*, with *Owein* nearest in date to the *Pedeir Keinc*, *Kulhwch*, and *Breudwyt Maxen*. As Sir Ifor Williams dated the *Pedeir Keinc* before 1100, Professor Foster *Kulhwch* not later than 1100, and Dr. Richards *Breudwyt Ronabwy c.* 1220–5, this line of reasoning would place our text early in the twelfth century.

Taking these points together it may be suggested with some confidence, slight though the evidences are when considered singly, that this romance already had a written form in Welsh, pretty certainly by the middle, and perhaps by the beginning of the twelfth century. It should be noted that orthographical evidence of the kind we have been considering in this section can show only that a text cannot have attained written form for the first time later than a given date; it cannot show how much earlier a written version, much less an oral version, may have existed.

In connexion with this date it will be remembered that the

composition of the French *Yvain* is usually dated between 1170 and 1175. We shall examine below (pp. lxxi–lxxxiii) the question whether such an early date for the Welsh text agrees with other aspects of the language and with the contents of the story.

v. *Other Versions*

Substantially the same story as we have in *Chwedyl Iarlles y Ffynnawn* is found also in a number of other European languages. The first of these is the romance of *Yvain* or *li chevaliers au lyon*, composed in French octosyllabic rhymed verse by Crestien de Troyes about 1170 or 1175. The major edition, with the variants of many of the manuscripts is that of W. Foerster, *Der Löwenritter* (1st edn. Halle, 1887); the text of Foerster's *editio minor* of the same work has been utilized by T. B. W. Reid for his edition (Manchester, 1942) with English introduction, notes, and glossary. The most recent edition, based largely on a single manuscript, is that of M. Roques, *Les Romans de Chrétien de Troyes: IV. Le chevalier au lion* (Paris, 1960). The text runs to 6,818 lines (Foerster), 6,806 (Roques).

In German the story is told by Hartmann von Aue, also in octosyllabic rhymed verse, in his *Iwein*, completed by 1204. The older edition with manuscript variants is that of E. Henrici (Halle, 1891); most recently by Benecke and Lachmann (6th edn. Berlin, 1959). The length is 8,166 lines.

A much later version of the story, told by Ulrich Füetrer in his *Iban* at the end of the fifteenth century, and apparently still not published in full, varies from Hartmann and from Crestien and in some points agrees with *Owein*. On account of this, Zenker (*Yvainstudien* 212) was disposed to believe there once existed another Middle High German version, independent of Hartmann, and going back to the common source of *Yvain* and *Owein*.

INTRODUCTION

The romance is also extant in Old Swedish, in a version in rhymed couplets, dated in the metrical colophon to the year 1303 (lines 6431–4). First edited in 1845–9 by G. Liffman and G. Stephens, it was re-edited with variants by E. Noreen in the series published by Svenska Fornskrift-Sällskapet, vols. 164–6 (Uppsala, 1931), under the title *Herr Ivan*. It extends to 6,446 lines.

There is also extant a prose version in West Norse, entitled *Ivens saga*, edited by E. Kölbing, first in a volume of romances under the title *Riddarasögur* (Strassburg, 1872), and later separately as vol. 7 of the Altnordische Saga-Bibliothek (Halle, 1898). It dates from the first half of the thirteenth century. In Danish it appears in verse in C. J. Brandt's *Romantisk Digtning fra Middelalderen* i (Copenhagen, 1869), and in vol. ii (1870) from an older manuscript.

Kölbing, in his 1872 edition, pp. xii–xxxviii, examined the correspondence between the Swedish and French versions at some length and concluded (pp. xxxiv ff.) that either the Swedish had used both the French and Norse versions, or that the Swedish was based on a Norse translation now lost, of which the surviving Norse version is an Icelandic abridgement. He then preferred the latter conclusion. In his second edition, however, pp. xvi–xxii, he changed his mind and favoured the former; the assumption of a full-length prose translation in Norse, at first sight improbable, now no longer seems necessary.

In Middle English the romance is found in octosyllabic couplets under the title *Ywain and Gawain*. It was first edited by G. Ritson in the first volume of his *Ancient Engleish Metrical Romanceës* (London, 1802), subsequently by G. Schleich (Oppeln and Leipzig, 1887), and most recently by A. B. Friedman and N. T. Harrington (E.E.T.S. o.s. 254), London, 1964. The extent is 4,032 lines. The dialect is a northern one and the date of composition, like that of the only manuscript, is thought to fall in the first half of the fourteenth century.

Although there are two Irish prose romances with the title *Ridire na Leomhan* (The Knight of the Lions) neither has anything to do with the present story.

VI. *Comparison of the Versions*

A question of major interest for the student of the Welsh romance must be its relationship to the other versions, and the question of its and their immediate source (cf. Windisch, KB 250). The question of the remoter sources is dealt with in section IX below.

The Scandinavian versions admit their dependence on a French original, and the Middle High German and Middle English ones are clearly dependent on Crestien's *Yvain* likewise, but in the earliest period of the study of the subject it was assumed, as for instance by Villemarqué in his translations, and by Stephens in the introduction to his edition of the Swedish version, that the Welsh tale was the origin of all the rest. Once the relatively late date of the Red Book became known—and we may remember here that the existence of the White Book or any earlier fragments was hardly known except to Welsh scholars until Loth's second edition in 1913—this first view had to be abandoned. A fourteenth-century Welsh text could not be the source of a twelfth-century French one.

The reaction was extreme, and it was as confidently maintained that the Welsh romances were mere translations of the French poems of Crestien. This view was most influentially and rigidly asserted by W. Foerster in the introductions to his editions of Crestien's works, and by J. D. Bruce in his *Evolution of Arthurian Romance* (2 vols., Göttingen and Baltimore, 1923). The difference of length and scale, of course, showed that it would be an exaggeration to speak of the Welsh romances as translations without further qualification, and Foerster described *Owein* as 'eine freie, etwas gekürzte Übersetzung des französischen Werkes' (*Löwenritter* (1887) xxii), and Bruce, writing of the group as a whole (op. cit. i 46) said '. . . these tales are undoubtedly derived from French romances—either the extant romances of Chrétien (as the present writer believes) or lost French versions of the same stories . . .'. Foerster's motive here seems to have been a desire to exalt the genius of Crestien, and this he thought could best be done by claiming for him a high degree of originality, not merely so as to exclude Celtic sources, but almost so as to exclude sources of any kind, and make Crestien sole creator of his matter, even to dismissing the poet's own statements to the contrary as medieval commonplaces not to be taken literally (cf. Windisch, KB 271–2).

The first argument, then, which we have, if possible, to settle, is whether *Owein* is an abridgement of *Yvain* or not. In what follows we shall endeavour to restrict ourselves to the discussion of *Yvain-Owein*, despite Smirnov's criticism (RC 33. 130) of Edens's dissertation on the ground that he should not have restricted himself to a single text, but treated the group as a whole. We do this partly to avoid trespassing on the territory of other editors in this series, but chiefly because it is not at all certain that evidence of the relationship of one pair of romances means that the same relationship exists between the other two pairs. Though it is often assumed that, just as the three works of Crestien that have Welsh parallels are the work of one man, so those three parallels are the work of a single translator or adapter, and are based on a single French manuscript which contained these three and no other works of Crestien (cf. Loomis, AT 34), yet it may be noted that the three Welsh romances are not certainly a group. In the White Book they do not occur together, and although in the Red Book *Owein* and *Peredur* are juxtaposed, *Gereint* follows them at a long distance. If we assume, despite some doubts expressed above (pp. xv ff.), that R is a copy of W, then one or both must at one time have been bound differently: to the W grouping (1) *Pedeir Keinc*, (2) *Peredur, Breudwyt Maxen, Llud a Llefelys*, (3) *Breudwyt Ronabwy* (probably), *Owein*, (4) *Gereint, Kulhwch*, with other matter intervening between (1) and (2) and between (3) and (4), there corresponds in R the order (3), (2), (1), (4), but with other matter between the two items of (3). It is clear on this ground alone that, when the three romances were brought together into W, they came to it separately, and that any subsequent grouping in later manuscripts is an editorial act. Confirmation of this view may be found in the frequency in these three texts of spellings more archaic than the normal practice of the White Book scribe. In *Peredur* these are very few indeed, in *Owein* they are relatively few and occur slightly less frequently than in the *Pedeir Keinc*, whereas in *Gereint* they are considerably more frequent, about ten times as common as in *Peredur*, and three or four times as frequent as in *Owein*. If the three romances originated simultaneously and were transmitted together it is difficult to see how this different frequency of orthographic archaism could have arisen, for in the *Pedeir Keinc*, which evidently form a unit, the proportion of archaic spellings is almost steady throughout. It is therefore virtually certain that the textual history and probably the origin of each of the romances is different from that of the others, and that no conclusion drawn from one will necessarily be valid for the others.

The argument for dependence on Crestien is primarily an argument based on the similarity in incident and detail of the two texts. It was criticized as long ago as 1889 by W. H. Carruth in a review of Foerster, pointing out that the similarities are not really so striking that the differences can be ignored. 'Any one who reads the two works without prejudice will certainly question the correctness of the assertion that they bear a close resemblance one to the other' (*Modern Language Notes* 4. 163–6). A. C. L. Brown in 1912 expressed the same view; 'one need only glance through these versions to see that *Owein* bears a different relation to *Yvain* from any of the others' (*Romanic Review* 3. 143).

Several scholars have engaged in large-scale comparisons of pairs of texts, concentrating usually on attempting to ascertain which of the two is the more 'primitive' or 'original', in an endeavour to establish something about their relationships. Such have been K. Othmer *Das Verhältnis von Christian's von Troyes 'Erec et Enide' zu dem Mabinogion des roten Buches von Hergest 'Gereint ab Erbin'* (Bonn, 1889), and R. Edens *Erec-Geraint, der Chrétien'sche Versroman und das wälsche Mabinogi* (Rostock, 1910), both on *Erec-Gereint* (cf. Windisch, KB 255, on Othmer's work); W. Greiner, *Owein-Ivain* in ZCP 12 (1918) 8–120, and R. Zenker, *Forschungen zur Artusepik, I. Ivainstudien* in *Beihefte zur Zeitschrift für romanische Philologie* 70 (1921) 217–317, both on *Yvain-Owein*; and L. Mühlhausen on *Perceval-Peredur* in *Zeitschrift für romanische Philologie* 44 (1924) 465–543. All such comparisons of Welsh and French versions alone have lacked any evidence drawn from the undoubted translations into other languages which are the only means of providing a standard for judging whether the differences between the Welsh and French accounts are greater or less or the same as might be expected in a translation. The conclusions on such a question can never be completely objective, but without some standard of comparison they are necessarily unconvincing, and may do no more than rationalize the position the investigator has, by instinct or prejudice, already taken up. Cf. Windisch, KB 269.

The general impression that comes from reading the various versions of the *Yvain* story carefully and in parallel is that all are very close to the French except for the Welsh one. This is borne out in the more detailed comparison, episode by episode, that follows. It will be seen that in the case of the Middle English version (E), the Norse (N), and the Swedish (S), variations in detail do exist, though on a relatively trivial scale (sometimes paralleled by divergencies between manuscripts within the tradition of the French text), so that these variations can be adequately represented in footnotes. The German text has been omitted from the comparison as it amplifies considerably. It will be found that the Welsh version, while following the same sequence of events for the most part, cannot be adequately represented in the same way (except in a summary so slight as to gloss over every difference of detail) and demands a separate treatment. This fact seems to dispose of the argument quoted by Bruce, *Evolution* . . . ii 74 note 17: 'The analogy of these Norse sagas has often been cited in support of the view that Chrétien was, likewise, the only source of the three Welsh tales.' In case it should be suggested that this degree of difference between the French text (F) and the Welsh (W) is merely a normal difference between any Welsh translation and its original, i.e. that Welsh translators never did follow their original closely, it may be as well to add that the validity of our argument may be established by taking for comparison another Welsh prose text that is certainly a translation from French verse, and of which Norse prose and English verse translations also exist. Such a text is *Ystorya Bown de Hamtwn* (ed. Morgan Watkin, Cardiff, 1958); the parallel versions are edited by A. Stimming, *Der anglonormannische Boeve de Haumtone* (Halle, 1899), by E. Kölbing, *The Romance of Sir Beues of Hamtoun* (E.E.T.S. E.S. 46, 48, 65, London, 1885–94), by B. Vilhjálmsson, *Riddarasögur* (Reykjavik, 1949) i 285–398, with the text from Cederschiöld's edition (Lund, 1884); and a fragment of an Irish prose version, edited and translated by F. N. Robinson will be found in ZCP 6. A comparison of these versions, following the same method as is employed below, gives a clear indication that in this case the

INTRODUCTION   xxix

Welsh version is based directly on the French, for it shows no variations of any significance, and is about equally as close to the French as the Norse version is. The English versions are much less close, and actually contain more than one incident not paralleled in the French, but in each case followed by the Irish version. Cf. Windisch, KB 273.

If W were no more than a free prose abridgement of F, as Foerster held, it is difficult to see why it should differ so much from F, and that in a way and to a degree quite unlike the variations of N, which in insignificance are much more comparable with those of the ampler verse renderings, E and S.

Brief notes at the end of the summary of each episode indicate the major points of divergence: these are discussed more fully in the following section, together with some other kinds of evidence concerning the relationship of the versions.

VII. *Analysis of the Versions*

I. F 1–174, E 1–152, N I 1–9, S 1–158.

W 1–30.

Arthur, king of Britain (1), holds court at Whitsuntide at Carduel (2) in Wales. After dinner he retires to his chamber, followed by the queen, and falls asleep. Outside the door Dodinel, Sagremor, Kay, Gawain and Yvain gather (3) listening to a tale told by Calogrenant (4); the queen overhears it and comes out. Kay rails at Calogrenant for showing prompter courtesy than the rest. The queen begs him to continue and take no heed of Kay. He demurs, but Kay charges the queen on her

The emperor Arthur was holding court at Kaerllion ar Wysc; sitting in his chamber with Owein, Kynon, and Kei, Gwenhwyuar and her maidens sewing—Glewlwyt Gauaeluawr was acting as porter— Arthur proposes to take a nap before the meal, leaving the others to entertain themselves by conversation, and promising that Kei will provide a snack for them. Kynon demands the fulfilment of the promise from Kei, who demands the story first. They promise the story and Kei allegiance to command him, and Calogrenant reluctantly agrees. He appeals for an attentive and sympathetic audience.

goes for the food. When they have eaten Kei demands the promised tale in exchange. Owein bids Kynon tell the best he knows.

(1) king of England, conqueror of Wales and Scotland E, king of England and conqueror of Rome NS. (2) Kerdyf in Wales E, no name N, Karidol S. (3) Dedyne, Segramore, Gawayn, Kay, Ywaine E; Segremors, Walewan, Kalegrewanz, Iwan, Kæyæ S; Lancelot, Kalebrant, Sighamors, Valven, Iven, Kæi N. (4) Colgrevance E, Kalegrewanz S, Kalebrant N.

NOTE. Different location of events; perhaps different date; before dinner in W, after elsewhere; story begun and interrupted in F, queen present throughout in W; Kei's part very different. In W only speaking characters are named; elsewhere Dodinel, Sagremors, Gawain 'walk on'.

II. F 175–277, E 153–237, N II 1–13, S 159–250.

W 31–116.

Seven (1) years before Calogrenant had been wandering in search of adventure, and came through the forest of Broceliande to a tower (2), the master of which, standing on the drawbridge with his falcon, invited him in. A copper (3) gong in the yard (4) was struck by the host to summon his household. A maiden disarmed and clothed C. and led him to an enclosed meadow (5) whence the host summoned them for supper. Afterwards the host begged him to visit them again if he returned that way. He stayed the night.

Kynon, an only son, having accomplished every feat in his own country was seeking someone to test himself against. He chanced on a wooded valley with a river, which he followed till he came to a plain with a fortress at the end of it near the sea. Here he found two youths engaged in shooting practice, and an older man who invited him in. In the hall were 24 beautiful maidens who took charge of his horse, prepared a meal and provided fine clothing. The rest of the place seemed deserted. Half way through the meal his host asked K. where he was going and who he was. He told his ambition and was reluctantly directed to the wild herdsman (fully described). He stayed the night.

(1) six E, no number S. (2) Broceliande not mentioned ENS. (3) neither iron nor wood, unknown what it was made of E, *klukkumálmr* 'bell-metal' N, every kind of metal S. (4) hall N, not clear where E. (5) chamber E, NS suggest a garden.

NOTE. Different amount of detail and general proportion in this section. Kynon's motive more explicit than Calogrenant's. Two youths not in any version but W. *Tête-à-tête* not in W. No directions given in F, only request to return; no such request in W (though he does return).

III. F 278–407, E 238–348, N II 14–28, S 251–386.   W. 117–64.

Leaving the next morning C. came to a clearing where wild bulls (1) were fighting. Nearby he saw the black herdsman (described in detail), and enquired if he was human and what he was doing. The herdsman described his mastery over the beasts, and then directed him to the cold boiling spring (2), the evergreen tree, the chained iron basin and stone, and the chapel, and told him what would happen if he poured water on the stone. If he were to escape without trouble he would be more fortunate than anyone previously.

K. followed the directions next morning and found everything more remarkable than his host had told him. He greeted the herdsman and asked his occupation. He demonstrated his authority over the animals by striking a stag with his club and bringing serpents, lions, vipers, and others crowding round. They did homage to him and returned to their feeding. K. asked directions and was told how to reach the evergreen tree, the well with its marble slab, silver vessel, and chain. He was warned of the tumult, the storm, the black knight and his prowess. If he did not come to grief there he need never fear to do so again.

(1) leopard, lion, bear, bull, boar E; leopards and bulls N; wild bulls, lion, bear, panther S. (2) well (no details), tree (no type), gold basin, chapel, stone E; no tree (here), but other details and order as F, except material of basin not noted N; trees bear roses all the year and keep the sun from the spring; water does not boil; basin is of gold S.

NOTE. Animals differ in all versions, but W is distinct. Herdsman describes in F, demonstrates in W. Circumstances at spring differ, and W alone has no chapel. W goes further in warning what will follow storm. Closing formula similar in both traditions.

IV. F 408–580, E 349–456,
N II 29–49, S 387–536.

W 165–218.

C. came to the pine-tree (1), the chapel, the hanging gold basin, the spring and emerald stone, poured the water, endured the storm, heard the song of the birds (2) gathered in the tree, and the knight approaching. The knight protested against the damage and disturbance caused by the storm C. had raised; they fight, C. striking the knight's shield (3), but C. was quickly unhorsed. The knight rode off with his horse. C. disarmed himself and returned to his host of the previous night, where he received the same welcome. Everyone previously had been killed or taken prisoner.

K. followed his directions till he came to the tree, the spring with its marble slab and silver vessel. He poured the water, heard the tumult, suffered the hailstorm, heard the birds sing on the now leafless tree, until the black knight approached. The latter complained of the damage, they fought, and K. was unhorsed. The knight rode off with his horse, not deigning to notice K., who returned to face the ridicule of the herdsman, and spent the night at the same castle, where eveyone was tactfully silent about his adventure. The next morning a new palfrey was waiting for him, and this he still possessed.

(1) thorn E, vine N. (2) heard the nightingale and other birds, then when the sun came out saw them S. (3) helmet S.

NOTE. Tree is leafless in W, but in F is so thickly covered with birds that the branches are invisible. F takes C. back without meeting the herdsman. In F the host finds out where C. has been. Only W mentions giving him a new mount. In F C. dismisses the story as a foolish escapade, while in W K. tells it as an unexplained mystery.

V. F 581–722, E 457–564,
N III 1–8, S 537–638.

W 219–32.

Yvain chides C. for not having told this story before, and proposes to go and avenge his

Owein suggests they should go in search of the spring, but Kei hints he is more ready to

INTRODUCTION xxxiii

disgrace. Kay mocks him, hinting that his courage will not last till morning, and is reproved by the queen, while Y. disdains to bandy words with him. Arthur wakes and the story is retold for him by the queen. He swears (1) that within a fortnight he will lead an expedition to the spring. Y. sees his chance of distinguishing himself dwindling and resolves to set off alone immediately (2).

suggest than to perform. The queen reproves him. Arthur wakes up and asks if he has been long asleep. After the usual preliminaries they go in to dinner. After dinner O. slips away to his quarters and gets his horse and arms ready.

(1) by the soul of Utherpendragon his father, his son and his mother F, by his own crown and his father's soul E, not by anything N, by the souls of his father U., his mother and his brother S. (2) NS omit F 682–722, an enumeration of the things Y. expects to see on the way.

NOTE. O. suggests a general expedition, and then, when taunted by Kei, turns to the idea of going alone, while in F he proposes to go alone from the first. The story of K.'s adventure is not told to Arthur at this point (cf. 462, where it is already known to him) and he cannot therefore initiate an expedition to the spring. O.'s motive for slipping away is therefore simply Kei's innuendo, not the fear of being anticipated. In S C.'s adversary is twice named (566, 630) as *Wadein rødhe* (W. the Red), cf. 717.

VI. F 723–906, E 565–670, N III 9–28, S 639–772.

W 233–77.

Y. goes to his lodging, orders a squire with horse and armour to meet him outside the town, then rides out to wait for him. They meet, Y. arms himself, and rides off alone. He comes to the tower (1) and stays the night, meets the herdsman in the morning, and comes to the spring. He throws the water on the stone, the storm and the birds follow, and the

The next morning early O. arms himself and rides off, finally coming to the valley, the river, and the fortress K. had described. There were the two youths and the host, and the maidens sewing, much more beautiful than K. had said. O. was served as K. had been, and found the food even more excellent. Half way through the meal the host knight appears. They fight, first with lance, then with sword, on horseback, for a long time, till Y. wounds the defender in the head, and he retreats homewards, with Y. in hot pursuit (2), into the town and up to the palace-gate.

asked his business, and, when O. told him, reluctantly directed him to the herdsman. He stayed the night. The next morning he encountered the herdsman and found him even bigger than K. had done. The herdsman directed him to the spring. There O. threw water on the slab, heard the noise, suffered the storm, listened to the birds on the leafless tree. Then the knight came up, they broke two lances and came to close quarters. O. gave the knight a head-wound, and he turned and fled, O. pursuing him closely till they came to the fortress.

(1) E 603 speaks of seeing the chapel before he reaches the first lodging, apparently through a misunderstanding of F 770-6. (2) the knight's flight is seen from the town, the drawbridge is lowered for him and the town gate opened N, as soon as they saw who it was that was retreating they let him in immediately S.

NOTE. Main difference is one of scale. W goes over the ground again and compares with Kynon's account, while F gets to the fight as soon as possible. In F Y. seems to set off on the same day, in W the following morning.

VII. F 907-1054, E 671-762, N III 29-49, S 773-882.

W 278-309.

The gate had a rat-trap portcullis actuated by a spring underneath. It came down on Y. cutting the horse in two. Through another gate (1) beyond, the knight escaped (2). The door of an adjoining room admits (3) a maiden who expatiates on his predicament, but promises him aid in return

When they reached the gate the knight was let in but a portcullis was dropped on O. cutting his horse in two and leaving him imprisoned between the portcullis and the inner gate. Looking through a join in the gate O. saw a street and a row of houses, and a maiden calling for the

INTRODUCTION

for his courtesy to her at Arthur's court on a previous occasion. She gives him a ring of invisibility, and (4) seats him on a couch. Then she brings (5) him some refreshment from the side chamber.

gate to be opened. He explains he cannot get out or she in. She, taken with his appearance, promises her aid and gives him a ring of invisibility. She will wait on a horseblock for him to be released by the opening of the gate when those who seek him there find nothing. He is then to follow her.

(1) Apparently also a portcullis F and E; N has *hurð* which shuts not falls, and is perhaps therefore an ordinary gate. As F has *sale* for this place of captivity, so N uses *höllr*. (2) having passed the second gate Wadein explains matters to his followers, then falls dead from his horse, and they shut the inner gate S. (3) *een iomfrw kom tha gangande ther* 807—no explanation of how she got in S. (4) for which he returns thanks, and she then takes him into a *litin kofua* (865) where he is to rest; he stays there till she returns with food S. (5) the maiden takes Y. into her chamber, seats him on her bed, and there feeds him E.

NOTE. More than normal variation in FENS, possibly reflecting the translators' difficulties with the account in F. The existence of the side chamber, the splendid decoration, the beds, are all improbable in a gateway. W, even if not nearer the original account would deserve much more credit for imaginative reconstruction than ENS.

VIII. F 1055–1588, E 763–931, N III 49–IV 21, S 883–1152.

W 310–83.

Sounds of a search are heard; the maiden warns Y. not to stir from the couch, and then leaves him (1). The portcullises are raised but they find no one. While they are angrily searching (2) the distraught widow enters with the bier (3). Absolution (4) is pronounced and the wounds bleed again, stimulating a renewed

The men of the court come in search of O., but find nothing except the dead horse, and he slips away to the maiden, who leads him to a handsome upper room. She heats water for him to wash and provides an incomparable meal, which continues till late afternoon. A cry at the administering of extreme unction to the knight

search, during which the invisible murderer is addressed by the widow. The search proves fruitless, and (5) the burial proceeds. The maiden returns to Y., who begs a sight of the funeral procession. (6) The maiden, seeing Y.'s agitation at the sight of the widow urges prudence and restraint. She leaves him again, and the poet enlarges on the hopeless position in which Y. finds himself. The funeral over he continues to observe her, meditating the meanwhile on love and hate. The widow retires, the gates are shut, but Y. is now the captive of Love, and when (7) the maiden returns to promise an early escape he will have none of it. She understands the situation.

is heard, and O. goes to bed. At midnight a second cry betokens his death, and early on the morrow a third signals the passing of the funeral procession with a great concourse, the bier borne by his nobles, and following it the distraught widow. Love for her sweeps over O. as he watches from a window. The maiden tells him who she is and O. declares his love. The maiden washes and shaves O. and feeds him once more, then sends him to bed while she goes out to woo her mistress on his behalf.

(1) F implies she goes into her chamber, but E has *when sho come unto the yate*. (2) F implies they searched the one room, but E has also *in the maydens hall, in chambers, . . . and in solers on ilka side*. (3) Before the corpse rode an armed knight E. (4–5) omit E; in N no absolution is mentioned and the bleeding begins in the middle of the hall. (6–7) In E Y. is stricken with love for the widow; the others leave her after the interment except for her immediate attendants; Y. regrets what he has done to her and resolves to wed her; in N after the funeral the others leave the widow, whose swoonings and attempted suicide Y. witnesses; he falls deeply in love with her.

NOTE. The two accounts are notably different at this point. EN generally abbreviate the mental monologues, but S follows throughout. Only E omits the bleeding and only E adds the armed knight. Much more actually happens in 70 lines of W than in the 500 of F.

IX. F 1589–1878, E 932–1096,
    N V 1–30, S 1153–1382.   W 384–419.

The damsel presents her grief-stricken mistress with the

The maiden finds her mistress grief-stricken, and receiving

emergency produced by Arthur's impending approach and her own retainers' inability to defend the spring. Her advice is spurned as disloyal and she withdraws. While her mistress is reflecting that she may well be right (1), the damsel returns and reproaches her for her immoderate grief, urging that many knights must be superior to the husband she has lost—obviously the one who defeated him is one (2). The lady a second time bridles at the suggestion, and the damsel leaves her and returns to Y. During the night the lady turns over the situation in her mind, including (3) an imaginary dialogue with her husband's slayer, and when next morning the damsel reappears, she apologizes and is prepared to accept the advice if the man is suitable. On hearing Y.'s name, she urges the damsel to impossible haste (4) in fetching him from Arthur's court. Meanwhile she is to summon her vassals and get them to agree to allow her to marry a knight who will defend the spring.

no answer to her greeting, enquires what is wrong. The lady chides her for neglect. Lunet urges the necessity of looking to the defence of the spring by replacing her husband. The lady says he was irreplaceable, which L. denies. Her mistress breaks off the conversation with a sentence of banishment for suggesting such a thing. L. replies in kind, and is stalking out when her mistress recalls her with a cough, and forgives her, as she had her good at heart. L. urges that only a member of Arthur's court can effectively defend the spring, and offers to go in quest of one. The lady reluctantly allows her to try.

(1) She sat long in study, but no report of her thoughts E. (2) In FS the damsel draws this conclusion, in EN the lady draws it for herself. (3) ENS omit the imaginary dialogue. (4) unspecified F, third night E, in two days' time N, on the third day S.

NOTE. W briefer, over in a single (interrupted) interview, in contrast to F's three, but is less committed to future action. No haste or eagerness in W, as no urgency exists. In F the lady is quite clear she is marrying her husband's slayer, though trying to prevent general comment on the fact, but this is not so in W.

X. F 1879–2169, E 1097–1266, N VI 1–VII 20, S 1383–1660.   W 420–454.

The damsel retires to her pretended mission, and prepares Y. for his appearance before her mistress. She then informs her that her messenger has returned with Y., and is urged to bring him privately at once to see her. She tells Y. (1) he must now appear before her as her prisoner, promising him an easy captivity. He is at first bashful, but the damsel introduces him and he puts himself entirely in her mistress's hands. The lady accepts his plea of self-defence (2), and extracts from him a confession of love (3). She also obtains an assurance that he will do the job required of him. They are then reconciled, and the lady's vassals having already consented to her marriage with the new champion, she betroths herself to him (4). They present themselves before the council, all of whom, on seeing Y., wish them married. The seneschal (5) sums up the position, and, lest the custom of more than sixty years lapse (6), they press her to consent to immediate marriage. Laudine marries him and he is everywhere esteemed.

L. set off as if for Arthur's court, and stayed in her quarters with O. till it was time to return. Then she went and reported to her mistress that her mission had been successful, and was told to bring O. to her at noon the following day. When O. appears, finely dressed, she sees at once that he is not weathered, and is angered to discover that he must be her husband's slayer. L. points out his proven superiority. She sends them both home and takes counsel; her subjects prefer to let her marry a stranger, and she takes O. He defends the spring successfully for three years, sharing the profits with his vassals, and growing very popular with them.

(1) E omits that her lady knows she has concealed him and is angry with her for it. (2) E omits. (3) In ES Yvain offers the confession. (4) the lady goes alone to the barons to obtain their assent without a previous meeting, and then gives herself to him E. (5) steward E, *ráðgjafi*, *ráðsmaðr* N, *drozati* (ON *dróttseti*) S. (6) omit E, fully 200 years S.

NOTE. Damsel is supposed to have gone in person in W, but sent a messenger in F. Her mistress wishes to see Y. immediately in F, at noon the following day (no eagerness) W. The last stage of the argument (that he must be fit to defend the spring because he defeated the previous defender) is postponed till now in W. Three years elapse before the next episode in W, only a day or two in F.

XI. F 2170–2301, E 1267–1364, N VII 1–16, S 1661–1814.

W 455–547.

Meanwhile Arthur and his company reach the spring and Kay derides Y.'s evident cowardice in not being there, but is reproved by Gawain. Arthur pours the water on the stone, and after the storm Y. appears. Kay asks permission to engage him first, and at the first onset Y. unhorses him. He then returns Kay's horse to the king, who asks his name. The revelation of his identity shames Kay, but gives great pleasure to everyone else (1). Y. tells how he comes to be defending the spring.

As Gwalchmei is walking with Arthur one day at court he finds him sorrowful, and asks why. A. tells him it is because of O.'s long absence, and that Kynon's tale is responsible for that. G. suggests that A. and his household can go and avenge O. if dead, or release him if imprisoned. With a company of 3,000, not counting menials, and Kynon as guide, they come to the fortress with the youths, the host and the maidens, which easily accommodates them. The next day they meet the herdsman and come to the spring. Kei asks permission to fight first, and throws water on the stone; in the storm many of the menials perish. After the birds' song comes the knight and Kei is quickly overthrown. Both parties camp for the night. The next morning Kei requests a second chance and is again overthrown and badly wounded. A.'s followers go in turn to face the knight till only Gwalchmei and Arthur are left undefeated. A. is preparing to go forth in person when G. comes forward, wearing a *cwnsallt* that effectively hides his identity from everyone. The knight and he fight all day till evening without either getting the upper hand. A second day passes in the same manner. On the third day both are unhorsed at once and continue fighting on foot. Eventually the knight strikes off G.'s helmet and recognizes him. Each tries to declare the other victor, and A. intervenes, and they embrace one another. The household flocks to greet O., and all retire to their tents.

(1) F plays down Kay's disgrace, whereas NS and, to a lesser extent, E rejoice at it.

NOTE. Arthur's arrival is very differently motivated in the two versions. W at least outlines the stages on the journey to the spring. In F the king pours the water, in W Kei, as challenger, does so. The storm and other following circumstances are much abbreviated in F. From Kei's second encounter until the last of the household fights with O. is peculiar to W. The remainder of W, as far as the end of the fight between Owein and Gwalchmei, corresponds to a much later episode in F (XXIV below) under quite different circumstances.

XII. F 2302–2684, E 1365–1576, N VIII 17–37, S 1815–2090.

W 548–63.

Y. invites A. to stay with him and he agrees to do so for a

The following morning A. proposed to return home, but

INTRODUCTION

week (1). Y. sends warning to his wife who comes out to meet the king from a town decorated in his honour. She greets him and he embraces her. (2) An acquaintance is struck up between Lunete and Gawain (moon and sun), to whom she relates Y.'s adventures there. (3) Everyone is enjoying himself. Meanwhile the guests (4) beg to be allowed to take Y. back with them (5), G. particularly stressing the perils of degeneration after marriage if he stays with his wife and does not come on a round of tournaments. Y. asks permission of his wife, who grants him a year's (6) leave of absence, no more. He urges the possibility of sickness or captivity, for which she agrees to make an exception, and presents him with a ring as a talisman against both. The time passes all too quickly, and A. (7) is at Chester (8) in mid-August (9) of the following year.

O. invited him to stay and share the feast he had been preparing for this occasion. Thus they spent three months together. When A. left at the end of this time he begged the lady to allow him to take O. with him for a further three months, to which she reluctantly agreed. When he got back to A.'s court O. stayed three years instead of three months.

(1) fortnight E, but eight days and nights (1438); not specified N, but stays seven days (.24); 8 days S. (2–5) omit E. (3–5) omit N. (4) Arthur first broaches the subject, seconded by Gawain S. (6) twelve months and seven days N. (7) invited to a feast by the earl's sister (cf. Kölbing (1898) p. 61 note). (8) *Karidols heedh* S. (9) not specified E; twelve months and almost three half-years had elapsed (.35) N; one year gone, another begun S.

NOTE. The time-scale is very different (and more plausible) in W, as Yvain has been married only a week in F. The motif of uxoriousness or effeminacy is not present in W. In W Owein stays at Arthur's court, in F he wanders far and wide with Gawain. No ring is given in W, though it is taken back (568), and there is no suggestion of a talisman.

XIII. F 2685–2795, E 1577–1648, N VIII 37–IX 7, S 2091–2180.

W 564–73.

Y. and Gawain camp outside the town, where they are joined by A. (1). As they are sitting, Y suddenly remembers he has overstayed his leave, and while he is thinking about this, a damsel rides up, and gives greeting to A. and to all except Y., whom she denounces as a traitor to her mistress, reminding him of the term of his leave of absence (2) and demanding the return of the ring, which she takes from his finger, and rides off leaving Y. in deep distress.

As O. is sitting at table one day at Kaerllion a maiden rides in, splendidly dressed and equipped, comes up to him, takes the ring from his hand, and denounces him as a perfidious traitor. She rides off and O. remembers his adventure at the spring. He is distressed and, as soon as the meal is over, retires to his quarters and spends a miserable night.

(1) Earl Koozar (?) sees them, asks A. who they are; A. recognizes Y, and he and his go over to join them S. (2) F speaks of Y. having killed her mistress by stealing away her heart, and of the slow passage of time and the sleepless nights of lovers; N similarly talks of his having killed her and expands the rest into a statement that she is very ill and gets no rest.

NOTE. The two versions are very similar except for the last two points noted at the end of episode XII.

XIV. F 2796–2887, E 1649–1708, N IX 8–13, S 2181–2262.

W 574–81.

Y. immediately rises from the table, and rushes madly off, tearing off his clothes (1) and quickly outdistancing all pursuit. He takes a bow and five

The following morning O. arose and set off into the wilds. There he stayed till his clothes were worn out and he grew thin and was covered all

INTRODUCTION

arrows from a lad he meets, and lives for a while on raw venison. He comes to the house of a hermit who locks himself in but leaves barley bread and water outside for the madman. After this he returns daily for his bread and water, bringing presents of game (2).

over with hair. He kept company with wild beasts till he grew too weak to keep up with them, and descended from the hills to a valley in which lay the park of a widowed lady.

(1) not mentioned in E, but is naked below (1674). (2) E adds that this continued a full year.

NOTE. There is no hermit in W. The clothes are torn off in F, worn out in W. Madness is not explicit in W, though his physical condition worsens, and it is a consequence of his manner of life, not, as in F, a cause of it.

XV. F 2888–3141, E 1709–1868, N IX 14–33, S 2263–2494.

W 582–621.

One day Y. is found asleep in the forest by two (1) damsels and their mistress. One at length recognizes him by a facial scar. She tells her mistress this and shows how useful Y. might be, if restored to sanity, in her struggles with count Alier. The lady recalls that she has an ointment given her by Morgan the wise against delirium, and they ride home to the town (2) for it. It is to be applied only to the temples (3), and clothing and a palfrey are also sent. The maiden returns to Y., leaves the clothes by him, and anoints him all over, and then retires to watch. Y. awakes, sane but

This lady and her maidens walking by a lake in the park see O. and, examining him, find him alive but exhausted. They return to the castle; the lady sends one maiden with a box of ointment to be applied over the heart, clothing, and a spare horse. The maiden applies the whole of the ointment, leaves the clothes and horse, and retires to watch. O. recovers enough to crawl to the clothes, put them on, and struggle on to the horse. The maiden then appears and tells him where he is, and of the perilous position of her mistress. They come to the castle, where, despite the

weak, takes the clothes, but cannot walk. The maiden appears as if by chance, and lends him the palfrey she is leading, provided he will go where she takes him. On the way back the now empty box is dropped into a stream, as if by accident (4). The lady nevertheless takes Y. in, and he is carefully tended and given everything he wants, including a horse and arms (5).

apparent waste of the ointment, O. is tended for three months until the tufts of hair fall off him.

(1) three NS. (2) castle N, home ES. (3) not specified, but not to use it all E; head and neck N; head and hair S. (4) her lie about the loss of it is not anticipated here, as in F (and S), but told circumstantially below (1841–54); the loss of the box and the lie are omitted in N. (5) N omits mention of the horse and arms, but adds that he recovered in six weeks.

NOTE. Owein is not recognized in W. The ointment in W is used up but the container is not disposed of. The point of application differs, and no source for the ointment is given. In F only clothing, not the horse, is left for Y.; the horse and arms-giving belong to the immediate threat in W (cf. next episode), whereas in F it is part of the occupational therapy. In FNS (there is no mention in E) lying in the sun after the ointment has been applied seems to be part of the treatment, whereas in W it appears to be regarded as harmful. There is rather less fuss about pretending not to see Y before he is dressed in ENS than in F.

XVI. F 3142–3340, E 1869–1974, N X 1–22, S 2495–2690.

W 622–60.

One Tuesday (1) Count Alier came to the town burning and pillaging. (2) The citizens sallied and the count awaited them in a narrow pass (3). Y. sallied forth with the rest, slew one knight, then (4) four (4) more in attempting to clear the pass; this encouraged the

One day O. heard a great disturbance which the maiden told him was due to the appearance of the hostile earl. He asked her to obtain for him the loan of horse and arms, which her mistress allowed him to borrow without expecting him to make any good use

citizens to greater efforts. Those watching (6) from within the town praised Y.'s prowess and wished he were their lady's husband. The enemy fled with Y. pursuing the count closely till he overtook him and he yielded. Y. returns with his prisoner, whom he presents to his hostess. Restitution is to be made by the count and security given. The lady would willingly marry Y. (7) or be his mistress, but Y. insists on leaving.

of them. Accompanied by two armed squires he sets out; the squires tell him where in the army the earl is stationed, and he leaves them to wait at the gate while he penetrates the enemy, seizes the earl, and carries him by force back to his hostess. This is his return for the precious ointment. In exchange for the earl's life and liberty terms are agreed on, and the hostess recovers all her lands and possessions, with hostages as security. O. departs, despite her invitation to stay there, and wanders off again into the wilds.

(1) a day E, at that time N, one day S. (2–3) E stresses Y., 'with other succour that he had' is all the mention the rest get; similarly N (.2, .3). (4) the comparison with Roland at Ronceval occurs here in S, after the citizens' praise in F. (5) a second, third and fourth E, ten N, not mentioned S. (6) the citizens FN, the lady and a maiden. (7) N does not mention this till he has gone.

NOTE. The accounts differ in a number of details. Y. goes out with an army, O. with two squires; in F the count is captured alone, in W from the midst of his forces. The suggestion of marriage to the hostess in F is absent from W. The reference to repayment for the cure in W is absent from FNS, though alluded to in E (1898).

XVII. F 3341–3562, E 1975–2102, N X 23–38, S 2691–2880.

W 661–81.

As Y. is going on his way he hears a loud cry among the trees and finds in a clearing a lion held by the tail by a serpent (1), which is scorching his rear with flames (2). Y. considers the serpent is the one to attack first (3). He cuts

As O. is going on his way he hears a repeated cry in a wood and finds a white (black R) lion trapped by a snake issuing from a cleft in a rock. O. draws his sword and, as the snake darts out, cuts it in two, wipes his sword, and goes on his way.

it in two and then in tiny pieces, taking off the tip of the lion's tail to free him (4). The lion, instead of attacking Y., makes signs of surrender and gratitude, and accompanies him on his way. (5) Scenting game, he awaits Y.'s permission, and then brings down a deer (6), which he fetches back to Y. As it is now near nightfall, Y. lights a fire and roasts some of the meat, leaving the rest for the lion. He then goes back to sleep while the lion keeps guard over him and his horse. In this way they go on for a fortnight until they again come to the spring. Y. in distress swoons and, as he falls, his sword accidentally wounds him in the neck (7). The lion thinks he is dead and, seizing the sword, is about to commit suicide (8) when Y. revives, and bitterly reproaches himself for his unfaithfulness and the loss of his former happiness, and contemplates killing himself in earnest (9).

The lion follows, playing round him like a pet greyhound. They travel thus till evening. At nightfall O. dismounts, turns his horse out to graze in a wooded meadow, and while he is kindling a fire the lion goes off and returns with wood enough for three nights. He then goes off again and returns with a buck; O. flays it, spits some chops over the fire, and gives the rest of the carcass to the lion.

(1) dragon E. (2) and venom N; sim. S, and directed against Y., not the lion. (3) in E the choice is automatic, their merits are not weighed. (4) in S the tip of the tail is not cut off until after the lion has expressed its gratitude! (5) N condenses the following passage; they spent a fortnight in the forest and the lion hunted game for their food. (6) doe E, hart S. (7) both NS refer to a second wound in the breast (*ok undir geirvörtunum* N, *och j hans bryst eet annath* (*saar*) *var* S). (8) the lion removes the sword so that it can do no further harm, but does not attempt to kill itself S. (9) Y. would commit suicide but that the devil would win his soul S (the tone is pious throughout).

NOTE. All after the events of the first night is lacking in W, which has brought O. straight back to his wife's territory. The other differences are minor: the cutting of the lion's tail, the consideration which to assist, the lion killing game before the halt (in F) or afterwards (as W).

XVIII. F 3563–3769, E 2103–2206, N X 39–55, S 2881–3058.

W 681–710.

A damsel in the chapel overhears Y.'s complaints about his hard fate, and calling him over, tells him she is far worse off than he, and will be executed the next day unless she can find a champion to defend her cause in battle against three who accuse her of treason. Gawain or Y. would aid her, she is sure, especially Y., as he is the cause of her being accused. At this Y. tells her who he is, and recognizes her as Lunette. When he failed to return on time (1), the seneschal (2), jealous of L.'s influence with her mistress (3), accused her of having betrayed her by promoting the match with Y., and she rashly (4) undertook to find a knight to fight against three (5) by way of refutation. She had had 40 (6) days' grace to find one, but Gawain had gone off in pursuit of the abducted queen Guinevere, and no one knew where Y. was. Therefore she must suffer death the next day (7). Y. promises to aid her, but no one must know who he is (8). She argues that

As O. is thus engaged he hears a repeated groaning near him, and asks if it is a human being. The voice identifies itself as Lunet, imprisoned because of the young man who deserted her mistress, and whom she dearly loved. In her presence two of her mistress's chamberlains had slandered him as a traitor, and she had rashly said he could beat the two of them. Therefore she was imprisoned in a stone vessel and would be executed the next day but one unless O. came to rescue her; but she had no one to fetch him. O. asks if she is sure he would come if only he knew her plight; she is. O. shares his provisions with her and they spend all night in conversation. In the morning O. asks where he can find hospitality for the night, and she directs him to a nearby castle. The lion had watched over O. the previous night.

it is better to let her die than
that they should both perish,
but Y. rejects this course (9),
and goes off to seek shelter for
the night (10).

(1) S adds that her mistress grew angry with her. (2) steward E *ráðsmaðr* N, *drozati* S. (3) the counsellor hated L. because she knew of his dishonesty with her mistress's property N. (4) no such undertaking in N, suggestion comes from the *drozati* S. (5) i.e. himself and his two brothers ES. (6) not specified N, 14 S. (7) N omits this point. (8) need for anonymity not mentioned N. (9) L.'s proposal to sacrifice herself not mentioned EN. (10) no motive mentioned E.

NOTE. In W L. identifies herself at once, O. never does so: in F neither knows the other until Y. guesses from her story who she is. The hero is to fight against two in W, against three in F. There is a definite but rash offer of judicial combat in F, a mere thoughtless retort ('worth two of you, anyway') in W. It follows that in W no opportunity of finding her named champion is given, while in F she has forty days to find any champion. W has no reference to the abduction of Guinevere. The execution is fixed for the next day in F, the next but one in W; consequently Y spends that night elsewhere, O. the following one. O. does not reveal himself, and makes no promise of aid.

XIX. F 3770–4030, E 2207–2352, N X 56–XI 8, S 3059–3268.

W 711–38.

Y. travels on with the lion till he comes to a castle (1) the surroundings of which are razed (2). Seven (3) men come over the lowered drawbridge, but, frightened by the lion, beg him to leave it outside. Y. assures them they need not be afraid and he will not part with it. He is everywhere made welcome but grief keeps breaking in on their joy. Pressed by Y. the host explains that a giant, Harpin, demands his

O. saddles his horse and rides off till he sees the castle, where he is honourably received. The lion goes with the horse to the manger and lies there so that no one dare go near the horse. O. is well served, but everyone is as gloomy as death. O. sits between the earl and his daughter, and the lion comes between his feet under the table, and O. feeds him there. Half-way through the meal

daughter, and having been refused, has seized his six sons, has slain two already, and will kill the other four the next day unless the daughter is handed over (4) to be the plaything of his servants. The giant has laid waste all his domains except what lies within the fortifications (5). When Y. suggests recourse to Arthur's court for assistance, his host tells him that Gawain is his brother-in-law, but as he has gone in pursuit of the abductor of Guinevere, he cannot obtain his assistance. Y. offers to help provided the encounter is over early in the day (6). The host's daughter and her mother appear and are scarcely prevented from throwing themselves at Y.'s feet in gratitude. (7) He repeats the condition about an early encounter with the giant (8). Y. and the lion are taken to their room for the night.

the earl welcomed O., who asked the cause of their sadness. The earl had two sons caught out hunting by a cannibal creature in human shape and of gigantic size. The price of their ransom is the earl's daughter. O. asks whether he will choose to lose his sons or his daughter, and the earl assures him he will not give up his daughter to be defiled and ruined. They then talk of other things, and O. spends the night there.

(1–2) not mentioned in E. (3) four porters E, no number ES. (4–5) N omits. (6) he must be elsewhere by midday NS. (7–8) N omits.

NOTE. The daughter is introduced at the beginning in W, not till after the promise has been given in F. There is no mother, and no relationship to Gawain, and no attempt to enlist O.'s help in W. The number of sons is different, and none of them is dead yet in W. The daughter is not explicitly the giant's primary objective in W, nor is there any reference to her being abandoned to his servants. O. gives no promise in W, and consequently there are no expressions of gratitude or joy, and no reference to Gawain or Guinevere. The Welsh giant is nameless and perhaps not regarded as human.

XX. F 4031–4315, E 2353–2506, N XI 9–23, S 3269–3566.

W 739–57.

In the morning (1) Y. hears mass (2) and waits till prime (3) before announcing that he must go; he is held a little longer by the entreaties of the host and his daughter (4). While Y. is torn between the two courses (5), the giant appears, driving before him the four sons, bound and in rags, mounted on miserable horses, while a dwarf beats them with a scourge (6). The giant repeats his offer to take the daughter for the sons. While the father is hesitating (7), Y. goes out followed by the lion. They fight, and Y. wounds the giant in the breast with his lance, but is almost overcome by blows from his club. With his sword he cuts a slice from the giant's cheek (8). The giant gives him a severe blow with the club, but the lion tears away part of his thigh (9). Striking at the lion, the giant overbalances (10) and falls, and Y. cuts off one arm (11) and runs him through (12). He falls dead. The people try to detain Y. or make him promise to return. (13) He will only ask that Gawain should be informed of what has been done and they are to say that the Knight of the

The next morning O. hears a tremendous din at the approach of the giant. The earl proposes to abandon his sons but O. arms himself and goes out with the lion to fight the giant. The lion does him more harm than O., and the giant insists on the lion's being confined in the castle. O. does so, but as the fight continues, the lion climbs and leaps his way out of the castle, and with one blow of his paw disembowels the giant, who falls dead. O. restores his sons to the earl, refuses an invitation to remain, and rides off in haste to the meadow where Lunet is to be executed.

Lion did it. Refusing the aid of the four sons (14), he then makes haste towards the chapel.

(1–5) N omits. (2) a priest awakens Y. and summons him to a mass of the Holy Ghost S. (3) ENS omit. (4) host only, in E. (6) the dwarf leads the horses and the giant flogs them N, both giant and dwarf flog them S. (7) EN omit. (8) EN omit. (9) *fro his hals to hys cropoun* E, from neck to loin NS. (10–11) the lion dodges, and Y. cuts off the giant's left cheek and shoulder E; the giant strikes at the lion, misses, his club sticks fast in the ground, and Y. seizes his opportunity S. (12) cuts off his head N. (13–14) E omits.

NOTE. The lion is in the fight from the first and is sent off in W, but does not become active until his master is in danger in F. There is no dwarf or description of the sons in W. The wound inflicted by the lion is different in F from W (and ENS). There is no provision for telling Gawain in W (or E). There are no details of the fight with the giant or of his weapon in W.

XXI. F 4316–4702, E 2507–2742, N XII 1–XIII 4, S 3567–3962.

W 758–81.

Y. arrives in time to stop L. being thrown into the fire, sees his wife again (1), and hears the lamentations of L.'s friends (2). Y. then announces he is ready to do battle and L. formally protests her innocence. The seneschal and his brothers threaten Y., but he persists in his determination to defend her cause. They protest at the lion, and Y. tells it to lie down. At the first encounter all splinter their lances on Y.'s shield; at the second, Y. unhorses the seneschal and stuns him. His brothers engage Y. with the sword and he does well until the seneschal

There a large fire is burning and two young men are about to throw L. into it. O. asks what they charge her with and is given the same account as L. gave him. O. suggests that Owein has omitted to come only through ignorance of her situation, and offers to deputize for him. The young men accept, and they begin to fight. O. is getting the worst of it when the lion intervenes. They oblige O. to imprison the lion where L. had been confined, and continue the fight. O. continues to be in difficulty until the lion breaks out and kills both his adversaries. L. is

recovers and aids them. Then the lion intervenes and disembowels the seneschal. Y. tries to drive it off, but unsuccessfully, and it is itself badly wounded. Y. makes greater efforts and the two brothers yield, and are thrown into the fire. L. is now reconciled to her mistress, who tries to persuade Y. to stay. He cannot do so (3) until his lady ceases to be displeased with him (4). He gives as his name only 'The Knight with the Lion', and departs. L. sees him off and promises to lose no chance of recommending him to his wife while he is absent. He goes on, carrying the wounded lion in his shield, until they come to a castle where both stay until they have recovered, and then proceed.

saved, and she and O. go to her mistress. When O. came away again he brought his wife to Arthur's court and she was his wife as long as she lived.

(1) in E, his sighing at the sight of her he loved (so F) is referred to Lunete; NS omit. (2) N omits. (3–4) E omits. Lacuna in N corresponding to F 4692–5115.

NOTE. The fight has begun in W before any objection to the lion is made; in F the objection is a preliminary. In F one assailant is killed, two yield and are burnt; in W both are killed. There is no mention of the lion being wounded in W. The recognition and reconciliation between O. and his wife is not described in W (though it must have occurred); in F it is still to come. The W story ends at this point apart from one disjoined episode.

XXI. F 4703–5106, E 2743–2930, N lacuna, S 3963–4444. After this follows the story of two sisters quarrelling over their inheritance, within which occurs the story of the castle of Pesme Avanture. According to the former the knight of Noire Espine died, and his elder daughter refused any share of his lands to the younger, who announced her intention of seeking

INTRODUCTION

Arthur's arbitration. The elder sister arrived first at the court and secured Gawain as her champion, but anonymously. The younger sister reached the court just after Guinevere had been restored to Arthur, and on the day on which the news of the death of the giant Harpin reached there. No one was willing to aid the younger sister, and Arthur was unable to persuade the elder to relent; the younger asked respite for forty days to produce her champion, and went off in search of the Knight of the Lion. She fell ill at the home of a friend who took up the quest on her behalf, and who after being benighted in a storm, came to the castle where Y. had killed the giant. The next day they put her on the road that Y. had taken, and she came to the town where Y. had killed the seneschal and his brothers. Here Lunete gave her directions and she came to where he and the lion had convalesced. This castle he had just left, and she soon overtook him and secured his promise of assistance.

XXIII. F 5107–5809, E 2931–3358, N XIII 5–XIV 6, S 4445–5272.

W 782–817.

Y. and the messenger come to the town of Pesme Avanture, where the people murmur at them (1) and an old lady explains this by saying that he may lodge only at the castle, while she warns him not to do so (2). They are discourteously received (3); Y. turns to the porter, who refuses to let them out, for information, but gets none, and finds the entrance to a yard where they find 300 maidens in rags sewing costly stuffs—(4) their diet and wages are scanty. The maidens (5) tell him they are a yearly tribute of 30 (6) damsels paid by the king (7) of the Isle of Damsels to ransom himself from the

Then O. came to the court of the Du Traws, and fought him, and did not leave him till he was defeated. When he arrived he found in the hall twenty-four beautiful women in rags and sad. They told him they were earls' daughters, had come there with their husbands, been made drunk, their husbands slain, and themselves robbed of all they had; the corpses were in the same building. They feared O. would meet the same fate. He met the D. T., who received him warmly, but was told they were enemies. In the fight O. overcame him, and he promised to reform and become an hospitaller. The adventure in the castle, i.e. fighting with two devils (8). In a garden they find a gentleman (9) and his wife being read a romance by their daughter (10). They receive him kindly, but in the morning after mass (11), when he takes leave, the adventure is forced on him: if he wins he will become lord of the domain and have the daughter to wed (12). Y. refuses the prize but cannot evade the battle. The devils are armed with clubs and shields. The lion, they insist, shall be confined. Y. is in dire straits when the lion, having dug his way out under the threshold, comes to his aid and pulls down one devil. As the other goes to help his fellow, Y. strikes off his head, and the first, badly mauled, yields. The lord of the place takes offence at Y.'s renewed refusal of his daughter (13), but lets him go, with the maidens, who (14) then leave him to return to their homes.

next day O. took the twenty-four women and their property to Arthur's court, and each had the choice of staying there or going away.

(1-2) omit E, and probably N. (3) not at the gate as in FE, but in the hall N. (4-8) N omits. (5) *een gamul frugha* is their spokeswoman in S. (6) each devil was to have 150 (no mention of an annual tribute) S. (7) aged not yet 18 F, 14 E, not fully 10 S. (8) *geten of a woman with a ram* 3019 E, *jötunssynir tveir* (.11) but *djöflasonum* (.20) N, *thæn annar var fødder aff een kona, een annar thera aff eet faar* S. (9-10) and his daughter N. (11) N omits. (12) N may suggest that he offers his lands and daughter as a reward (not a prize) for overcoming the two giants. (13) Y. refuses the lordship, the daughter, and the offer of gold N. (14) no further information about them N.

NOTE. The differences are very numerous. In W no warning is given on approach; there are twenty-four women, not 300 maidens, in a hall not in a palisaded yard; there is no reception or porter; a different story is told to account for the women's presence; there is no hint of commercial exploitation; there are no devils, no wife, daughter, or romance. O. does not wait till the next day for the fight (though it may be implied that this was the normal procedure); the lion is not present, and O. appears to be travelling alone. The story of the reformation of the Du Traws with its play on words is possible only in W. The women go home direct in F, via Arthur's court in W. The contrast in F between the friendly host and the hostile champions corresponds to two different attitudes of the D. T. himself in W.

XXIV. F 5810–6818, E 3359–4032, N XIV 7–XVI 28, S 5273–6430. Y. and his guide and his lion hurry back to join the younger sister, and arrive on the thirty-ninth day; they stay the night outside the town. Gawain returns in disguise to champion the elder sister, who presses Arthur to give judgement in her favour. The younger sister presents her champion (they have left the lion in their lodgings), and makes a further plea to the elder for justice, but she remains obdurate and the battle begins. The two are well matched and the struggle is prolonged so far that the general opinion turns against the elder sister, and Arthur is pressed to impose a settlement, but declines. Each combatant is astonished at the powers of the other, and cannot imagine who it can be that opposes him so long. The contest continues till nightfall, and while they are pausing to recover their breath, Y. expresses his admiration of his opponent's valour, and asks his name. On discovering he has been fighting Gawain he throws away his arms and, declaring his own name, admits defeat. Gawain refuses to accept the victory, and they are still arguing when Arthur intervenes. He leads the elder sister to convict herself of injustice, and by threatening to declare her champion defeated, forces her to deal justly with her sister. The lion arrives on the scene as Yvain and Gawain are disarming, and shows that Y. is the same as the Knight of the Lion of whom they have heard.

Once he is recovered from the fight with Gawain, Y. returns with the lion to the spring, where he provokes the usual storm. Lunete advises her mistress to secure the services of the Knight of the Lion, of whose prowess they have heard, to defend the spring in future, but adds that this cannot be done unless he is first reconciled to his lady. This her mistress is led to swear to assist in to the utmost. Lunete rides off in search of him and finds him beneath the tree at the spring; she takes him to her mistress, and bids her discharge her oath, for she herself is his unforgiving wife. Aided by Y.'s promise not to stray again, the reconciliation is brought about, and here the story ends.

W 817–21, adds that O. stayed in Arthur's court as his *pennteulu* till he went to his own domain, the swords and the flight of ravens, in company with which he was ever victorious.

NOTE. Most of this matter is unparalleled in W, but the fight between Y. and G. has already occurred in W 518–37, when Arthur first came to the spring. There is some difference in the way in which Y. recognizes G., but the motif of each trying to yield to the other is common to both. The non-participation of the lion in the fight with G. is natural enough in W, as O. had not then met it, but is rather lamely contrived in F.

In the opinion of the present writer, at least, there can be no doubt, in the light of the foregoing summary of the versions, that Brown was right in saying that W bore a relationship to F different from that of any other version, that Carruth was justified in claiming that the similarities between W and F are not great enough to eclipse the differences, and that Foerster and Bruce were wrong in asserting that W is simply a free translation and abridgement of F.

The view that appeared as the contemporary alternative to Foerster's, that of Gaston Paris (*Histoire littéraire de la France* (Paris, 1888) 30. 13) that W was based on lost Anglo-Norman or other French verse narratives, need not detain us long. Since no such Anglo-Norman or French texts have survived, and as even the probability of their existence is generally doubted, no comparisons are possible and the hypothesis is unverifiable. It was in the first instance a by-product of a particular theory of the transmission of Arthurian material to Crestien, which, in the absence of any positive evidence, is now abandoned.

INTRODUCTION lvii

VIII. *The 'Common Source' Theory*

That this view of the non-dependence of W upon F is now thought consistent with the highest regard for Crestien's work appears from the comments of J. Frappier. In his lectures on *Le Roman breton: Yvain ou le Chevalier au Lion* (Centre de documentation universitaire, Paris, 1952) 31, he said:

> On a beaucoup discuté sur les rapports du *Chevalier au Lion* avec le conte gallois, mais on peut admettre aujourd'hui . . . que de l'un à l'autre il n'existe pas de dépendance directe; *Owein et Lunet* est un texte relativement tardif qui ne semble pas antérieur au début du XIIIème siècle; il n'est donc pas la source de Chrétien; mais les différences de structure—pour ne rien dire de l'esprit, du ton et de l'art—sont telles entre les deux œuvres qu'il semble invraisemblable que le *Chevalier au Lion* ait servi de modèle à l'auteur gallois. . . . Comme, cependant, *Owein et Lunet* porte des traces incontestables d'une influence française, la conclusion la plus plausible qu'on puisse tirer de ces apparentes anomalies, c'est que le *Chevalier au Lion* et le conte gallois dépendent l'un et l'autre d'une source commune, écrite en français, et du reste inspirée elle-même par des traditions celtiques; œuvre qui devait être un de ces 'contes d'aventure' dont Chrétien parle avec dédain dans le prologue d'*Erec*.
> On peut penser qu'*Owein et Lunet* reproduit sans changement considérable, et en tout cas avec des changements moins considérables que ceux de Chrétien, la structure de cette source commune.

A little earlier, in his *Introduction, des origines à Chrétien de Troyes* to the same subject (ibid., 1950) 40, Professor Frappier was more explicit on two points:

> Malgré d'indéniables ressemblances, les différences restent trop considérables. Les raffinements courtois du poète champenois, les belles manières de ses héros ne se retrouvent pas dans les romans gallois, dont le ton garde quelque chose d'abrupt et de sauvage. Et pourtant ils nous transportent dans un monde qui n'est pas purement celtique, où beaucoup de traits matériels

et moraux révèlent l'influence de la civilisation française du XIIème siècle.

Tout en adaptant des sources françaises, les auteurs gallois de *Gereint* d'*Owein* et de *Peredur* ont probablement renoué avec des traditions indigènes, ce qui expliquerait qu'ils aient curieusement juxtaposé des éléments tout français et des traits nettement celtiques.

Similar conclusions are briefly stated in his *Chrétien de Troyes; l'homme et l'œuvre* (Paris, 1957) 156.

Professor R. S. Loomis in his *Arthurian Tradition and Chrétien de Troyes* (New York, 1949) deals with the relationship of F and W as follows:

Were the Welsh tales the source of Chrétien? Was Chrétien the sole source of the corresponding portions of the Welsh tales? Was Chrétien only one of the sources of the Welsh tales? Was there a common source for each of the three pairs of romances? (p. 33).

All this [six points where W appears to be independent of F] makes an impressive case for the independence of the French and Welsh authors, their reliance on what was substantially a common original, written in the French language. Chrétien and the one or two Welsh authors treated the sources with considerable freedom as to details. Sometimes it is difficult to see any rational or artistic motive for their departures from their common original; . . . At other times it is quite easy to perceive Chrétien's purpose and mannerisms in the alterations and additions. Comparison with the Welsh tales, when carried out with discrimination, can be of great value in estimating the degree of Chrétien's originality and detecting his methods of work (p. 37).

Happily there is now agreement on certain points. Everyone recognizes that the Welsh tales are not, like *Kulhwch* and *The Dream of Rhonabwy*, of pure, or nearly pure, native inspiration, but are based in the main on French or Anglo-Norman originals. Everyone, I believe, agrees that the Welsh tales are somewhat later in date than Chrétien's poems, probably compositions of the thirteenth century. There is no one now, therefore, to contend that they are the sources of Chrétien, and the first of the four alternatives is thus abandoned (p. 33).

INTRODUCTION lix

The theory of a common source may be summarized in the following five points:

A. W and F are derived not from each other (i.e. neither W from F, nor F from W) but from a common source (Loomis's Y);
B. the common source was a written one and in French;
C. the structure of this common source has been better preserved by W than by F;
D. W shows French influence in a number of ways;
E. W is an adaptation of Y into Welsh, modified in the light of native Welsh tradition.

We may now discuss these points in turn.

A. The evidence drawn from the divergence between W and F, illustrated in section VII, above, tends to show only that W cannot be derived from F, not the reverse (on which see below, lxiv ff.). The only evidence adduced here against the derivation of F from W is the date of W: if the date is reliable, this evidence is conclusive; but we have already seen (above, section IV) that there are reasons for thinking it may not be reliable, and that W may already have been in existence before Crestien began to compose his version.

B. It is reasonable to conclude that a written source may have been in French, or possibly in Latin, since it would hardly be intelligible to Crestien in Welsh or Breton. This argument is a little weakened if we assume that Crestien was not the first to tell this tale in French, and that he may have taken it from a previous narrative in his own language. This in turn could be the production of a bilingual Breton or, less probably, Welshman. Alternatively, the tale might have come orally to Crestien. The primary argument against this is the amount of detailed correspondence between W and F, which may be thought to make a written source more likely, but this may be unjust to Crestien's powers of memory.

INTRODUCTION

Conclusive evidence that the Welsh romances are derived immediately from a written French text is hard to find. Loomis (AT 34) cites the arguments of Loth (Mab. i 55–), according to whom the evidence for the Welsh tales having as their immediate origin French prose *contes* is held to lie in some examples of mistranslation and the presence of some foreign names. Mistranslation cannot, of course, be established between the Welsh tales and the hypothetical French prose *contes* simply because the latter are hypothetical, and comparison once more is between W and F. Windisch, in criticizing the assumption that W was derived from F, denied emphatically that any examples of direct translation occurred or that any French loanword was found in both texts at the same point. This argument has great force as long as we are considering the possibility of direct translation from Crestien; its value is much diminished in connexion with a common source. Windisch made a more valuable point in that connexion when he said 'Ich habe bis jetzt keine Stelle gefunden an der ein kymrischer Ausdruck und eine kymrische Konstruktion die genaue Wiedergabe des französischen Ausdrucks und der französischen Konstruktion wäre' (KB 273), i.e. that there is nothing unidiomatic or translation-like in the Welsh.

Loth alleged as proof the case of *y llestyr maen hwn* (694) in which Owein finds Lunet imprisoned. In F Lunete is imprisoned in the chapel at the spring to which chance has brought Yvain and the lion (3490– Tant qu'avanture a la fontainne Desoz le pin les amena; 3564– Une chetive une dolante Estoit an la chapele anclose Si vit et oï cele chose Par le mur qui estoit crevez), and they converse through a crack in the wall: after promising to return, Yvain rides off to find shelter for the night. In W Owein hears a groan in the darkness as he is sitting down to supper by his camp-fire, and goes on to converse with the voice, which mentions being imprisoned *yn y llestyr maen hwn*, but there is no more precise description of the situation. Owein, however, is able to share his supper with her, and they stay talking till dawn. The 'stone vessel' thus plays the same part in the story as the chapel, and Loth suggested that the Welsh translator must have mistaken the sense of Old French *chapele*, which means both 'lieu secret, prison' and 'vase'. The Welsh version never mentions a chapel at the spring, and the implication is that such a meaning for 'chapele' never crossed the translator's mind here. Yet in W the scene is not the storm-producing spring at all, and the translator had therefore no reason to exclude the meaning 'chapel' on the ground that no such building existed at that spot. According to Tobler-Lommatzsch, *Altfranzösisches Wörterbuch*, there are three words of this general shape: (1) *chapel* m. 'head-covering, hat', which we may disregard; (2) *chapel* m. Schuppen (i.e. shed), Räucherkammer (room for smoking meat), which, as appears from the quotations, is the same word as Godefroy defined as 'lieu obscur ou secret', though neither lexicographer gives the meaning 'prison'; and (3) *chapele* f. which means both 'chapel' and 'alembic' (for distilling). It is intrinsically most improbable that a translator, confronted with *chapel(e)*, should, without any prompting from the context, think of a kippering-shed or an alembic rather than a chapel, and even if he had done so, it is not clear how he could put down *llestyr maen* as their Welsh equivalent. There is certainly something obscure in W, but the reading is one on which, unfortunately, the three available manuscripts agree. It is far from certain that it is due to a mistranslation of any kind. When Owein confines the lion in the same place (772) it is described simply as being *yn y lle y buassei y uorwyn yg karchar*; we may note the identity of the first few letters with *yn y llestyr maen hwn*, and guess that the latter may be the result of an unhappy conjecture by a puzzled copyist very early in the history of the text. A parallel phrase would be *yn y lle yd yttwyf yr awron*, or something of the kind, but a palaeographically easy correction would be *yn y lle yscymun hwn* 'in this accursed place'.

Loth also suggested that the spelling *geol* in *Peredur* (WBM 172. 16, RB i 238. 2) must be copied, not phonetic. He seems to have assumed here *ge-* for [dʒ], but a glance at *NED* under *Jail* will show that Middle English had both [g] and [dʒ] forms of the word from Norman and Central French respectively. Welsh *geol* is clearly the Anglo-Norman type, still represented in Modern English by the spelling *gaol*.

A similar type of argument to that about *chapele* concerns a passage in *Gereint*, and was advanced by Loomis (AT 35–36). According to this the name *Ynywl*, that of Enid's father, is dependent on a failure to recognize Old French *uials* 'old', but the suggestion is rightly rejected by both Mrs. Bromwich in TYP 475 note 1, and R. M. Jones in *Llên Cymru* 4. 216.

Lastly, the presence of foreign names in the text has been proposed as evidence of translation from a French source. There are two items here in *Owein*, the name of *Lunet* and the passing reference to *Rangyw*, no doubt for *yr Angyw* 'Anjou'. Despite Philipot's assertion (*Annales de Bretagne* 8 (1892) 55) that 'le nom de Luned est un nom celtique' and the assumption of the same view by Loth (Mab. ii 2 note 2), who proposed an etymology from *llun* 'image', the fact remains that the invariable initial *L*- in permanent lenition suggests a loan-word never fully assimilated in Welsh; the references to the name in the Welsh poets are later than the romance (cf. Loth, ibid., TYP 345; all three references belong to the second half of the fourteenth century, and have *L*-, though ordinary lenition cannot always be excluded). MS. Llanstephan 58, however, regularly has *Elined* or *Elyned*, and a similar form *Eluned* occurs in TYP 241, from MS. Peniarth 77; the same reading is possible in *Gutun Owain* vi 31–32 (ed. E. Bachellery (Paris, 1950)), printed *Och am y Lvned ddedwydd A'm kvddiai pen ddelai yn ddydd*, but not in vii 30 *Lvned wen* (vocative).

Examples of *Eluned*, or spellings which may be interpreted as lenited forms of *Llunet*, seem therefore always to be later than the White Book's *Lunet*; T. Gwynn Jones's examples of *Eluned* from the poetry of the Gogynfeirdd (*Aberystwyth Studies* 8. 45) are interpretations, and the texts from which his examples are taken have only *L-*. Mrs. Bromwich (TYP 345) and Mr. Jones (*Llên Cymru* 4. 219) therefore agree in acknowledging a borrowing of the French name Lunette, thus confirming the opinion of Windisch (KB 279) as long ago as 1912. His explanation was that the name was a later importation into the story, but the occurrences of the name are quite numerous (unlike the solitary instance of the name Laudine, given by Crestien to the *iarlles*), and it might be difficult to imagine the circumstances in which a Welsh storyteller, discovering that his unnamed character was by Crestien called Lunete, would introduce this name throughout his story. R. M. Jones's explanation, based on the case of Gwiffret petit who, we are told in *Gereint*, was called by this name by the French (and English), whereas the Welsh knew him as *y brenhin bychan*, is that in this bilingual community in Glamorgan the same originally Welsh tales were told in both languages. This, however, hardly helps. If the story of *Gereint* was originally Welsh and contained a character called *y brenhin bychan* how does the French version come to give him the name of Gwiffret? Similarly, if Lunet was, like her mistress, unnamed in *Owein*, why does the French version call her Lunete?

In comparing the two names, Lunete and Lunet, it is difficult to decide whether Lunete is a modified form of a Welsh name, with a transparent French etymology, or whether Lunet is a Cymricized form of the French name. Crestien introduces Lunete as *une dameisele* at line 973, and so describes her on a dozen occasions, as well as calling her *pucele* once, but not until 2414 does he give her a name. There seems little point in this merely as an exercise in suspense, and it is probable that he invented the name to crown his fanciful comparison of her and Gawain with the moon and the sun, lines 2393-2414. In the Welsh tale Lunet appears for the first time at line 290 as *morwyn*, and is first named, without explicit identification, when she goes to see her mistress after the latter's husband's funeral, line 386, a much earlier point in the story than in the French version. A point comparable with F would be about line 556.

The second foreign name, Rangyw, is not specially significant, as it has no part in the structure of the plot, and at the point at which it occurs any place-name would fill the bill. In MS. Llanstephan 58 the corresponding word is *Kyrniw*, i.e. *Kernyw* 'Cornwall'. There is a distinct possibility of a misreading in either direction, and there is nothing corresponding in F. If *Kernyw* were the original reading it would explain why *yr Angyw* is misdivided and the remains of the article suppressed; *Rangyw*, however, is the reading of R only (W is wanting at this point), beside *Angyw* in MSS. Llanstephan 171, Cwrtmawr 20, and Llanover B 17, all three without the article, so that it looks as if *Kyrniw* may be only a substitute for an unfamiliar name.

C. On the point that W preserves the structure of the common source (Y) better than F does, no very certain conclusions can be drawn from the comparison of F with W, for the decisions must all be on matters of probability rather than certainty.

If we adopt the hypothesis that Crestien based his romance on a narrative similar in general outline to W, that is, that they had a common source to which W is nearer than F, much less difficulty arises in explaining the actual state of the two versions than if we try to explain W as a derivative of F. On this hypothesis Crestien would have made many small changes of detail, both of addition and omission, but his first major contribution will have been to tighten up the chronology of the first part of the story (episodes I to XI). Thus Yvain's hasty departure for the adventure of the spring is necessitated by Arthur's intention to attempt it in person with only a slight delay, and this in turn necessitates Arthur's having been told Calogrenant's story immediately after he has recounted it to the rest. Unfortunately, in making these 'improvements' Crestien would involve himself in two difficulties that are not present in W: first, the wooing of Laudine must progress at breakneck speed towards marriage because of the imminent arrival of Arthur, and second, Yvain is dragged away from his bride of only a few days (not, as in W, of fully three years). Gawain's recall to a life of martial valour under these circumstances is rather forced.

Crestien's second major contribution in retelling the story would be to remove the combat between Yvain and Gawain from the middle of the story to a position better suited to set it off as the grand climax of the romance. This meant that Yvain must reveal his identity as defender of the spring immediately after overthrowing Kay. Crestien would now be obliged to engineer a new climax, and this we may suppose he did by introducing the story of the quarrelling sisters. An interesting piece of evidence in favour of this supposition's being correct is that in the duel of Yvain and Gawain the lion takes no part; it would, of course, not have been appropriate to have Gawain savaged by a wild beast in the same way as cannibal giants and devils in human shape or even false accusers like the seneschal and his brothers, yet so attached is the lion to Yvain and so eager to assist him in all his difficulties that the explanation in F, that they slipped away in the morning and left it asleep, with the implication that it did not awake and track down its master till almost the end of the day, must sound remarkably feeble. The truth of the matter, as Brown saw (*Romanic Review* 3 (1912) 143), is that, at the point at which the combat between Yvain and Gawain occurred in Y, Yvain had not yet met the lion, and Crestien therefore had no ready-made explanation of its tardiness.

The third major contribution of the French poet would be the insertion of the Pesme Avanture episode within the quarrelling sisters story. It is not integrated in the romance at all in W, and might have been jettisoned without difficulty. That it is not rejected, and that Crestien, unwilling to use it in its original form, nevertheless worked it into his completed account, is strong evidence for its having been connected with the rest of the story from the time of Y. Similar disjointed episodes occur at the end of *Peredur*, though in that case comparative material from French is lacking. Crestien may have been encouraged to retain this episode because it plays an important part in establishing an artistic parallelism between Yvain coming to rescue Lunete and Yvain coming to do battle for the younger sister, in both cases building up an almost intolerable atmosphere of suspense.

Some minor details will also fall into place if this hypothesis is accepted; the youths in episode II, who are superfluous to the story, are simply omitted—the addition of such matter in an abridgement would be peculiar; the twenty-four young ladies who minister to Kynon are reduced to one, but the castle is supplied with a normal complement of servants; the alleged rationalization of the portcullis episode in W would be odd, when nothing like it takes place in the other versions—in some the improbabilities are even greater than in F; the absence of the chapel in W must surely be original, or why does no one think to shelter in it during the storms? It is obviously better that the lady of the spring should not be aware who it is that she is proposing to marry, and freed from the forced pace of Crestien's sequence of events, she is able to show a proper indifference, and not be in any hurry to see her champion when he arrives; before Lunet springs the surprise upon her, she has had a little longer to recover from her first grief at the loss of her husband and to come to terms with the realities of her situation.

We may conclude then that while much of the difference between F and W could be attributed to a particularly able abridger and adaptor, it is scarcely conceivable that such a person should have reversed the three major contributions, as we have called them, made by Crestien, and that therefore, while F could be drawn from W or something like it, W could not be drawn from F.

It should be noted that this argument from the possibility of conversion in one direction and the impossibility of the reverse is quite different from the argument, so strongly put by Zenker (*Ivainstudien* 213) from the greater logicality, coherence, or probability of one version: that type of argument is highly subjective as Windisch (KB 269) noted, and we may see its weakness displayed in the rival views held by Brown (*Romanic Review* 3 (1912) 146–50) and Smirnov (RC 34 (1913) 337 ff.) of the portcullis episode.

But the exact content of Y is not so easy to establish. According to the methods one adopts for reconstructing it, the nature of Y will itself vary, and its relationship to W and F must therefore vary too. At every point where they disagree the comparison of W with F leaves us without guidance as to which is the aberrant version. It is presumably for this reason that Loomis has cast his net wider and included in the comparison a large number of other texts which may be versions of the same themes. He gives no complete or systematic account of the content of Y (which is unfortunate, as the plausibility of the hypothesis of a common source must largely depend on our ability to reconstruct it and explain convincingly how the differences between it and the extant versions came into being), but from time to time in AT he drops some hints. There seem to be eleven of these hints:

1. 'It must have been at this stage [i.e. 'an early stage in

Continental Arthurian tradition' when 'there was some confusion between the names of Guenievre and Winlogee, Guenloie, and Guendoloena'] that one version of the eavesdropping lady attached itself to Guenievre and another version to Winliane' (p. 277). Since the incident is not in W it is by no means certain that it was in Y. When we see that of the three points (p. 276), which, according to Loomis, were drawn from the Ford Combat tradition, only one, and that the least distinctive (Kynon's loss of his horse), is present in W, we may legitimately doubt the truth of his hypothesis.

2. After suggesting that the Yellow and Terror episodes in *Bricriu's Feast* are the source of W and F in their Hospitable Host episodes, Loomis proceeds (p. 281): 'Thus it would seem that Calogrenant's sojourn with the Hospitable Host combines two Irish accounts of the testing of the Ulster warriors, the Welsh *Owain* retaining clear traces of the stay at the house of Yellow, while Chrétien retains a trace of Blathnat's hospitality in the fortress of Curoi.' On this showing Y would have to have both. It is far more likely that the host's daughter in F is Crestien's work, part of his rationalization of the folk-tale elements preserved in W.

3. 'Thus we are led to the conclusion that Escalados' castle preserves, in the dropping portcullis, a curiously modernized relic of Curoi's fortress' (p. 283). But the important question is when it was modernized and how. The similarity of W and F suggests it was already in this state in Y, but this is by no means certain, for Crestien would hardly have used the motif in its older form, and it may therefore be part of the supposed process of contamination with F when it appears in W. Pre-W or Y might then have the Irish version of the incident. Loomis does not discuss the question.

4. On p. 295 there is a rather obscure argument about Aranrot being a moon-goddess, and her mythical nature descending to Lunete; 'there is no difficulty in supposing that

the naming of Lunete and Chrétien's likening her to the moon reveal the original nature of her divinity.' The mechanism of this is not explained. Aranrot is scarcely possible in a Welsh story, and would in any case have been meaningless to Crestien. It is far more likely, in view of the point at which the name Lunete is introduced in F, that it was Crestien's own invention, perhaps even on the spur of the moment.

5. Pp. 308–9. Loomis regards the author of Y as responsible for the series of adventures designed to enhance the reputation of the hero, between the loss of his faery wife and their reconciliation, and therefore it was necessary that he should first be cured of his madness. This, however, is largely because Loomis thinks of these adventures as having no earlier connexion with each other and not being inherited from any earlier version of the story. There is a tale which provides a better explanation of their presence and especially of their form. It should be noted that there is no hermit in W, and that Owein is nowhere stated to be mad.

6. P. 313. The rescue of the lion was in Y.

7. Pp. 314–15. Loomis compares the parallels of the Irish beasts fighting for their masters with the lion defending Yvain; 'would not the story of a monstrous horse which came to the aid of his master in a prolonged conflict recall to the mind of a twelfth-century Frenchman the familiar story of the grateful lion, and suggest the substitution of a lion for the hybrid creature? Would not a fusion of the two traditions be natural?' The rhetorical question expects agreement, but in this case rather deserves a negative answer. Loomis has agreed that the rescue of the lion was in Y, and presumably its subsequent adventures with the hero must have been in Y also. A direct transplantation of the Irish form of the story into French is highly improbable, and it is much easier to assume that Y here follows a Welsh tale, parallel to the Irish one, but in which the substitution of the lion has already taken place.

8. P. 317. 'The theme of the rescue of a woman from death by fire cannot have a Celtic provenance.' This is a matter of the remoter sources; the first question is whether it was in Y.

9. P. 319. Loomis agrees that in Y the fight with Gwalchmei occupies the position it does in W, not that in F.

10. P. 321. 'Such a tale [Pesme Avanture] was included in Y since it is found in *Owain* as an awkward appendage and in Malory's Book of Gareth.'

11. Pp. 329–30. Y contained the duel of Owein and Gwalchmei and their magnanimous willingness each to confess that the other had overcome him; it must have been in Y since it is in W as well as F.

It may not be going too far to wonder whether Professor Loomis went about this comparison in the right way. In a book entitled *Arthurian Tradition and Chrétien de Troyes* it may seem natural to begin all comparison from Crestien's own account of each episode, but it should be realized that such a method is justifiable only if there is no other version of the romance as a whole that can be shown to be independent of Crestien. This is exactly what Brown did in his *Iwain* (in 1903, before he had studied the Welsh version), comparing Crestien directly with Irish stories, but after he had given reasons for the independence of the Welsh version in 1912, it should have become impossible to take Crestien as representing all versions of the romance. There are four stages in a validly based comparison: (*a*) to establish whether W (or any other version) is independent of F, and if it is, then (*b*) to use the independent versions to reconstruct Y (as Loomis seems to imply, in points 10 and 11 above, is the correct procedure); then (*c*) to explain the changes made in Y by W and F; and (*d*) to discuss the origins of whatever in W and F is in excess of Y. It is at this last stage, primarily if not exclusively, that discussion of other versions of the same motifs and incidents in other texts becomes appropriate.

To maintain, as both Frappier and Loomis do, that W is independent of F, that both derive from a common source (Y), and that W preserves this source better than F does, though all, in the opinion of the present writer, quite true, is not a fully satisfactory final conclusion. For if W is much closer to Y than F is, what is there to prevent us supposing that Y in reality was only a French translation of the Welsh tale? It cannot, of course, have been translated from our earliest copy in MS. Peniarth 4, but we have seen above (section IV) that there is good reason to think copies of the tale existed as far back as the twelfth century, and we may suppose that the text was not substantially different at that time from our W.

We should thus return to the oldest view of the relationship of the versions, albeit in a more elaborate and critical form, namely that the Welsh tale is in effect, though not quite directly, the source of the French romance. Before we can embrace this conclusion, however, we must first consider the signs of foreign influence which have been seen in the text by most scholars.

D. Three kinds of foreign influence have been suggested: (*a*) that the plot is not Celtic but classical; (*b*) that the story is too well told to be an unaided native production, and is in other ways unlike the native tales; and, (*c*) that there are evident signs of acquaintance with French or Norman vocabulary, manners, customs, building, armour, and the like.

On (*a*), which was the original view of Foerster (*Yvain* (1887) xxi), endorsed by Bruce (*Evolution* i 112), and carried to absurd lengths by C. B. Lewis (*Classical Mythology and Arthurian Romance*, London, 1932), the most effective answer is still that of A. C. L. Brown in 1903; parallels between particular incidents in *Yvain-Owein* and particular classical sources are numerous, but no known classical source shows these motifs already combined in the way in which *Yvain-Owein* combines them, whereas amongst Celtic sources it is possible to find the same set of motifs combined in the same way and at an earlier date (see below, section IX). It would be too much of a coincidence for Crestien to have put together from classical sources in the twelfth century a plot which already existed in Irish several centuries earlier.

Bruce puts his argument on point (*b*) thus: 'The French origin of the three Welsh tales . . . is indicated unmistakably by their coherent structure . . .' (*Evolution* i 46), and again: 'The differences, however, in style and construction between the three Welsh tales . . . and the unquestionably native tales in the *Mabinogion*, such as *Kulhwch and Olwen* or *Branwen, Daughter of Llyr*, are too plain to deny. Instead of the incoherence and ineffectual rambling of the latter, we have here organization and order' (ibid. 70). He also suggests that the romances show a lack of geographical precision uncharacteristic of the native tales: 'instead of the precise localization of the genuine Welsh stories, which makes it possible even at the present day to follow with substantial exactness the movements of their heroes in Wales, everything is vague and shadowy' (ibid. 47); again, Arthur's standing in the romances differs from his position in the native Welsh sources, 'Arthur in the three tales is the *roi fainéant* of the French romances, not the active hero of Welsh saga' (ibid. 70).

In choosing *Kulhwch* as an example of a native tale to contrast with the superior organization and coherence of the three romances, Bruce selected the one amongst the surviving Welsh prose narratives that is least well executed, but he did not make any allowance either for its plan being systematic enough (the framework-story enclosing a number of contributory incidents, first enumerated and then described in detail) or for the fact that such a plan, while it may hold together a number of separate tales, of very unequal size and complexity, cannot and does not attempt to fuse them into a unified plot. *Kulhwch* does not provide a sound basis for

INTRODUCTION lxxiii

comparison, since, unlike the romances, it does not pretend to be a single story. Comparison with the Four Branches or the other native tales is much more apposite, and gives a much less unfavourable picture of the 'incoherence and ineffectual rambling' of Welsh story-telling. It is interesting to note here that not every student of the subject has found F more to his taste than W: T. Gwynn Jones (*Aberystwyth Studies* 8 (1926) 82) writes: 'In the poems of Chrétien de Troyes, the narrative is long and tortuous, with many unnecessary and cumbersome deflections, so that even if the Welsh versions are composite redactions, then the Welsh writers were incomparably the best storytellers, judged by any standard.' Even Loth can say (*Mabinogion* i 70):

> Il est même remarquable que dans l'ensemble, *Owen et Lunet*, *Peredur*, *Gereint et Enid* sont supérieurs aux romans français correspondants. Au point de vue artistique, la supériorité des écrivains gallois est également incontestable. On ne peut que souscrire au jugement d'Alfred Nutt. Comme il le dit, aucun écrivain français du temps de Chrétien, ni en France ni en Angleterre, ne saurait lutter contre les Gallois comme conteurs. Chez les Français, l'histoire se déroule lentement, terne, incolore, embarrassée de maladroites répétitions, de digressions oiseuses. Chez les Gallois, la narration est vivante, colorée, mettant en relief avec un sûr instinct artistique, les traits de nature à produire un effet pittoresque et romantique.

In the following footnote he adds: 'A l'appui, Nutt compare le début de la *Dame de la Fontaine* jusqu'à la fin du récit de Kynon, au début de Chrétien. Il est certain que la comparaison est tout à l'avantage du conteur gallois.'

When Bruce argues that the geographical vagueness of the romances is like that of Crestien and unlike the precision of the native tales, he rather oversimplifies the contrast. Despite the absence of place-names the descriptions of routes are, if anything, more precise in W than in F, while in the use of place-names Crestien made some unfortunate gaffes (cf. Loth,

Mab. i 53–54). We have to remember that these stories are originally folk-tales, and that though they have become attached to historically real people, the people themselves all belong to Brythonic territories outside Wales and had not yet, at the time the romances attained a fixed form, been relocalized in Wales. Perhaps it is for this reason that the story-teller is prepared to accept Geoffrey's localization of Arthur's court at Caerlleon-on-Usk, whereas *Kulhwch* and *BR* still connect him with Cornwall.

Bruce also exaggerates the contrast in speaking of Arthur as an active hero in native tradition and a *roi fainéant* in the romances. Though in *Kulhwch* he takes part in the rescue of Eidoel and Mabon and hunts Twrch Trwyth in person, most of the adventures are regarded as too trivial for a person of his eminence to engage in (WBM 489. 28–30). Only when the others fail does he step in, as when he kills the witch with Carnwennan (WBM 506. 20–24). It is interesting, too, to note that Arthur should be represented as saying, 'Ydym wyrda hyt tra yn dygyrcher. Yd yt uo mwyhaf y kyuarws a rothom, mwyuwy uyd yn gwrdaaeth ninheu ac an clot ac an hetmic' ('We are noble men so long as we are resorted to. The greater bounty we show, all the greater will be our nobility and our fame and our glory' J & J), for here is the germ of the idea of his court as the great centre and resort of heroes. We may notice, too, that Kei in *Kulhwch* is already ungracious in not wishing to admit the late-comer Kulhwch (WBM 458. 24), and touchy, as in his reaction to the englyn that Arthur composed about him after the adventure with the giant Dillus (WBM 495. 32), though still retaining his traditional preeminence in arms. The less attractive side of his character is hinted at also in his father's description of him as *kyndynnyawc* (WBM 465. 1).

The third point, (*c*) above, the belief that the romances are pervaded by French elements in language, dress, etc., is

INTRODUCTION lxxv

worthy of more serious consideration in connexion with the question of dating the composition as we now have it, though it has no direct bearing on the question of origins. The suggestion that Medieval Welsh prose literature reflects a French milieu has most recently and most fully been dealt with by Emeritus Professor Morgan Watkin in his *La Civilisation française dans les Mabinogion* (Paris, 1963), not with respect to the romances, where he may have thought his case was already conceded by general consent, but with regard to BR, PKM, BM, and K & O, where it is likely to be contested, to judge from previous criticism of his views on the subject by Loth (RC 39. 227–40 and 40. 442–51), by S. J. Williams (*Llên Cymru* 5. 90), and by T. Jones (*Bulletin* 13. 17–19). He adduces evidence under a number of headings, conveniently summarized CFM 428–34, and concludes that since so much of the detail of life and manners in these texts is an imitation of twelfth-century or later French civilization, in their present form none can be earlier than the thirteenth century.[1]

[1] Professor Watkin would date BR to the end of the thirteenth century (CFM 102), PKM to the first half or middle of the thirteenth century (294), BM to the first half of the fourteenth century (349), and K & O to the middle of the thirteenth century (426). He is careful to make clear that he is dealing only with the final forms of these texts: 'Nous ne devons toutefois en aucun cas perdre de vue que la conclusion que nous développons ci-dessus s'applique seulement à la version des Mabinogion telle qu'elle nous est parvenue. Elle ne s'applique pas aux versions dans lesquelles ils ont pu paraître dans le passé.' But we cannot so easily evade the consequences of his conclusions. The early dating of these texts depends primarily on orthographic evidence, and such evidence cannot exist without there having been a continuous tradition of copying and imperfect modernization between the date of the extant manuscripts and the date implied by the sporadic archaic spellings. Thus the whole text virtually in every detail except orthography, occasional modernizations in vocabulary, and perhaps some minor ones in syntax, must go back to the earliest date suggested by the oldest stratum of orthography surviving in it. Professor Watkin, on the other hand, is arguing that these texts reflect a Welsh milieu so deeply penetrated by French and Anglo-Norman civilization that they cannot have attained their

Professor Watkin is in danger of trying to prove too much, and makes too little allowance for the folk-tale elements in these stories. It is unwise to assume that mention of magnificent buildings, costly fabrics, gold and silver plate, and an abundance of good food and drink, can only be the result of seeing the exterior and interior of Norman castles in Wales. A. C. L. Brown made a good point in this connexion when he noted (*Romanic Review* 3. 160) that this magnificence is found only in the description of what was originally an other-world scene or fairy landscape. BR illustrates very well this contrast between sordid realism in the description of this world and the brilliant colourful fantasy of the dream-world. Similarly, from an Irish source we may compare SCC 109–10, 449–52, 486–9, 494–501, 512–13, 561–4.

The names of fabrics and materials, *pali, cordwal, bliant, ysgarlat, gra, syndal, seric, eliffant*, as luxury items of foreign provenance naturally have foreign names, and in such cases it is usual for the name used in the last country the new material has passed through to be adopted, though here the last two are probably Latin. The presence of only the first three in PKM may suggest the conclusion that *Owein* is a more recent composition. The names of items of clothing and the like, other than those of native or Latin origin, viz. *swrcot, orffreis*,

present form before the dates he suggests, that our scribal tradition cannot therefore go any further back than these dates, and that before these dates the tales circulated orally, open to continuous modification under the pressure of French civilization, and that no manuscript now surviving preserves the uncontaminated versions. The two views are thus too much opposed to be reconciled in the way he suggests. Either his thesis must be unsound in detail, in that he exaggerates the quantity and the lateness of the French elements in the tales, or else the system of dating by orthographic archaism must be unreliable, as would be the case, for example, if it could be shown that the 'archaic' spellings are not to be related to date but to location, and proceed not from different periods in the development of a unitary Welsh orthography, but from different and contemporaneous schools of orthography. This is a subject to which I hope to return elsewhere.

twel, cwnsallt, are not easy to date; all except the last occur in Middle English, none recorded earlier than about 1300, but this reflects the shortage of documents rather than telling us when the words were introduced, and there is in any event no reason to think they entered Welsh from English rather than from Norman French.

The fair curly hair with which Lunet and the two young marksmen are endowed is taken by Watkin as a clear case of Norman influence. He assumes that such a preference must develop among a fair-haired people, but it is not at all certain that those of darker colouring may not admire fair hair, and there is some evidence that they do. More to the point, the fact that Olwen is fair, in a tale whose linguistic antiquity, despite Watkin's efforts, shows it can hardly be post-Conquest, suggests that the admiration of fair hair is older than Norman fashion. The Saxons, if one dare mention it, were also fair. As regards shaving, Watkin quotes evidence (CFM 49) that from 1230 to 1314 French gentlemen were clean-shaven, and assumes that the same practice in Welsh literature must be an imitation of this French fashion. We may note that Olwen's father was going to shave for his daughter's wedding, but perhaps this is too much in the nature of a special occasion to count as evidence of a general practice. But there is no need to wait until 1230; in the Bayeux tapestry almost everyone except King Edward is clean-shaven, though the English have moustaches, and, according to recent studies (cf. *The Bayeux Tapestry, a Comprehensive Survey* (London, 1957), 11), the work is to be dated 1070–80.

The names of weapons and the like are mostly native or else much older borrowings from Latin or Old English. Medieval Welsh did not create a distinct word for 'armour', but used the pl. *arueu*, which also means 'weapons'; occasionally the reference seems to be to armour, as when Kynon's *arueu* are cleaned by six of the twenty-four maidens

(66), though this applies to chain-mail such as the Saxons used as much as to plate-armour, or when Owein is given *dogyn o arueu gwr a march* (637), where the mention of armour for the horse suggests a rather late date, perhaps the second half of the thirteenth century, as does the statement that Gwalchmei's *cwnsallt* covered both himself and his horse. The *penngwch pwrqwin* (274) worn by the knight of the spring next his scalp is presumably made of Burgundian cloth; the name of the region is already found in BM (WBM 188. 32). In his edition Sir Ifor Williams quotes (p. xxi) Nutt's opinion that BM was redacted about 1150, but adds that the traditions on which it is founded are older than Geoffrey of Monmouth and quite independent of him. Sir Ifor's text is that of RB; had he then (1908) taken into account the orthography of Peniarth MS. 16, he might well have found in it additional reason for preferring an earlier date than Nutt's.

The practice of fighting on horseback with lances (Medieval Welsh uses the ordinary word for 'spear') has often been seen as an instance of continental influence on the Welsh stories, for Saxon and Scandinavian practice was to use horses for transport but to dismount to fight. The practice is also found in PKM, as in Pwyll's encounter with Hafgan (*Pwyll* 112–16); it is possible, of course, that we have here a tradition from earlier times, rather like the Irish references to fighting from chariots continuing long after the practice—attested by classical historians—had ceased. The regularity with which, in such encounters, the opponents unseat one another without inflicting other serious injury, does, however, require rather substantial protective armour. The two names of types of horses mentioned, *gwascwyn* and *palffrei*, are both clearly loan-words. Watkin argues (CFM 341) that the latter cannot go back beyond 1250 because of the loss of the medial *-e-* and final *-d* of OFr *palefreid*. It should, however, be noted that the lost second syllable comes in the weakest possible position for

INTRODUCTION lxxix

survival, whether in French or Welsh; in the former it is situated between the two more strongly stressed syllables, and immediately before the main stress; in the latter, if the borrowing could have taken place before the Welsh stress-shift it might well have been eliminated as being the weak syllable immediately before the stress, and if, as is much more likely, it was borrowed after the shift to penultimate stressing in Welsh, it would be the French secondarily stressed first syllable that would become the Welsh stressed syllable, and the weak second (French) syllable would be syncopated to preserve the penultimate nature of the Welsh stress. The second syllable was obviously too weak to attract the stress in Welsh; the same fate, for similar reasons, befell it in English before 1300. On the loss of -*d* through a spirant stage, cf. Pope, §§ 347, 1175, 'both sounds [θ, ð] seem to have become obsolete in the beginning of the twelfth century' in AN and earlier on the continent. We should perhaps amend Professor Watkin's 1250 to 1100, a perfectly acceptable date. The only other word for which phonological arguments have been advanced (CFM 97–98) is *ystondard*, the -*on*- of which is explained as a development of AN -*aun*-, which appears not earlier than 1200 (cf. Pope, § 1152, 'in the early thirteenth century'), with -*on*- rare until after 1250. In this case we seem rather to have to do with an English than a French development, and *standard* is one of the very early French loan-words in Middle English. In the West Midland area -*on*- for OE -*an*- is normal (cf. R. Jordan, *Handbuch der mittelenglischen Grammatik*, Heidelberg, 2 edn. 1934, § 30), and in this area French -*an*- would be assimilated to the same pronunciation. This explanation is confirmed by the evidence for Welsh -*o*- for OE and ME -*a*- collected in EEW § 7, pp. 52–53; it is from the West Midland dialects that English loan-words most easily pass into Welsh.

The word *ysparduneu* 'spurs' is of French origin, but, as it occurs in the Laws in the Black Book of Chirk about 1200, it is presumably already well established. Their *troelleu* or 'rowels' are apparently more datable: Sir Guy Laking in his *Record of European Armour and Arms* (London, 1920–2) iii 164 writes: 'We mention the rowel spur of this [thirteenth] century because, though it was certainly used, it is but rarely represented.' He illustrates it, fig. 969, from an early thirteenth-century brass, and notes that it also occurs on the first Great Seal of Henry III.

Some traces of a feudal society may be discerned in the words *barwn* and *parc*. The former is found in Middle English texts perhaps even before 1200, but its introduction was no doubt much earlier; *parc* is rather uncertain, for though the form is closer to ME and OFr, it is not impossible that it should represent OE *pearroc*. The execution of Lunet by burning, and her rescue by Owein in what may be interpreted as a judicial battle, can also be seen as reflections of continental legal practice; for the former see the discussion by J. R. Reinhard in *Speculum* 16. 186–209. Burning does seem at one time to have been countenanced by Welsh law, if we may rely on the passage in the Black Book of Chirk (129. 26) *ay dyhenyd ew yn ewyllys yr argluyd nay grogy nay losgy a uynno* 'and the manner of his execution is at the discretion of the lord, whether he wishes to hang him or burn him', with reference to cases of poisoning. Cf. too AL 2. 230 (MS. Z), 486, 624, but these may be no more than misconstructions of the main text at 230. References to burning occur in Irish legendary material, but Reinhard (art. cit. 208) quotes Thurneysen for the opinion that such traditions might go back to before the period of the Laws. For the references to *yspytty*, see note on 809.

Building in stone and the presence of turrets or towers may reflect Norman castle architecture, but we may note some earlier instances than those in the romances, e.g. K & O *kaer uaen gymrwt* (WBM 486. 7) and *y maendy hwnn* (492. 35), or in PKM *kaer uawr aruchel a gueith newyd arnei yn lle ny welsynt na maen na gueith eiryoet* (55. 20), and in BM *a phrif tyroed amyl amliwawc a welei ar y gaer* (WBM 180. 1). It would be strange if Welsh tradition preserved no memories of the glory of Roman buildings, when the Anglo-Saxon poets could be stirred by the contemplation of their ruins.

The upper room in which Lunet entertains Owein is called *llofft*, a Norse loan-word. In the description of its decoration the passage 318–20 has been seen, e.g. by Foerster, as a direct reminiscence of Crestien's lines 963–6 *la sale . . . Qui tote estoit cielee a clos Dorez et peintes les meisieres De buene oevre et de colors chieres*; but the details are interchanged, for in *Owein* it is the nails that are coloured and the panels gilt. The relationship between the two accounts is uncertain; it is the only descriptive feature that W and F have in common, so that it is hardly sufficient to prove dependence of one text upon the other, and yet it is hard to regard it as pure coincidence.

The portcullis (*dor byrchauat*) which just misses Owein and bisects his horse is also likely to be regarded as a sign of the narrator's acquaintance with Norman fortifications, and such a conclusion is the more damaging to our assumption of an early date in that this detail is an essential part of the story. While it is perfectly true that the portcullis itself is likely to be a rationalization of something more magical (see above, p. lxviii, and below, section IX), the form that rationalization takes is not unimportant. Nevertheless, though Brown naturally enough thought of the portcullis that was to be seen at every castle gate, this is very likely another instance of the survival in Welsh tradition of the memory of Roman buildings and fortifications. The portcullis without and the gate within is precisely the Roman arrangement, as well as the defensive towers to prevent attacks on the walls. We may read about them in the fourth-century *De re militari* of Vegetius iv 4— 'Cauetur praeterea, ne portae subiectis ignibus exurantur. Propter quod sunt coriis ac ferro tegendae; sed amplius prodest, quod inuenit antiquitas, ut ante portam addatur propugnaculum, in cuius ingressu ponitur cataracta, quae anulis ferreis ac funibus pendet, ut, si hostes interauerint, demissa eadem extinguantur inclusi'; and for the towers in iv 2—but in the tradition of the *kyuarwyd* they were still alive, transplanted into a faery landscape.

The exotic animals, the serpents and lions round the giant herdsman, and the serpent and lion whose struggles Owein interrupted, form another possible piece of evidence for dating. A good deal of attention has been given to the grateful lion, which has generally been seen as an oriental importation in Crestien's work, perhaps drawn from the Androcles story, but, more usefully for dating, probably as based on the experience of some crusader. The fullest discussion is by A. G. Brodeur in *Publications of the Modern Language Association of America* 39. 485–524; he traces the theme from Gellius and Pliny, showing the gradual evolution in it of chivalric features, and believes that it did not attain the form it has in *Yvain-Owein* before the early twelfth century. Another important contribution is that of Th. M. Chotzen in *Neophilologus* 18. 51–58 and 131–6, in which he draws attention to the Celtic parallels to beasts, like Owein's ravens in BR, the wolf-dogs of the ancient Gauls, the steeds of Cuchulain and Conall, which fought for their masters. (There is some argument whether we are to look for parallels to helping or guiding or fighting animals.) Both *sarff* and *llew* are Latin, not French, loan-words in Welsh, and whatever help the lion incidents may give in dating *Yvain* they do nothing, in view of the evidence for guiding and fighting beasts in Celtic legend, to fix the date of *Owein*. The freedom with which the lion is introduced in the giant herdsman episode also suggests that it was quite at home in Welsh story-telling (cf. *Peredur* WBM 146. 1), as it was in early Welsh poetry (cf. *Llên Cymru* 4. 213 note 47); it appears at this point in French only in one manuscript, probably suggested by the words *lieparz* (leopards), itself a misreading, like *ors* (bears) for *tors* (bulls) in the same line (280), as is shown by the reference (348) to their having *corz* (horns). For most of the points mentioned above, cf. also KB, chap. 51.

We have now completed our survey of the evidence for the proposition that *Owein* could not have the form it has unless it had been influenced by the *Yvain*, or else composed in a milieu thoroughly steeped in French civilization. At first sight there is quite a considerable amount of such evidence, but on closer inspection a good deal of it, as we have just seen, turns out to be open to other interpretations. We are left with two points suggesting a date in the thirteenth century, the rowels of Owein's spurs and the armour for the horse as well as the rider, and two which may indicate a dependence on or knowledge of the *Yvain*, the decoration of the room in which Owein is concealed and the name of Lunet. While these are not insuperable obstacles to our adopting the mid-twelfth-century date for *Owein* which we have proposed on other grounds, they await a more convincing explanation than we are at present able to offer.

E. The common-source theory concludes by assuming that the hypothetical, and as yet unreconstructed, common source Y is translated from French into Welsh, and perhaps slightly modified in the light of existing Welsh tradition. The details supposed to be added or altered at this stage from native tradition have not been specified, but we may suppose they include all those points in which W is fuller than Y—in the absence of any satisfactory delimitation of Y we can hardly be more precise—and for which parallels can be produced. It has been left for R. M. Jones to point out in *Llên Cymru* 4. 208–27 the improbability of a theory that necessitates the assumption that the Welsh story upon which Y is founded (as is now generally agreed) had survived long enough to be picked up in its homeland by Breton conteurs before 1100, carried back to the continent for processing during the twelfth century, and re-exported before the end of that century, and that meanwhile the native tale had died out on its own ground. This notion that the local version could go out of currency in so short a time is difficult to accept. The reason for this assumption of obsolescence and replacement appears to be that there would otherwise be two competing, and perhaps in some points contradictory, versions circulating at the same time. But we have already concluded from the difficulty of seeing W as an adaptation, however free, of F, that Y must be much closer to W than to F. We have also seen that there are very few features in W that demand either a knowledge of F or a date as late as the thirteenth century, and that their number may be reduced even further. In short, we suppose on these grounds that Y was simply the Breton conteur's French (prose?) version of W as it existed in the eleventh century. If we can agree that there was no substantial difference between W and Y but the points mentioned at the end of section D above, then there is no need to assume that the story died out in Wales after it was exported to France, because there is no conflicting variant version retranslated from French for it to contend with. It simply survives, possibly with a few touches added later.

IX. *Remoter Sources*

The view that Crestien de Troyes invented the whole plot of his *Yvain* out of his own head or put it together for himself from a number of classical stories may now be regarded as untenable. That it can be so regarded is in large measure due

INTRODUCTION

to the work of A. C. L. Brown. In his *Iwain* he expressed dissatisfaction with Foerster's view of the plot as consisting of four motifs: a story about a spring, Gyges ring, the matron of Ephesus, and Androcles and the lion, and with his belief that the easily consoled widow is the central theme, showing how different is the anti-feminine satire of that story from the *Yvain*. He preferred to regard the tale as basically a fairy-mistress story, and illustrated from a number of Irish and Welsh sources the character of such fairy-mistresses, as beings distinctly superior to their mortal lovers, whom they choose and summon to them, and showed too that the journey to their abode often involved crossing water. The most notable parallel to the scenario of *Yvain-Owein* is the Irish tale of *Serglige Con Culainn* (ed. M. Dillon (Dublin, 1953) to which references below relate; Professor Dillon has also translated the text in *Scottish Gaelic Studies* 7. 47–75).

Brown sums up the resemblances as follows (*Iwain* 39 ff.):

(i) 'It is the account given by a previous adventurer Loeg that stirs Cuchulainn to undertake the Other-World Journey', just as Calogrenant's account provokes Yvain.

(ii) 'In both stories the encounter with the Other-World folk is provoked by going to a particular spot and performing a particular act'; Cuchulainn sits against the pillar-stone, Yvain pours the water.

(iii) 'In both there is a tree from which a flock of birds sings with harmony, while close at hand is "a noble well".'

(iv) 'There is a dangerous passage on the way to the Other World, according to the *Serglige*, from which Loeg is told that he will not return alive unless a woman protects him. Liban therefore takes him by the shoulder at this point. Similarly in the *Ivain* the hero escapes from the peril at the falling gates by the aid of a woman, Lunete, who is, like Liban, the messenger and *confidante* of the lady.'

(v) 'In both stories the hero must be the victor in a combat before he secures the lady's hand. Cuchulainn slays Eochaid Iúil and Senach Síabortha. Iwain slays Escalados the Red.'

(vi) 'In both the hero marries the lady. In both he leaves her to return to his own land.'

(vii) 'In both, for a slight offense (in the *Serglige*, because of his having revealed to his wife the appointed place of meeting; in the *Ivain* for having overstayed his time), he loses her.'

(viii) 'In both, the result is the madness of the hero, who runs wild in the forests or on the mountains.'

(ix) 'In both cases he is cured by a marvellous remedy: Iwain by an ointment of "Morgue la sage", Cuchulinn by a druidical "drink of forgetfulness".'

Beyond this point in the two stories there seemed to Brown to be no similarity in the adventures of the two heroes, and at this date (1903) he was reduced to suggesting that 'the remaining incidents of the romance are most of them evidently of Chrétien's own introduction. . . . A probable explanation of Chrétien's extensive insertions and additions toward the end of the romance is that he desired to bring his piece up to the length of his *Erec*, *Cligès*, and *Lancelot*. He may also have been unwilling to close without including a little of the knightly service to ladies which was a convention of his time.'

In addition to a general similarity in the incidents and the order in which they occur in these two texts, Brown was able to point (*Iwain* 70–94) to parallels to the Giant Herdsman, the Perilous Passage, and the Otherworld Landscape at the spring. We may briefly notice these:

(i) Parallels to the Giant Herdsman are found in a number of passages in *Immram Curaig Maíle Dúin* (ed. A. G. van Hamel in *Immrama* (Dublin, 1941) 20–53 (prose) and 54–77 (verse); see p. 24 for dating). Brown noted six points about Crestien's herdsman: he is (1) 'a hideous beast-like giant', (2) 'perched upon a tree-trunk', (3) 'guarding a herd of animals', (4) which are 'savage beasts who fight each other arrogantly', yet

(5) 'the monster herdsman is able to seize any one of them in a terrible way', and finally (6) 'he points out to the traveller the road to a marvellous land'. In § 23 of the *immram* items 1, 2, 3, and 5 of this series are combined, in § 13 items 1, 3, and 6, and in § 9 there is a parallel to item 4. The reader will find that these parallels are not very close, but they are perhaps no more remote than the distance in time and space of the two texts would lead us to expect. Brown had to admit too that 'they [the six items] do not all, to be sure, occur united in one incident', but he thought that 'enough of them are so joined to make the parallel hold good. Everything, therefore, seems to indicate that this is a stock episode of the Celtic Other-World Journey, which has been preserved by Chrétien in his *Ivain*, with but little change from its more primitive form.'

(ii) Quotations suggestive of a Perilous Passage: (1) in the same *immram* § 17, line 401 f., there is a glass bridge on which no one could keep his feet (and a bronze door with pillars, see van Hamel's variants, p. 127) leading to a *dún*; (2) the description in the poem *Preideu Annwn* of 'the isle of the strong door' (on which see now R. S. Loomis in *Wales and the Arthurian Legend* (Cardiff, 1956) 131–78; (3) a revolving door or barrier in the same *immram* § 32, line 791 f., and a locked door in § 27, line 593; (4) another revolving rampart in *Fled Bricrend* (Irische Texte (Leipzig, 1880)) 1. 295, § 80, line 12 f., also ed. and trans. G. Henderson, Irish Texts Society vol. 2 (London, 1899), § 80, adopting the reading *déinithir* for LU's *demithir*). Brown concluded: 'It is perfectly clear, then, that a revolving barrier, or an active door of some kind, was a widespread motive of Celtic Other-World story. *A priori*, therefore, we have reason to believe that it must have been present in the material that Chrétien used when he was writing his *Ivain*. What could he do with the motive, supposing he decided to keep it at all? Would he not naturally rationalize it into the familiar portcullis, to be seen at every castle gate?'

(iii) The chief feature of the Other-World landscape in *Ivain* are: 'there is (1) a magnificent tree, (2) whose leaves do not fade summer or winter, and (3) whose foliage is so dense that rain cannot pass through it, (4) standing by a fountain. (5) The tree is full of birds, who sing not in unison, but in harmony, and (6) their song is really a divine service.' In *Immram Brain maic Febail* (van Hamel's *Immrama* 1–19) st. 7 we have the birds singing in harmony, and the word *tráth* used here (ll. 35, 37) can mean 'canonical hour' as well as 'time' in general; in the same text, st. 43 (ll. 186–7), there is a wood without decay and without defect and with golden foliage; in *Immram Curaig Maíle Dúin* § 18 there are the psalm-singing birds, in § 19 many trees and birds and a well, and in § 20 another, more remarkable well; in *Immram Snédgusa* (van Hamel's *Immrama* 78–85 (prose), 86–92 (verse)) § 4 a similar passage about birds, trees, and singing like that of psalms occurs; and finally in SCC, § 33, ll. 494–506, we find again associated wonderful trees, birds, and a well. Only point 3, the density of the foliage, is not paralleled.

Brown concludes: 'It is only on Celtic ground that stories written before the time of Chrétien can be pointed out that contain all of the important features of the landscape at the Fountain Perilous. Few things are, therefore, more certain than that the marvellous landscape of Chrétien's Fountain is derived from Celtic sources.'

A further parallel to the *Yvain* is to be found, according to Brown, in Malory's seventh book, interspersed with other adventures; it is the story of Gareth, for the relevant parts of which see E. Vinaver's edition of *The Works of Sir Thomas Malory* (London, 1954), 215 f., 232 f., 236 f., 241 f. Its antecedents are unknown, but Brown regarded it in some respects as a more primitive account than Crestien's. Thus in

Malory a messenger really does come to summon the hero, Lynet is sister to the mistress of the castle, the red knight is challenged by blowing a horn, and there is no lion. He accordingly regarded it (*Iwain* 144) as 'a late and extremely confused form of an ancient Celtic Other-World tale which some transcriber, noticing its resemblances to the *Ivain*, has worked over to make the resemblance still closer, and that this redactor has named the lady's messenger Lynet'. There are some points of similarity to *Owein* also in this version, e.g. in the assurance that Arthur will come in search of him (*Malory* 246, *Owein* 552), in the series of combats with Arthur's knights before his identity is known (*Malory* 259–60, *Owein* 510–12), and in his fight with Gawain (*Malory* 267, *Owein* 518–37); there is also a curious verbal parallel in the description of a thunderstorm (*Malory* 263) 'as hevyn and erthe should go togydir', while one later manuscript (S) of *Owein* has *y nef ar dhayar yn dyfod yng-hyd* in connexion with the noise made by the mourners at the Black Knight's funeral, and *y Nef ar ddayar yn dwad ynghyd* of the noise that follows pouring water on the slab at the spring (*Owein* 347, 151).

Despite our feeling that some of Brown's comparisons are inadequate or somewhat forced, in general we may agree with his conclusion that 'parallels to every important incident of the main portion of Chrétien's *Ivain* [from the beginning to the appearance of the lion] are found in ancient Celtic stories belonging to one clearly defined type. Most of the themes thus traced appear united in a single Irish Other-World tale, the *Serglige Conculaind*.' Since there is evidence that SCC goes back to at least the ninth century in part, it would certainly be a striking coincidence for Crestien about 1170 to have combined so many of the same motifs in the same way. The reader will observe, of course, that it is only in terms of this kind of analysis into motifs that there can be said to be a striking similarity between the plots of SCC and the *Yvain*;

the unprepared reader will no more observe it than he will notice the similarities which Professor Carney finds (*Studies in Irish Literature and History*, Dublin, 1955, chap. iii) between *Beowulf* and *Táin Bó Fraích* simply on reading the two texts. 'Any other theory', says Brown, speaking of Crestien's source, 'is compelled to regard the entire romance as essentially a jumble of incidents, arranged without any definite thread of connexion.'

In 1905 he complemented his discussion of the first half of the *Yvain* by an article on the 'Knight of the Lion' in PMLA 20. 673–706. SCC does not provide a satisfactory parallel to the second part of the poem, from the point at which the hero realizes he has lost his wife, for the remainder of the Irish tale is contained in two short paragraphs (§§ 47–48, ll. 826–43). Cu Chulainn runs wild in the mountains without food or drink for a long time, till at his wife Emer's suggestion Conchobar sends poets, learned men, and druids from Ulster to bring him home. He attacks them, but the druids put a spell on him and give him a drink of forgetfulness, and his wife's jealousy of his fairy mistress, Fand, is dealt with in the same way.

The theme of madness or a period of existence alone in the forests or mountains followed by some sort of cure is common to both the Irish and French tales, though greatly elaborated in the latter. It may be noted in passing that madness is not actually mentioned in either the Irish or the Welsh stories, and that the 'woodnesse' of Gareth in Malory (243) is a madness of rage at the abduction of his dwarf, not of frustrated passion.

In the events after the hero's loss of his wife Brown sees a parallel or repetition of the first part of the story: the hero again sets out alone through a tangled wilderness, is kindly received (in the first part by the hospitable host, in the second by the lady who cures him), is guided on his way (in the first part by the herdsman, in the second by the lion), is successful in a combat (in the first part with Escalados, in the second with the seneschal), and as a result gains or regains Laudine. This parallelism is, of course, far from exact: the Earl Alier episode and that of Harpin de la Montagne are not accounted for. Brown had, however, taken cognisance of the Welsh version by this time, and regarded its arrangement as more primitive than Crestien's, so that he was able to dispense with any obligation to explain the quarrelling sisters, the *pesme avanture*, and the fight with Gawain, as original constituents of the second part. His parallelism, while not perfect, is much more nearly so than it could have been if he had accepted the *Yvain* as the primary version.

In the absence of any help from SCC Brown turned to another Irish story, again from the Ulster cycle, and concerned with the adventures of Cu Chulainn, to support his belief that there was a Celtic story, or stories, behind Crestien's narrative. The Irish tale is *Tochmarc Emire* (ed. van Hamel in his *Compert Con Culainn and other stories* (Dublin, 1933) 16–68, translated in Eleanor Hull, *The Cuchullin Saga in Irish Literature* (London, 1898) 55 ff. a revised abridgement of a translation by Kuno Meyer in *Archæological Review* 1 (1888)). The relevant portion is § 63 f. (transl. 73 ff.) in which Cu Chulainn, on his way to study warfare under Scáthach, and separated from his companions, is accosted by a large and fearful creature like a lion, which keeps in front of him whichever way he goes, and keeps its flank turned toward him as if inviting him to mount it. He does so, but has to be content to let it take him where it will. It carries him for four days until they reach an inhabited region, and there he dismounts and they part. He comes next (§ 64) to a big house in a great glen where he is received by a maiden who surprises him by knowing his name—they had been fostered and educated together—and who gives him refreshment. On leaving her, he meets (§ 65) a youth who directs him on his way across the plain of ill-luck, and gives him a wheel and an apple to follow across it. Beyond that lies a great valley with a thin rope (or narrow path, according to whether one reads *tét* or *sét*) across it and monsters waiting to destroy him. He passes the plain and the valley and comes (§ 67) to the camp of Scáthach's pupils, who point out to him the bridge leading to the island where she is. It is low at the ends and high in the middle, and when trodden on at one end the other rises and throws the traveller down. Cu Chulainn makes three unsuccessful attempts to gain a footing on it (§ 68), and finally makes his salmon-leap on to the middle of it and gets across. He forces his way into the fortress, and is met by Scáthach's daughter Úathach, who falls in love with him on sight. He kills Scáthach's champion Cochair Cruibne (§ 69), and consoles her for his loss by taking his place as champion and captain of the host. The reader will notice that there are some further parallels here to the first part of the *Yvain* as well as to *Peredur*.

Parallel to this guiding lion there is the mule in Païen de Maisières's *La Damoisele a la Mule*, also known as the *Mule sans Frein*, ed. B. Orlowski (Paris, 1911), from a manuscript of the late thirteenth or early fourteenth century. It exhibits a number of other parallels to *Yvain*: 'here occur the damsel messenger [ll. 20 f., not in *Yvain*], the failure of the first adventurer [ll. 112–281, Kay, Calogrenant], the solitary journey [l. 117], the dense forest [ll. 131, 358], the savage beasts [ll. 135, 361], the narrow path [ll. 160, 377], the fountain [ll. 216, 383], the perilous passage [ll. 169, 381], the cutting off of half of the mule's tail [ll. 439–70], . . . and lastly the successful combat(s) with the creature(s) of the fay.' Again we may note that this story, like the extract from *Tochmarc Emire* above, is, apart from the guiding beast motif and the partial loss of its tail, parallel to the first half of the *Yvain*, so that Brown presumably meant it as a proof that the second part was in some sense a repetition of the first. The notable parallels between *Tochmarc Emire* and *La Damoisele a la Mule* are the dangerous valley infested with serpents in the latter, like the plain and dangerous valley in the former, the fact that the lion-like creature and the mule both know the way and will not be guided, and the dangerous bridges in both stories. Brown considered the evidence as showing that it was 'almost certain that the entire romance [of *Yvain*] was derived from some one particular tale', and also that it was 'almost certain . . . that a helpful lion must have been an integral part of the original used by Chrétien'.

Brown's case for regarding *Tochmarc Emire* as a close parallel to the second half of the *Yvain* would have been strengthened had he not abandoned his comparison with the end of § 69.[1] In what follows Cu Chulainn extorts from Scáthach instruction in the use of arms (§ 71). She is at war with other tribes led by the famous female warrior Aife (§ 74); she binds and drugs Cu Chulainn, but what would hold another for twenty-four hours holds him only for one, and he joins her two sons in battle, slaying the three sons of Ilsúanach on the first day and the three sons of Éss Énchenn on the next (§ 75). Aife challenges Scáthach to combat, and Cu Chulainn undertakes it; she breaks her sword on him, he distracts her attention, seizes her, throws her over his shoulder and carries her back to his own lines. In exchange for her life he demands three things, two of which are a permanent cessation of hostilities and a giving of hostages to Scáthach (§ 76). Then he sets off for Ireland, and comes (§ 80) at Hallowe'en to the house of Rúad, King of the Isles, where there is great lamentation because the king's daughter (Derbforgaill, § 84) is to be given as tribute to the Fomori (giant sea-demons). He slays

[1] In OGL 51 he continued the summary to the end of the story, but without explicit reference to *Owein*.

the three of them (§ 81) and rescues her, and her father offers her to him in marriage (§ 82). Finally, Cu Chulainn succesfully performs all the feats that Emer named at the beginning of the story (§ 86), and carries her off, defeating all the pursuers (§ 87), and bringing her to Conchobar's court (§ 88), where they were married (§ 90), and never parted as long as they both lived.

The parallels here with *Yvain-Owein* are notably: (1) the training (F), or giving arms (W), by a woman; (2) going out with two squires (W); (3) overcoming her enemy (in W, by carrying the enemy off by main force); (4) exacting terms of peace and hostages from the enemy; (5) the rescue of a maiden from giants, and (6) having her offered in marriage, and finally (7) a combat leading to the obtaining of a wife, with whom (8) the hero returns home. As with the parallels in Malory's seventh book, though not to anything like the same extent, other matter intervenes here and there.

It is apparent, therefore, that from the point at which the hero is cured of his madness (F) or restored to health and strength (W), down to the end of the story—assuming the Welsh order of the incidents, i.e. the absence of the quarrelling sisters and the fight with Gawain, and the treatment of the *pesme avanture* or Du Traws episode as an appendix— *Tochmarc Emire* provides parallels to all the main incidents in the same order. There is, however, one important difference, that the lion-like beast has entered and left the Irish story before Cu Chulainn reaches Scáthach, whereas the lion in Owein enters only after he has rescued his hostess from her oppressive neighbour, and never leaves him, though it plays no part against the Du Traws.

In view of all this the importance of *Tochmarc Emire* for our purpose seems to lie not in its providing a parallel to the guiding, helping lion, which, despite Brown's suggestion that 'we see from it [the Welsh story], though no explanations are given, that the lion guided Iwain back to the Castle of the Fay', it does not really do, but rather in the similarity between its sequence of events and the latter part of *Owein*.

Subsequent work on the subject, notably by R. S. Loomis, first in his *Celtic Myth and Arthurian Romance* (New York, 1927), and most fully in AT, of which pp. 3–58, 269–331, and 463–75 are specially relevant to our text, has reared upon Brown's simple foundations an immensely elaborate structure of sources and analogues for every incident and sometimes for almost every detail of Crestien's poem. If we sometimes feel that the superstructure has become too elaborate to be fully credible, it is largely because the hunt for sources has tended to lose sight of Brown's great advantage over previous investigators, that he postulated a unitary origin for X, the common source of *Yvain* and *Owein*, and found it in one Irish tale, *Serglige Con Culainn*.

If we accept A. C. L. Brown's views, whether in simple or elaborated form, we must, of course, realize that we have at most penetrated only a little way into the antecedents of *Yvain-Owein*. An Irish origin for the story would at most carry us back three or four centuries to a period already Christianized and in which tales originally mythological were in process of euhemerization. What the underlying myths were may be, as Sir Thomas Browne said of the sirens' song, 'not beyond all conjecture' but they are most certainly beyond our direct knowledge. Therefore, whether the conflict at the spring is, as R. M. Jones holds, a myth about the storm god—whence the fact of his being a black knight in *Owein*—probable as it is that some myth of this kind existed in Celtic territory (cf. G. L. Hamilton in *Romanic Review* 2. 355–75 and 5. 213–37, and Louise B. Morgan in *Modern Philology* 6. 331–41), this is the kind of question to which we can give no final answer.

There remains one important question: how did such a story reach Crestien de Troyes? If we were able to say above that he could not have known a tale of *Owein* in the original language, we may be even more certain that he could not read the Irish narratives. Some intermediary there must have been, and it is generally agreed, as a first step, that the Irish stories must have been current in Britain. They may have belonged to a common Celtic fund of story-material, attached in each country to different heroes, and localized in different places; but even if this is not so (and it is in general an assumption that scholars seem unwilling to entertain), there is still ample evidence of cultural contact between Ireland and Wales to make such a transference of themes between the two lands perfectly credible.

After being a considerable time current in Wales, or at least in Brythonic territory, these tales would pass in post-Conquest (perhaps already in pre-Conquest) times into French, and so become available to Crestien or his predecessors. This second transition may have been by one of two routes, and there has been a great deal of dispute about which was in fact used. The earlier view regarded the translation as being from Welsh in Wales and on the borders into Anglo-Norman, and thus to France, but Zimmer and Loomis especially have strongly advocated a different route, in which the intermediaries would be the bilingual Bretons who accompanied Duke William in large numbers to this country, and would have acquired these stories from their Welsh, and perhaps also Cornish, fellow Brythons, and then put them out again in French in both England and France. The main argument in favour of Anglo-Norman transmission is that it is so obviously a possible route; in favour of Breton intermediaries there are the French 'Breton lays', the references to 'as the Bretons say', the fact that the names of characters are sometimes Breton rather than Welsh, and that events may be localized in Brittany, and that the belief in Arthur's return was lively there, as in Cornwall.

There is no reason to exclude either route; what is needed

is a situation in which some Welsh speakers learn French or some French speakers learn Welsh or are already bilingual in a cognate dialect. The offspring of mixed Norman and Welsh parentage fulfil these conditions just as well as the Bretons do; but if rapidity of transfer is important, the Bretons are better placed in the initial stages.[1]

[1] For a summary of the generally accepted views on the questions dealt with in sections IV to IX see I. Ll. Foster in Loomis's *Arthurian Literature in the Middle Ages*, chap. 16. The typescript of this book was almost complete when *Llên Cymru* 6, parts 3 and 4, ostensibly for January and July 1961, actually August 1964, reached me. In an article on *Peredur* (ibid. 138–53) Glenys Goetinck states a number of theses relevant to the discussion earlier in this Introduction. It is encouraging to find that she, and R. M. Jones in his introduction to his modernization of the romances, should propose a date of composition as early as 1100, and that she should maintain that the source of Crestien's French source was an early form of *Peredur*, as I have suggested was the case with *Owein*; and this despite the generally accepted view, stated by Loomis (AT 33): 'Everyone, I believe, agrees that the Welsh tales are somewhat later in date than Chrétien's poems, probably compositions of the thirteenth century. There is no one now, therefore, to contend that they are the sources of Chrétien.' Similarly Professor Foster (op. cit. 192), and (ibid. 205) 'there is good orthographical and linguistic evidence for an exemplar dated about 1200', though he wisely expresses no view about the date of composition. Glenys Goetinck's dating appears to be based on uncertain foundations: (*a*) unitary authorship for the romances, (*b*) a patriotic purpose in the author, and therefore (*c*) composition in a period when political and social conditions are appropriate. I have given some reasons above for doubting (*a*), and without this premise the rest is unconvincing.

In her paper *Professional Interpreters and the Matter of Britain* (Cardiff, 1966) Dr. Constance Bullock-Davies has thrown important new light on the old controversy over transmission by demonstrating the existence in Britain of professional interpreters, and showing that these men could be persons of high rank and broad culture, and so eminently suited to the transmission of Welsh native tradition to a French-speaking audience in their own language.

x. *Literary Qualities*

It may seem that we have spent in fanning the embers of an ancient controversy too much energy that we ought to have devoted to discussing the merits of the Welsh story. Yet in so doing we have only reflected the dominant interest of most of those who have written most on the subject. Medieval literature all too easily becomes a source of problems rather than a source of pleasure, and on a text which has for the most part been studied and cited in translation, we need not expect much in the way of literary appreciation.

Comparison with Crestien's *Yvain* has given rise to some useful observations, as we have already seen, but the two works are too different in the aims of their authors and the interests of their audiences to take us very far. It seems unlikely that either the *kyuarwyd* or Crestien would have much appreciated the work of the other: the former we might expect to echo the sentiments of T. Gwynn Jones and J. Loth quoted above, while the latter might have stigmatized *Owein* as just another of those stories mangled by ignorant *conteurs* which he deplored in *Erec* 20–22.

The first thing that strikes the reader who comes to this story from PKM or K & O is the amount that is familiar in the language and vocabulary; in the notes below and in R. M. Jones's article in *Llên Cymru* 4. 226 some of these are pointed out, and although neither collection is at all complete, sufficient examples have been noted to make the point that *Owein* is composed in what may be called the *kyuarwyd* style. It is essentially an oral style, simple and direct in expression, with no subtleties or obscurities to distract the contemporary hearer from following the story, and helpful to the memory of the story-teller by reason of the set phrases and standard formulas for every frequently recurring situation. This is not to say, of course, that it is a transcript of a particular telling of the story, but rather that whoever gave it a written form for the first time was steeped in this oral style. The contrast with works which are translations, passing from book to book, unspoken, through the mind of the translator, is quite marked, for though in them a certain number of the *kyuarwyð*'s formulas and clichés occur, they do not pervade the whole. Detailed studies of the style of the various kinds of medieval Welsh prose have yet to be written, but I believe they will confirm this impression.

This simplicity and uniformity of language and expression is matched by a simplicity of grammatical structure common to all these prose works in the native tradition. By far the most common conjunction is the co-ordinating 'and', and subordinate clauses are relatively few. Even where the grammarian finds difficulties of analysis, these arise from closeness to natural speech-order being preferred to the artificial effect of a more closely articulated structure. It is part of the directness of the style that reported speech is rare and almost all conversation is re-enacted by the story-teller.

Both simplicity of diction and a speech-like quality have their dangers: prolixity, diffuseness, monotony, digression, incoherence. Our narrator is remarkable for the skill with which he avoids these pitfalls.

His chief safeguard is brevity or conciseness, not carried to excess as we feel it occasionally is in Irish prose tales, so that we are left with notes for a story rather than the story itself, but nevertheless implying a firm resistance to the charms of digression; in Kynon's account of his adventure there are only two short digressions, one on the office of porter at Arthur's court, one on the power of the giant herdsman, neither by any reckoning irrelevant. He is brief, too, in conversation; apart from the usual courtesies nothing is reported but what is to the point, and nothing is repeated or elaborated. The audience was expected to give the *kyuarwyð* their full attention.

The narrator also adheres carefully to the sequence of the story, even to the extent of making it entirely self-contained. He does not, like Crestien, tell us that, of course, Owein and Lunet had met before at Arthur's court, or that the hospitable hostess who spent her precious ointment in restoring him to health recognized him by a scar, or refer to the abduction of Arthur's queen. Yet this adherence to the sequence of the story does not mean that he pushes ahead at one pace and without relief or change of tempo. In a number of ways the narration is varied, and these may be illustrated from Kynon's tale within a tale.

Kynon begins with the reason for his journey and the route he took—all progress in the narrative; then comes the description of the castle, the young men shooting, the host, the twenty-four young women—the inward eye of the imagination is satisfied by the colour and movement, the curiosity is stimulated, but not immediately satisfied. Then come the formal elements of welcome, seating at table, the formulaic praise of the food, and the long silence that gives curiosity a keener edge. Then, at last, the formula of inquiry about the guest and his business sets the story moving again, but our satisfaction that Kynon is on the right road is tempered by vague anxiety stirred by his host's hints of danger, and his apparent unwillingness to tell more. We still do not know what the adventure is, for the host has directed Kynon only to the next stage, the herdsman, and all we have been told is that it lies beyond that point. So Kynon proceeds, but the narrator does not merely repeat what the host had described, for we find that everything has been understated and must now be magnified. In attempting to make friendly advances to the herdsman Kynon inquires about his power over his herd; meanwhile we remain in suspense about his adventure and its outcome. At length the herdsman is persuaded to give Kynon the directions he asks for, culminating this time in

INTRODUCTION

a warning more explicit than that of the host, and at the same time with a note of promise. Kynon presses forward eagerly; the scene is this time shown to have been accurately described by the herdsman, and then comes the climax, his encounter with the Black Knight, over in a single sentence. We are both glad and sorry; sorry that he has not achieved what he hoped for, glad that his fate has been so much less calamitous than the forebodings of the host and the herdsman seemed to portend. Curiosity is now largely allayed, the tension relaxed, and Kynon ruefully recounts his slow return on foot, the withering mockery of the herdsman, and the tactful silence of his hosts. And now the story told by Kynon arouses Owein's interest, and what began as pastime is suddenly serious, so that the one who urged the telling of the story is the one most concerned when once it has been told.

And so it goes on: we know what lies ahead of Owein, and we follow with interest the succession of events leading him to the spring, condensed by the narrator to spare our impatience but without omission, and, as before, with some heightening of details—the beauty of the maidens, the excellence of the food, the size of the herdsman, all are greater than Owein had imagined when Kynon described them, just as Kynon's imagination had fallen short when the herdsman and the storm were described to him. This time the fight with the Black Knight is more equal, and the scale tips the other way. So far Owein has been following a way known to him and to us, but here the familiar ground ends, and the story moves forward into new territory. For the moment we are elated at Owein's victory; then he is caught between the gates, and he seems to have triumphed only to end in a worse plight than Kynon.

Lunet extricates him, however, and once he is safe again we have the quiet, relaxed scenes in her chamber—there is no further hint of pursuit or discovery. He is roused by the three outcries (the narrator is fond of threes, for there are in all three journeys to the spring and on three occasions Owein expresses regret and then puts things right), and the story takes a new turn, with Owein falling in love.

So we might continue, but enough has been said to show how the narrator, especially in the first part of the story (1–218), blends action and conversation, narration and description, in a varied pattern arousing in turn curiosity and concern, satisfaction and delight. Mr. Saunders Lewis does not exaggerate when he describes the three romances as 'perhaps the highest achievement of our prose in the Middle Ages' in his *Braslun o Hanes Llenyddiaeth Gymraeg* (Cardiff, 1932) 44, and bearing in mind, as he does, the Laws and the rest of the Mabinogion, this was no measured praise. There are few places in medieval literature where the modern reader can so easily get so much pleasure in so little space, as from this well-proportioned and well-told tale.

ABBREVIATIONS

AB	Edward Lhuyd, *Archæologia Britannica* (Oxford, 1707).
AT	R. S. Loomis, *Arthurian Tradition and Chrétien de Troyes* (New York, 1949).
B	MS. Llanover B 17 (see Introduction, section I).
BBC	*The Black Book of Carmarthen*, ed. J. Gwenogvryn Evans (Pwllheli, 1906).
BD	*Brut Dingestow*, ed. Henry Lewis (Cardiff, 1942).
BM	*Breudwyt Maxen* (ed. Ifor Williams, Bangor, 1908); cited by column and line of WBM.
BR	*Breudwyt Ronabwy*, ed. Melville Richards (Cardiff, 1948).
Branwen	*Branwen uerch Lyr*, ed. Derick S. Thomson (Dublin, 1961; Mediaeval and Modern Welsh Series II).
Bulletin	*The Bulletin of the Board of Celtic Studies*, University of Wales (Cardiff, 1921–).
C	MS. Cwrtmawr 20 (see Introduction, section I).
CFM	Morgan Watkins, *La Civilisation française dans les Mabinogion* (Paris, 1963).
E	The English poem corresponding to *Owein* (see Introduction, sections V–VII).
EEW	T. H. Parry-Williams, *The English Element in Welsh* (London, 1923; Cymmrodorion Record Series X).
ELIG	Henry Lewis, *Yr Elfen Ladin yn yr Iaith Gymraeg* (Cardiff, 1943).
Essai	Mary Rh. Williams, *Essai sur la composition du roman gallois de Peredur* (Paris, 1909).
Evolution	J. D. Bruce, *The Evolution of Arthurian Romance*, 2 vols. (Göttingen and Baltimore, 1923).
E & L	T. P. Ellis and John Lloyd, *The Mabinogion, a New Translation*, 2 vols. (Oxford, 1929).

F	Crestien's *Yvain*, the French poem corresponding to *Owein* (see Introduction, sections V–IX).
GBGG	J. Lloyd-Jones, *Geirfa Barddoniaeth Gynnar Gymraeg* (Cardiff, 1931–).
GCC	D. Simon Evans, *Gramadeg Cymraeg Canol* (Cardiff, 1951); enlarged English edn., *A Grammar of Middle Welsh* (Dublin, 1965).[1]
Ger.	*Gereint*, cited by column and line of WBM.
GMWL	Timothy Lewis, *A Glossary of Mediaeval Welsh Law* (Manchester, 1913; Publications of the University of Manchester, Celtic Series III).
GOI	Rudolf Thurneysen, *A Grammar of Old Irish* (Dublin, 1946).
GPC	*Geiriadur Prifysgol Cymru*, ed. R. J. Thomas (Cardiff, 1950–).
IEW	John Strachan, *An Introduction to Early Welsh* (Manchester, 1909; Publications of the University of Manchester, Celtic Series I).
Ir	Irish.
Iwain	Arthur C. L. Brown, *Iwain, a Study in the Origins of Arthurian Romance*, (Harvard) Studies and Notes in Philology and Literature VIII (1903) 1–147.
J	MS. Jesus College Oxford 20 (see Introduction, section I).
J & J	Gwyn Jones and Thomas Jones, *The Mabinogion* (London, 1949).
KB	Ernst Windisch, *Das keltische Britannien bis zu Kaiser Arthur* (Leipzig, 1912; Abhandl. der phil.-hist. Kl. der königl. sächsischen Gesellschaft der Wissenschaften, vol. 29, no. 6).
K & O	*Kulhwch and Olwen*, cited by column and line of WBM.
L	MS. Llanstephan 171 (see Introduction, section I)
L.	Latin.
LHEB	Kenneth Jackson, *Language and History in Early*

[1] References to the new edition are added in brackets.

ABBREVIATIONS

	Britain (Edinburgh, 1953; Edinburgh University Publications, Language and Literature 4).
LlB	*Llyfr Blegywryd*, ed. Stephen J. Williams and J. Enoch Powell (Cardiff, 1942).
LlIor	*Llyfr Iorwerth*, ed. Aled Rhys Wiliam (Cardiff, 1960; Board of Celtic Studies, History and Law Series XVIII).
L & P	Henry Lewis and Holger Pedersen, *A Concise Comparative Celtic Grammar* (Göttingen, 1937).
Mab.	J. Loth, *Les Mabinogion*, 2 vols. (Paris, 1913).
ME	Middle English.
MIr	Middle Irish.
MW	Medieval Welsh.
N	The Norse prose tale corresponding to *Owein* (see Introduction, sections V–VI).
NED	*A New English Dictionary on Historical Principles*, ed. James A. H. Murray (Oxford, 1888–1928).
OE	Old English (Anglo-Saxon).
OFr	Old French.
OGL	Arthur C. L. Brown, *The Origin of the Grail Legend* (Cambridge, Mass., 1943).
OIr	Old Irish.
Per.	*Peredur*, cited by column and line of WBM.
PKM	*Pedeir Keinc y Mabinogi*, ed. Ifor Williams (Cardiff, 1930).
PMLA	*Publications of the Modern Language Association of America* (Baltimore, 1884–).
Pwyll	*Pwyll Pendeuic Dyuet*, ed. R. L. Thomson (Dublin, 1957; Mediaeval and Modern Welsh Series I).
R	The text of *Owein* in RB.
RB	*The Text of the Mabinogion . . . from the Red Book of Hergest*, ed. John Rhŷs and J. Gwenogvryn Evans (Oxford, 1887).
RC	*Revue celtique*, 51 vols. (Paris, 1870–1934).
S	(1) The Swedish poem corresponding to *Owein* (see Introduction, sections V–VI).

ABBREVIATIONS

	(2) MS. Llanstephan 58 (see Introduction, section 1).
SCC	*Serglige Con Culainn*, ed. Myles Dillon (Dublin, 1953; Mediaeval and Modern Irish Series XIV).
TBC	*Táin Bó Cuailgne*, the Stowe version ed. Cecile O'Rahilly (Dublin, 1961).
TC	T. J. Morgan, *Y Treigladau a'u Cystrawen* (Cardiff, 1952).
TYP	Rachel Bromwich, *Trioedd Ynys Prydein* (Cardiff, 1961).
W	(1) The text of *Owein* in WBM. (2) The Welsh version of the story (see Introduction, sections V–IX).
WBM	*The White Book Mabinogion*, ed. J. Gwenogvryn Evans (Pwllheli, 1907).
WG	J. Morris Jones, *A Welsh Grammar* (Oxford, 1913).
Y	The hypothetical common source of F and W.
YBH	*Ystorya Bown de Hamtwn*, ed. Morgan Watkin (Cardiff, 1958).
ZCP	*Zeitschrift für celtische Philologie* (Halle, 1897–).

CHWEDYL IARLLES Y FFYNNAWN

Yr amherawdyr Arthur oed yg Kaer Llion ar Wysc. Sef yd oed yn eisted diwarnawt yn y ystauell, ac y gyt ac ef Owein uab Uryen, a Chynon uab Clydno, a Chei uab Kyner; a Gwenhwyuar a'e llawuorynyon yn gwniaw wrth ffenestyr. A chyt dywettit uot porthawr ar lys Arthur, nyt oed yr vn. Glewlwyt Gauaeluawr oed yno hagen ar ureint porthawr y aruoll ysp a phellennigyon, ac y dechreu eu hanrydedu, ac y uenegi moes y llys a'e deuawt udunt; y'r neb a dylyei vynet y'r neuad neu y'r ystauell, o'e venegi idaw; y'r neb a dylyei letty, o'e venegi idaw. Ac ym perued llawr yr ystauell yd oed yr amherawdyr Arthur yn eisted ar demyl o irvrwyn, a llenn o bali melyngoch y danaw, a gobennyd a'e dudet o bali coch dan penn y elin.

Ar hynny y dywawt Arthur, 'Ha wyr, pei na'm goganewch,' heb ef, 'mi a gyskwn tra uewn yn aros vy mwyt; ac ymdidan a ellwch chwitheu, a chymryt ysteneit o ved a golwython y gan Gei.' A chyscu a oruc yr amherawdyr.

A gofyn a oruc Kynon uab Klydno y Gei yr hynn a adawssei Arthur udunt. 'Minneu a vynnaf yr ymdidan da a edewit y minneu,' heb y Kei. 'Ha wr,' heb y Kynon, 'teckaf yw itti wneuthur edewit Arthur yn gyntaf, ac odyna yr ymdidan goreu a wypom ninneu, ni a'e dywedwn itti.' Mynet a oruc Kei y'r gegin ac y'r vedgell, a dyuot ac ysteneit o ved gantaw, ac a gorvlwch eur, ac a lloneit y dwrn o vereu a golwython arnadunt. A chymryt y golwython a wnaethant, a dechreu yvet y med.

The text begins at R, col. 627, and J, f. 16a; W is wanting, 1–35.
1 *a oed* J.   2 *yn y stauell* J.   3 *Kynyr* J.   6 *hagen oed yno* J.
6 *erbynnyeit ysp* J.   8 *y neb* J.   8–9 *dylyey lety o'e venegi idaw y neb a dylyei vened y'r neuad neu y'r stauell o'e venegi idaw. Ac* J.
11 *pali melyn* J.   12 *a'r gobennyd* J.   13 *Arthur a dywawt* J.
13 *goganawch* J.   16 *oruc Arthur* J.   18 *heb y Kei* after *vynnaf* J.
21–22 *y'r vedgell ac y'r gegin* J.   22–23 omit *ac* twice J.   24 *A chymryt*: *Kymryt* J.

'Weithon,' heb y Kei, 'chwitheu bieu talu y minneu uy ymdidan.' 'Kynon,' heb yr Owein, 'tal y ymdidan y Gei.' 'Dioer,' heb y Kynon, 'hyn gwr wyt a gwell ymdidanwr no mi, a mwy a weleist o betheu odidawc; tal di y ymdidan y Gei!' 'Dechreu di,' heb yr Owein (628), o'r hynn odidockaf a wypych.' 'Mi a wnaf,' heb y Kynon.

'Namyn vn mab mam a that oedwn i, a drythyll oedwn, a mawr oed vy ryvic. Ac ny thybygwn bot yn y byt a orffei arnaf o neb ryw gamhwri. A gwedy daruot im goruot ar bob camhwri o'r a oed yn vn wlat a mi, ymgywe[i]raw a wneuthum a cherdet eithauoed byt (225) a diffeithwch; a dywanu yn y diwed a wneuthum ar y glyn teccaf o'r byt, a gwyd gogyfuch yndaw, ac avon redegawc a oed ar hyt y glyn, a fford gan ystlys yr avon. A cherdet y fford a wneuthum hyt hanher dyd, a'r parth arall y kerdeis hyt pryt nawn. Ac yna y deuthum y vaes mawr, ac yn diben y maes y gwelwn kaer vawr llywychedic a gweilgi yn gyfagos y'r gaer. A ffarth a'r gaer y deuthum, ac nachaf deu was pengrych melyn, a ractal eur am pen pob vn onadunt, a ffeis o bali melyn am bop vn onadunt, a dwy wintas o gordwal newyd am traet pob vn, a gwaegeu eur ar vynygleu eu traet yn eu kau; a bwa o ascwrn eliffant yn llaw pob vn onadunt, a llinyneu o ieu hyd arnadunt, a saetheu ac eu peleidyr o askwrn morwil gwedy eu haskellu ac adaned paun, a ffenheu eur ar y

25–26 *yr ymdidan a edewit ym* J.   27 *wyti* J.   27 *miui* J.
29 *heb yr Owein* omit J.   31 *i* omit J.   32 *bot* J.   33 *ac wedi* J.   35 *ac yn y diwed dywannu* R.   36 *yn y byt* RJ.
36 *gogyfuch hydwf yndaw* J.   38 *y ford a gerdeys y hed* J.   39 *a gerdeis* RJ.   40 *y gwelwn* WJ, *yd oed* R.   41 *nachaf y gwelwn deu* RJ.
41 *velyn* RJ.   42 *o eur* J.   42 *ar penn* J.   42 *onadunt* WJ, *ohonunt* R.   42–43 *a ffeis . . . onadunt* omit J.   43 *bop* R, *ben pop* W.   43–44 *a dwy . . . pob vn* omit R.   43–44 *gordwal newyd* W, *gordwan writh newyd* J.   44 *o eur* J.   44 *am vynygleu* R.
44–45 *yn eu traet* R, *yn y eu cau, a pheis o pali melyn newyd am pob vn onadunt a saetheu ac eu peledyr* J.   45–46 *a llinyneu . . . arnadunt* omit J.   45–46 *ac eu llinyneu* R.   46 *arnadunt* omit R.   46 *a'e saetheu* R.   47 *pawin* R.   47 *paun, a llinynnyeu o ieu hyd arnadunt, a phenneu eureit arnadunt* J.

peleidyr; a chyllell a llafneu eureit udunt ac eu carneu o askwrn moruil ym pob vn o'r deu not, ac hwynteu yn saethu eu kyllyll.

'A rynnawd y wrthunt y gwelwn gwr pengrych melyn yn y dewred, a'y waryf yn newyd eillaw, a ffeis a mantell o bali melyn ymdanaw, ac ysnoden eurllin yn y vantell, a dwy wintas o gordwal brith am y draet a deu gnap eur yn eu kau. A ffan weleis i efo, dynessau a wneuthum attaw a chyuarch gwell idaw; ac rac daet y wybot, kynt y kyuarchawd ef well y mi no miui idaw ef. A dyfot (226) gyt a mi a oruc parth a'r gaer. Ac nyt oed gyuanhed yn y gaer namyn a oed yn y neuad. Ac yno yd oed pedeir morwyn ar ugeint yn gwniaw pali wrth fenestyr. A hyn a dywedaf ytti, Gei, vot yn debic genhyf bot yn degach yr haccraf onadunt hwy no'r vorwyn deckaf a weleist eiroet yn Ynys Prydein; yr anhardaf onadunt, hardach oed no Gwenhwywar gwreic Arthur pan uu hardaf eiryoet duw Nadolic ne duw Pasc wrth offeren. A chyfodi a orugant ragof; a chwech onadunt a gymerth vy march ac a'm diarchenwys inneu; a chwech ereill onadunt a gymerth vy arueu ac a'e golchassant y mywn role hyny oedynt kyn wynhet a'r dim gwynhaf; a'r dryded chwech onadunt a dodassant lieni ar y byrdeu ac a arlwyassant bwyt; a'r petweryd chwech a diodassant vy lludedwisc a dodi gwisc arall ymdanaf, nyt amgen, crys a llawdyr o'r

---

48 *chylleill* R, *chyllyll* J.   48 *eureit* WJ, *eur* R.   48 *ac eu carneu* JR.   49 *ym pob vn or deu not*: *yn nodeu vdunt* JR.   48–49 *ac hwynteu . . . kyllyll*: *yw saetheu*. J.   50 *kylleill* R.   51 *wr* R.   52 *a baraf newyd* J.   53 *a chysnoden eurllin yn* W, *ac ysnoden o eurllin ym penn* R, *ac orffreis lydan o eurllin ar y penn yn* J.   54 *gordwan* J.   54 *o eur* R.   54–55 *phan y gweleis* R.   55–56 *gwell a wneuthum idaw* R.   56 *daet oed y* J.   56 *wybot ef* R.   57 *miui* RJ, *mi* W.   57 *y gyt* J.   58 *yn vn* RJ.   58 *Ac yna* J.   59 *hugeint* R.   61 *hwy* omit J.   61 *weleist ti* R, *weliesti* J.   62 *a'r anhardaf* J.   63 *neu* RJ.   64 *a wnauthant* J.   65–66 *vy march . . . a gymerth* omit J.   65 *inneu* R.   67 *rol* R, *roly* J.   68 *trydyd* R.   68 *onadunt* R.   68 *llieineu* RJ.   69 *yn bwyt* J.   69 *petwared* J.   69–70 *lludeticwisc* RJ.   70 *a dodi* RJ, *ac y dodi* W.

bliant, a ffeis a swrcot a mantell o bali melyn ac orffreis lydan yn y vantell. A thynnu gobennydeu amhyl a thudedeu o'r bliant coch udunt y danaf ac y'm kylch. Ac eiste a orugum yna. A'r chwech onadunt a gymerth vy march a'y gorugant yn diwall
75 o'e holl ystarn yn gystal a'r ysweineit goreu yn Ynys Prydein.

'Ac ar hynny nachaf kawgeu aryant a dwfyr y ymolchi yndunt, a thweleu o wliant gwyn (227) a rei gwyrd; ac ymolchi a orugam, a mynet y eiste y'r bwrd a oruc y gwr gynheu, a minheu yn nessaf idaw, a'r gwraged oll is vy llaw inheu, eithyr
80 y rei a oedynt yn gwassanaethu. Ac aryant oed y bwrd, a bliant oed lieineu y bwrt, ac nyt oed vn llestyr yn gwassanaethu y bwrt namyn eur neu aryant neu uuelyn. An bwyt a doeth yn, a diheu oed ytti, Gei, na weleis i eirmoet ac nas kigleu bwyt na llyn ny welwn yno y gyfryw, eithyr bot yn well kyweirdeb y
85 bwyt a'r llyn a weleis i yno noc yn lle arall eiryoet.

'A bwyta a orugam hyt am hanher bwytta, ac ny dywawt na'r gwr nac vn o'r morynnyon vn geir wrthyf i hyt yna. A ffan uu debic gan y gwr bot yn well genhyf i ymdidan no bwytta, amowyn a oruc a mi pa ryw gerdet a oed arnaf, a ffa ryw wr
90 oedwn. A dywedut a orugum inheu bot yn vadws ym kaffel a ymdidanei a mi, ac nat oed yn y llys bei kymeint ac eu drycket

71 *a gorffoys llydan* R. 71–72 *lydan o eurllin yn* J. 73 *y danam ac yn kylch* R. 73 *orugam* R. 74 *a'e gwnauthant* J. 74–75 *diwall ef o'e holl prouant* J. 75 *ysweineit* R, *ysweinyeit* J, *ysgweineit* W. 75 *yn Ynys* RJ, *ym* W. 76 *nachaf y morynnyon yn dybot a chaugeu* J. 77 *thyweleu* R. 77 *gwyrd a rei gwynnyon* R. 77 *a'r rei* J. 78 *a wnaetham* J. 78 *gwr* R, *gwyr* J, *gwyr* corr. to *gwr* W. 79 *a'r morynnyon* J. 79 *oll* RJ. 79 *inheu* omit J. 81 *oed lieineu* R, *oedynt y llieinyeu* W, *oedynt . . . ieinnyeu* J. 81–82 *y bwyt* J. 82 *uuelyn* W, *vueli* R, *vual* J. 82 *doeth* W, *deuth* RJ. 83 *oed* omit J. 83 *i* RJ. 83 *eirioet* J. 83 *ac nas kigleu* omit R. 84 *gyfryw* W, *gyffelyp* R, *gyffelip* J. 85 *i* RJ. 85 *arall* RJ. 86 *wnaetham* J. 86 *hanner bwyt* RJ. 87 *na'r vn* J. 87 *i* R. 88 *i* omit R. 89 *gerdet . . . ffa ryw* omit R. 89 omit *a* before *oed* J. 90 *a wnaethaf neu a wneuthum* J. 90 *inheu* omit J. 90 *yn da gennyf i* R. 90–91 *kaffel ymdydan a mi* J. 91 *nat* R, *nac* W, *na* J.

ymdidandynnyon. "Ha vnben," heb y gwr, "ni a ymdidanem a thi er meitin ony bei lesteir ar dy vwytta; ac weithon ni a ymdidanwn a thi." Ac yna y manegeis i y'r gwr pwy oedwn, a'r kerdet a oed arnaf; a dywedut vy mot yn keisaw a orffei arnaf, neu vinheu a orffei arnaw.

'Ac yna edrych a oruc y gwr arnaf i, a gowenu, a dywe(228)dut wrthyf, "Pei na thebyccwn dyfot gormod o ouut ytti o'y venegi yt, mi a'e managwn yt yr hyn a geissy." A chymryt tristyt a goueileint ynof a wneuthum am hynny; ac adnabot a oruc y gwr arnaf hynny, a dywedut wrthyf, "Kanys gwell genhyt ti," heb ef, "menegi ohonaf i ytti dy afles no'th les, mi a'e managaf. Kwsc yma heno," heb ef, "a chyfot yn vore y uynyd, a chymer y fford y dodwyt ar hyt y dyffryn vchot hyny elych y'r koet y dodhwyt trwydaw. Ac yn rynawd yn y koet y kyveruyd gwahanfford a thi ar y tu deheu yt. A cherda ar hyt honno hyny delych y lannerch vawr o vaes, a gorssed ym perued y llannerch. A gwr du mawr a wely ym penn yr orssed ny bo llei no deuwr o wyr y byt hwnn; ac vn troet yssyd idaw, ac vn llygat yg knewillyn y tal; a ffon yssyd idaw o hayarn, a diheu yw ytti nat oes deuwr yn y byt ny chaffo eu llwyth yn y ffon. Ac nyt gwr anhygar efo: gwr hagyr yw ynteu. A choydwr ar y koet hwnnw yw. A thi a wely mil o aniueileit gwyllt yn pori yn y

93 *er meitin* omit RJ. 93 *dy vwyt* R. 93–94 *ni amdidanwn* J. 94 *i* omit J. 95 *kerdet oed* RJ. 96 *a orffwn ar bawb* J, *a orffei ar bawp* R. 97 *i* RJ. 98–99 *o'y venegi yt* omit R. 98–99 *yt o venegi yt yr hynn yr wyt yn gisiaw mi a'e managwn*. J. 99 *a uanagwn* R. 99 *hynn yd wyt yn y geissaw* R. 100 *a wneuthum ynof* R. 100 *am hynny* RJ. 100-101 *a wnaeth y* R. 101 *arnaf i* J. 101 *yw gennyt* R. 102 *heb ef* omit J. 103 *y bore* J. 104 *fford yd wyt ar* R. 104 *yny delych* R, *hyny delych* J. 105 *doethost* R, *deuthost* J. 105–6 *ef a gyferuyd* R. 106 *Kerda* J. 107 *gorsed yn y pherued*. J. 108 *penn* RJ, *perued* W. 108 *llei o dim* R, *llei dim* J. 109 (second) *ac* omit J. 110 *knewillyn* R, *knewillin* J, *gnewillin* W. 110 *idaw: yn y law* J. 110 *dieu yt* J. 111 *yn y byt* RJ. 112 *anhegar ef* RJ. 112 *agyr yawn* J. 112 *ac wtwart yw* R, *a choedwr yw ef* J. 113 *yw* omit RJ. 113 *gwyllt* omit J.

gylch. A gouyn idaw ef fford y uynet o'r llannerch. Ac ynteu a
vyd gwrthgroch wrthyt, ac eissyoes ef a venyc fford y ti mal y
keffych yr hyn a geissy."

'A hir uu genhyf i y nos honno. A'r bore drannoeth kyfodi
a orugum a gwiscaw ymdanaf ac eskynnu ar vy march a cherdet
ragof ar hyt y dyffryn (229) a'r koet, ac y'r wahanfford a venegis
y gwr y deuthum hyt y llannerch. A ffan deuthum yno hoffach
oed genhyf a welwn yno o aniweileit gwyllt no thri chymeint a
dywawt y gwr. A'r gwr du a oed yno yn eisted ymphen yr
orssed. Mawr y dywawt y gwr y mi y vot ef: mwy o lawer oed
ef no hynny. A'r ffon hayarn a dywedassei y gwr vot llwyth
deuwr yndi, hyspys oed genhyf i, Gei, vot yndi llwyth petwar
milwr. Honno a oed yn llaw y gwr du.

'A chyuarch gwell a orugum i y'r gwr du, ac ny dywedei
ynteu wrthyf namyn gwrthgroched. A gowyn a wneuthum
idaw pa wedyant a oed idaw ef ar yr aniweileit hynny. "Mi a
dangossaf ytti, dyn bychan," heb ef. A chymryt y ffon yn y
law, a tharaw karw a hi dyrnawt mawr hyny ryd ynteu vreiuat
mawr. Ac wrth y vreiuat ef y doeth o aniueileit gwyllt hyny oed
gyn hamlet a'r ser ar yr awyr, ac hyny oed kyuyg y mi seuyll
yn y llannerch gyt ac hwynt, a hynny o seirff a llewot a gwiberot

---

114 *ef* omit J.   114–15 *fford, ac ef a vynic fford ual* J.   114 *llannerch* R, *lannerch* W.   115 *wrthyt ti* R.   115 *eissyoes* omit R.
117 *hir yawn* J.   117 *i* omit J.   117 *y kyuodeis* J.   118 *esgynn vy* J.   119 *y'r coet* R.   121–2 *a dywawt* WJ, *ac y dywawt* R.
121 *yno* omit J.   123 *mwy . . . ef* R, *mwy llawer oed ef* J, *mwy oed ef lawer* W.   124 *gwr y mi uot* R.   125 *deuwr yndi . . . yndi llwyth* omit J.   125–6 *uot llwyth . . . yndi* R.   126 *a honno oed* RJ.   127 *a chyuarch . . . gwr du* omit R.   127 *wneithum y'r* J.   128 *wrthyf i* RJ.   128 *gwrthgloched* R, *gwrthgoched* J.
129 *vedyant oed* RJ.   129 *ef* omit R.   129 *hynny* RJ.
129–30 *mi a'e dangossaf* R.   130–1 *a dyrchawel y ffon hayarn a tharw* J.   130 *ynn y* W.   131 *dyrnawt mawr* omit J.   131 *vreuarat* R, *vre . . . eraf* J.   132 *ac yna y deuthant o* J.   132 *vrefarat* R.   132 *gwyllt* omit RJ.   132 *yny yttoedynt* R.   133 *gyn hamlet . . . hyny oed* omit J.   133 *syr yn* R.   134 *gyt ac wynt yn y llannerch, a riuedi . . . dybygwn y syr ar yr awyr* J.   134 *y gyt ac wynt* R.   134 *a llewot* omit RJ.

ac amryual aniueileit. Ac edrych a oruc ynteu arnadunt hwy, ac erchi udunt vynet y bori. Ac estwng eu penneu a orugant hwynteu ac adoli idaw ef val y gwnaei gwyr gwaredawc y eu harglwyd. A dywedut wrthyf i, "A wely dy yna, dyn bychan, y medyant yssyd y mi ar yr aniveileit hyn?"

'Ac yna gouyn fford a wneuthum (230) idaw ef. A garw uu ynteu wrthyf i, ac eissoes gouyn a oruc ef y mi pa le y mynnwn vynet. A dywedut a wneuthum idaw pa ryw wr oedwn a ffa beth a geisswn. A menegi a oruc ynteu y mi. "Kymher," heb ef, "y fford y dal y llannerch, a cherda yn erbyn yr allt vchot hyny delych y ffen. Ac odyno ti a wely ystrat megys dyffryn mawr, ac ympherued yr ystrat y gwely pren mawr a glassach y vric no'r fenitwyd glassaf. Ac y dan y pren hwnnw y mae fynhawn, ac yn emhyl y fynhawn y mae llech wawr, ac ar y llech y mae kawc aryant wrth kadwyn aryant mal na ellir y gwahanu. A chymer y kawc a bwrw kawgeit o'r dwfyr am ben y llech. Ac yna ti a glywy twrwf mawr, a thi a debygy orgrymhu y nef a'r dayar gan y twrwf. Ac yn ol y twrwf ef a daw cawat adoer, ac a vyd abreid ytti y diodef hi yn vyw, a chynllysc vyd. Ac yn ol y kawat hinon a vyd. Ac ny byd vn dalen ar y pren nyr darffo y'r kawat y dwyn. Ac ar hynny y daw kawat o adar y discynnu ar y pren, ac ny chlyweist y'th wlat dy hun eiryoet kerd kystal ac a ganant hwy. A ffan vo digriffaf genhyt y gerd, ti a glywy tuchan a chwynuan mawr yn dyfot ar hyt y dyffryn

    136 *wnaethant, a diolch yr gwaredawc* J.   137 *y gwnaei* omit R.   138 *ac yna y dywawt y gwr du wrthyf* RJ.   138 *lly[ma], dyn* J.   138 *yna* omit R.   139 *y mi ar* omit J.   140 *y fford* J.   140 *ef* omit R.   140-1 *garw ... eissoes* omit J.   141 *wrthyf i* omit R.   141 *ef* omit J.   142 *orugum* R.   143 *heb ynteu* R.   145 *o'e phenn* RJ.   145 *odyna* RJ.   146 *ac y glan yr* J.   146 *ti a wely* RJ, *y gwelei* W.   147 *yw y vric* RJ.   147 *no'r dim* J.   148 *llech varmor* R.   151 *ergrynu* R.   152 *y daw* R.   153 *ac abreid vyd itti* R.   153 *chenllysc vyd y gawat* R.   154 *prenn ny* R.   155 *eu dwyn* R.   155 *adar a* R.   156 *prenn a wnant* R.   156 *eiryoet y'th wlat dy hun* R.   157 *hwy* omit R.   157 *gennyt gerd yr adar* R.   158 *mawr* omit R.

parth ac attat. Ac ar hynny ti a wely varchawc y ar (231) varch
purdu, a gwisc o bali purdu ymdanaw, ac ystondard o vliant
purdu ar y wayw. A'th gyrchu a wna yn gyntaf y gallo. O ffoy
di racdaw, efo a'th ordiwed; os arhoy ditheu efo, a thi yn varchawc, ef a'th edeu yn bedestyr. Ac ony cheffy di yno ouut nyt
reit ytti amouyn gouut tra vych vyw."

'A chymryt y fford a orugum hyny deuthum y ben yr allt; ac
odyno y gwelwn val y managassei y gwr du ym. Ac y emhyl y
pren y doethum, a'r ffynhyawn a welwn dan y pren, a'r llech
varmor yn y emhyl, a'r kawc aryant wrth y gadwyn. A chymryt
y kawc a orugum a bwrw cawgeit o'r dwfyr am ben y llech. Ac
ar hynny nachaf y twryf yn dyfot yn wwy yn da noc y dywedassei y gwr du, ac yn ol y twryf y gawat. A diheu oed genhyf i,
Gei, na diaghei na dyn na llwdyn o'r a ordiwedei y gawat yn
wyw, kany orssauei vn kynllyskyn ohonei nac yr croen nac yr
kic hyny attalei yr ascwrn. Ac ymchoelut pedrein vy march ar
y gawat a orugum, a dodi swch vyn taryan ar ben vy march
a'e wwg, a dodi y baryflen ar vymphen vy hun, ac y velly porth
y gawat.

'Ac val yd oed vy eneit yn mynnu mynet o'r corff y peidyawd
y gawat. A ffan edrychaf ar y pren nyt oed vn dalen arnaw. (232)
Ac yna yd hinones. Ac yna nachaf yr adar y discynnu ar y pren
ac yn dechreu canu. A hyspys yw genhyf i, Gei, na chynt na
gwedy na chigleu gerd gystal a honno eirmoet. A ffan vyd
digrifhaf genhyf gwarandaw ar yr adar yn canu, nachaf tuchan
yn dyfot ar hyt y dyffryn parth ac attaf, a dywedut wrthyf, "Ha

159 *tu ac* R.   159 *varchawc ar* R.   159 *y ar* (231) *y ar* W.
165 *hyt pan deuthum* R.   169 *wneuthum* R.   171 *du im,* R.
172 *llwdyn yn vyw* R.   172 *gawat allan,* R.   173 *genllysgen* R.
173 *nac* (first) R, omit W.   174 *hatalyei* R.   175 *wneuthum* R.
176 *porthi* R.   178–9 *Ac val . . . y gawat* omit R.   179 *edrycheis*
R.   180 *Ac ar hynny nachaf* R.   180 *adar yn* R.   181 *yn
kanu* R.   182 *chiglef i kerd kystal* R.   182 *eiryoet* R.   182 *phan
oed* R.   183 *yn canu* omit R.   184 *yn dyuot parth* R.   184 *ac
yn dywedut* R.

warchawc," heb ef, "beth a holut ti y mi? Pa drwc a digoneis i ytti pan wnelut titheu y mi ac y'm kyfoeth a wnaethost hediw? Pony wydut ti nat edewis y gawat hediw na dyn na llwdyn yn vyw y'm kyuoeth o'r a gafas allan?"

'Ac ar hynny nachaf varchawc ar varch purdu a gwisc purdu o bali ymdanaw, ac arwyd o vliant purdu ar y vayw. Ac ymgyrchu a orugam, a chyn bei drut hynny ny bu hir hyny'm byrywyt i y'r llawr. Ac yna dodi a oruc y marchawc arllost y vayw trwy awwyneu ffrwyn vy march i, ac ymdeith yd aeth ef a'r deu varch ganthaw, a'm hadaw inheu yno. Ny wnaeth y gwr du o vawred ymdanaf i kymeint a'm karcharu inheu; nyt yspeilwys ynteu vi.

'A dyfot a orugum inheu tra'm kefyn y'r fford y deuthum gynt. A ffan deuthum y'r llannerch, yd oed y gwr du yndi; a'm kyffes a dygaf ytti, Gei, may rywed na thodeis yn llyn tawd rac kywilyd gan a gefeis o vatwar gan y gwr du. Ac y'r gaer y buasswn y nos gynt y deuthum y noss honno. (633) A llawenach uuwyt wrthyf y nos honno no'r nos gynt, a gwell y'm porthet, a'r ymdidan a vynnwn gan wyr a chan wraged a gaffwnn. Ac ny chaffwn i neb a gyrbwyllei wrthyf i dim am vyg kyrch y'r ffynnawn. Nys kyrbwylleis ynneu wrth neb. Ac yno y bum y nos honno.

'A phan gyfodeis y vynyd y bore trannoeth yd oed balffrei gwineudu a mygen burgoch idaw kyngochet a'r kenn yn barawt gwedy y ystarnu un gywei[r]. A gwedy gwisgaw vy arueu ac adaw vy mendyth yno, a dyuot hyt vy llys vy hun. A'r march hwnnw y mae gennyf i etto yn yr ystauell racko, ac y

185 *a hut ti* R.   185 (second) *a* omit R.   185 *inheu* R.
186 *kyf byth* R.   189–90 *gwisc o bali purdu* R.   190 *purdu ymdanaw* R.   191 *orugam* R, *orugum* W.   192 *y'r llawr* omit R.
193 *avwyn* R.   193 *i* omit R.   193 *ef* omit R.   195 *du* omit R.   195 *ymdanaf i o vawred* R.   195 *inheu* omit R.
197 *drachefen* R.   197 *y fford* R.   201 *buasswn* R, *buassam* W; from the end of this sentence to l. 538 W is wanting except for some fragmentary marginal readings.

rof a Duw, Gei, nas rodwn i euo ettwa yr y palffrei goreu yn
Ynys Prydein. A Duw a wyr, Gei, nat adeuawd (634) dyn arnaw
e hun chwedyl vethedigach no hwnn eiryoet; ac eissoes rac
215 odidocket gennyf i na chiglef eirmoet na chynt nat gwedy a
wypei dim y wrth y chwedyl hwnn namyn hynny y dywedeis,
a bot defnyd y chwedyl hwnn yg kyfoeth yr amherawdyr
Arthur heb dywanu neb arnaw.'

'Ha wyr,' heb yr Owein, 'ponyt oed da mynet y geisaw
220 dywanu ar y lle hwnnw?' 'Mynn llaw vyg kyfeillt', heb y Kei,
'mynych y dywedut ar dy dauawt yr hynny peth nys gwnelut
ar dy weithret.' 'Duw a wyr,' heb y Gwenhwyfar, 'oed gwell dy
grogi di, Gei, no dywedut ymadrawd mor warthaedic a hwnnw
wrth wr mal Owein.' 'Myn llaw vyg kyfeillt, wreicda,' heb y
225 Kei, 'nyt mwy o volyant y Owein a dywedeist di no minneu.'

Ac ar hynny deffroi a oruc Arthur, a gofyn a gysgassei
hayach. 'Do, arglwyd,' heb yr Owein, 'dalym.' 'Ae amser ynni
vynet y'r byrdeu?' 'Amser, arglwyd,' heb yr Owein. Ac yna
kanu korn ymolchi a wnaethpwyt, a mynet a wnaeth yr am-
230 herawdyr a'e deulu oll y vwytta. A gwedy daruot bwytta difflan
a oruc Owein ymdeith, a dyuot y letty a pharattoi y varch a'e
arueu a oruc.

A phan welas ef y dyd drannoeth gwisgaw y arueu a oruc, ac
ysgynnu ar y uarch a cherdet racdaw a oruc eithafoed byt a
235 diffeith vynyded. Ac yn y diwed y dywanawd ar y glynn a
uanagassei Gynon idaw ual y gwydyat yn hyspys panyw hwnnw
oed. A cherdet a oruc ar hyt y glynn gan ystlys yr auon, a'r
parth arall y'r auon y kerdawd yny doeth y'r dyffrynn. A'r
dyffrynn a gerdawd yny welei y gaer, a pharth a'r gaer y deuth.
240 Sef y gwelei y gweision yn saethu eu kylleill yn y lle y gwelsei
Gynon, a'r gwr melyn bieuoed y gaer yn seuyll ger eu llaw. A
phan yttoed Owein yn mynnv kyuarch gwell y'r gwr melyn,
kyuarch gwell a oruc y gwr y Owein, a dyuot yn y vlaen parth
a'r gaer. Ac ef a welei ystauell yn y gaer, a phan deuth y'r

216 *y dywede*[*is*] W. 218 *neb* omit W. 222 *oed* W, *ys oed* R.

ystauell ef a welei y morynyon yn gwnyaw (635) pali y mywn kadeireu eureit. A hoffach o lawer oed gan Owein e tecket ac eu hardet noc y dywawt Kynon idaw. A chyfodi a wnaethant y wassanaethu Owein mal y gwassanaethassynt Gynon. A hoffach vu gan Owein y borthant no chan Gynon, ac am hanner bwytta amofyn a oruc y gwr melyn ac Owein py gerdet oed arnaw. Ac y dywawt Owein gwbyl o'e gerdet idaw—'ac yn ymgeissaw a'r marchawc yssyd yn gwarchadw y ffynnawnn y mynnwn vy mot.' A gowenu a oruc y gwr melyn a bot yn anhawd gantaw menegi y Owein y kerdet hwnnw, mal y bu anhawd gantaw y uenegi y Gynon. Ac eissoes menegi a oruc y Owein gwbyl y wrth hynny. Ac y gysgu yd aethant.

A'r bore drannoeth y bu barawt march Owein gan y morynyon, a cherdet a oruc Owein racdaw yny deuth y'r llannerch yd oed y gwr du yndi. A hoffach uu gan Owein meint y gwr du no chan Gynon. A gofyn fford a oruc Owein y'r gwr du, ac ynteu a'e menegis. A cherdet a oruc Owein y fford ual Kynon yny doeth yn ymyl y prenn glas. Ac ef a welei y ffynnawn a'r llech yn ymyl y ffynnawn, a'r kawc erni. A chymryt y kawc a oruc Owein a bwrw kawgeit o'r dwfyr ar y llech. Ac ar hynny nachaf y twryf, ac yn ol y twryf y gawat. Mwy o lawer noc y dywedassei Gynon oedynt. A gwedy y gawat goleuhau a oruc yr awyr, a phan edrychawd Owein ar y prenn nyt oed vn dalen arnaw. Ac ar hynny nachaf yr adar yn disgynnu ar y prenn ac yn kanu. A phan oed digrifaf gan Owein gerd yr adar, ef a welei varchawc yn dyuot ar hyt y dyffryn. A'e erbynnyeit a oruc Owein, ac ymwan ac ef yn drut, a thorri y deu baladyr a orugant, a dispeilaw deu gledyf a wnaethant ac ymgyfogi. Ac ar hynny Owein a drewis dyrnawt ar y marchawc trwy y helym a'r pennffestin a'r penngwch pwrqwin, a thrwy y kroen a'r kig a'r asgwrn yny glwyfawd ar yr emennyd. Ac yna adnabot a oruc y marchawc duawc ry gaffel dyr(636)nawt agheuawl ohonaw, ac ymchoelut penn y varch a oruc a ffo.

275 *a wnaeth* W.

A'e ymlit a oruc Owein, ac nyt ymgaffei Owein a'e vaedu a'r
cledyf; nyt oed bell idaw ynteu. Ac ar hynny Owein a welei
280 gaer uawr lywychedic. Ac y porth y gaer y deuthant, ac ellwng
y marchawc duawc a wnaethpwyt y mywn, ac ellwng dor dyrchauat a wnaethpwyt ar Owein. A honno a'e medrawd odis y
pardwgyl y kyfrwy yny dorres y march yn deu hanner trwydaw,
a throelleu yr ysparduneu gan y sodleu Owein, ac yny gerda y
285 dor hyt y llawr, a throelleu yr ysparduneu a dryll y march y
maes, ac Owein y rwng y dwy dor a'r dryll arall y'r march. A'r
dor y mywn a gaewyt ual na allei Owein vynet odyno.

Ac yg kyfyg gyghor yd oed Owein. Ac ual yd oed Owein
uelly, sef y gwelei trwy gysswllt y dor heol gyfarwyneb ac ef, ac
290 ystret o tei o bop tu y'r heol. Ac [ef] a welei morwyn benngrech
uelen, a ractal eur am y phenn a gwisc o bali melyn ymdanei,
a dwy wintas o gordwal brith am y thraet, ac yn dyuot y'r
porth. Ac erchi agori a oruc. 'Duw a wyr, unbennes,' heb yr
Owein, 'na ellir agori ytti odyma mwy noc y gelly dithau waret
295 y minneu odyna.' 'Duw a wyr,' heb y uorwyn, 'oed dyhed
mawr na ellit gwaret itti; ac oed iawn y wreic wneuthur da
ytti. Duw a wyr na weleis i eirmoet was well no thidi wrth
wreic. O bei gares itt, goreu kar gwreic oedut; o bei orderch
itt, goreu gorderch oedut. Ac wrth hynny,' heb hi, 'yr hynn a
300 allaf i o waret itti, mi a'e gwnaf. Hwde di y votrwy honn a dot
am dy vys, a dot y maen y mywn dy law, a chae dy dwrn am
y maen, a thra gudyych ti euo, euo a'th gud ditheu. A phan
hambwyllont hwy o'r lleon y deuant wy y'th gyrchu di y'th
dihennydaw am y gwr. A gwedy na welont hwy dydi, drwc
305 vyd gantunt. A minneu a vydaf ar yr esgynuaen racko y'th aros
di; a thydi a'm gwely i kyny welwyf i dydi. A dyret titheu a dot
dy law ar penn (637) vy ysgwyd i, ac yna y gwybydaf i dy dyfot
titheu attaf fi. A'r fford yd elwyf i odyno, dyret titheu gyt a mi.'
Ac ar hynny mynet a oruc odyno y wrth Owein.

310 Ac Owein a wnaeth a erchis y vorwyn idaw oll. Ac ar hynny

278 *erlit* W.   301 *y maen hwnn* R.   306 *kany* R.

y deuth y gwyr o'r llys y geisaw Owein o'e dihenydu. A phan deuthant y geissaw ny welsant dim namyn hanner y march, a drwc yd aeth arnunt hynny. A difflannu a oruc Owein oc eu plith, a dyuot att y vorwyn, a dodi y law ar y hysgwyd; a chychwyn a oruc hitheu racdi, ac Owein y gyt a hi, yny deuthant y drws llofft uawr delediw. Ac agori y lloft a oruc y vorwyn, a dyuot y mywn, a chaeu y llofft a orugant.

Ac edrych ar hyt y lloft a oruc Owein: ac nyt oed yn y llofft un hoel heb y lliwaw a lliw gwerthuawr, ac nyt oed un ystyllen heb delw eureit arnei yn amryual. A chynnu tan glo a oruc y vorwyn, a chymryt kawc aryant a oruc hi a dwfyr yndaw, a thwel o vliant gwynn ar y hysgwyd, a rodi dwfyr y ymolchi a oruc y Owein. A dodi bwrd aryant goreureit rac y vronn, a bliant melyn yn lliein arnaw, a dyuot a'e ginyaw idaw. A diheu oed gan Owein na welsei eiryoet neb ryw vwyt ny welei yno digawn ohonaw, eithyr bot yn well kyweirdeb y bwyt a welei yno noc yn lle arall eiryoet. Ac ny welas eiryoet lle kyn amlet anrec odidawc o vwyt a llynn ac yno, ac nyt oed vn llestyr yn gwassanaethu arnaw namyn llestri aryant neu eur. A bwytta ac yuet a oruc Owein yny oed prytnawn hir.

Ac ar hynny nachaf y clywynt diaspedein yn y gaer, a gofyn a oruc Owein y'r uorwyn, 'Py weidi yw hwnn?' 'Dodi olew ar y gwrda bieu y gaer,' heb y uorwyn. Ac y gysgu yd aeth Owein, a gwiw oed y Arthur dahet y gwely a wnaeth y uorwyn idaw o ysgarlat a gra a phali a syndal a bliant. Ac am hanner nos y clywynt diaspedein girat. 'Py diaspedein yw hwnn weithon?' heb yr Owein. 'Y gwrda bieu y gaer ys(638)syd uarw yr awr honn,' heb y vorwyn.

Ac am rynnawd o'r dyd y clywynt diaspedein a gweidi anueitrawl eu meint, a gofyn a oruc Owein y'r uorwyn, 'Pa ystyr yssyd y'r gweidi hwnn?' 'Mynct a chorff y gwrda bieu y gaer y'r llann.' A chyuodi a oruc Owein y vynyd a gwisgaw ymdanaw, ac agori ffenestyr ar y llofft, ac edrych parth a'r gaer. Ac ny weiei nac ymyl nac eithaf y'r lluoed yn llewni yr heolyd,

313 *oaruc* R.

a hynny yn llawn-aruawc, a gwraged llawer y gyt ac wynt ar
ueirch ac ar traet, a chrefydwyr y dinas oll yn kanu. Ac ef a
tebygei Owein bot yr awyr yn edrinaw rac meint y gweidi, a'r
utkyrnn, a'r crefydwyr yn kanu.

   Ac ym perued y llu hwnnw ef [a welei] yr elor, a llenn o
vliant gwynn arnei, a physt kwyr yn llosgi yn amyl yn y chylch.
Ac nyt oed vndyn dan yr elor lai no barwn kyuoethawc. A diheu
oed gan Owein na welsei eiryoet niuer kyhardet a hwnnw o bali
a seric a syndal. Ac ar ol y llu hwnnw y gwelei ef gwreic velen
a'e gwallt dros y dwy ysgwyd, ac a gwaet briw amyl yn y brigeu,
a gwisc o bali melyn ymdanei gwedy y rwygaw, a dwy wintas o
gordwal brith am y thraet. A ryued oed na bei yssic penneu y
byssed rac dyckynet y maedei y dwylaw y gyt. A hyspys oed
gan Owein na welsei ef eiryoet gwreic kymryt a hi, beyt uei ar y
ffuryf iawn. Ac uch oed y diaspat noc a oed o dyn a chorn yn y
llu. A phann welas ef y wreic ennynu a wnaeth o'e charyat yny
oed gyflawn pop lle yndaw.

   A gofyn a oruc Owein y'r uorwyn pwy oed y wreic. 'Duw a
wyr,' heb y uorwyn, 'gwreic y gellir dywedut idi y bot yn
deckaf o'r gwraged, ac yn diweiraf, ac yn haelaf, ac yn doethaf,
ac yn vonhedickaf. Vy arglwydes i yw honn racko, a Iarlles y
Ffynnawn y gelwir, gwreic y gwr a (639) ledeist di doe.' 'Duw
a wyr,' heb yr Owein, 'arnaf, mae mwyhaf gwreic a garaf i yw
hi.' 'Duw a wyr,' heb y uorwyn, 'na char hi dydi na bychydic
na dim!'

   Ac ar hynny kyuodi a oruc y vorwyn a chynneu tan glo, a
llanw crochan o dwfyr a'e dodi y dwymaw, a chymryt twel o
vliant gwynn a'e dodi am vynwgyl Owein, a chymryt gorflwch
o ascwrn eliphant, a chawc aryant, a'e lanw o'r dwfyr twym,
a golchi penn Owein. Ac odyna agori prenuol a thynnu ellyn
a'e charn o asgwrn eliphant a deu ganawl eureit ar yr ellyn, ac
eillaw y uaraf a oruc, a sychu y benn a'e vynwgyl a'r twel. Ac
odyna dyrchafel [bwrd] a oruc y uorwyn rac bronn Owein a

CHWEDYL IARLLES Y FFYNNAWN

dyuot a'e ginyaw idaw. A diheu oed gan Owein na chafas eiryoet kinyaw kystal a honno na diwallach y wasanaeth. A gwedy daruot idaw y ginyaw, kyweiryaw a oruc y uorwyn y gwely. 'Dos yma,' heb hi, 'y gyscu, a minneu a af y orderchu itti.' A mynet a oruc Owein y gysgu. A chaeu drws y llofft a oruc y vorwyn a mynet parth a'r gaer.

A phan deuth yno nyt oed yno namyn tristyt a goual, a'r iarlles e hun yn yr ystauell heb diodef gwelet dyn rac tristit. A dyuot a oruc Lunet attei a chyuarch gwell idi, ac nys attebawd yr iarlles. A blyghau a oruc y uorwyn a dywetut wrthi, 'Py derw ytti pryt nat atteppych y neb hediw?' 'Lunet,' heb yr iarlles, 'py wyneb yssyd arnat ti pryt na delut y edrych y gofut a uu arnaf i? Ac ys gwneuthum i dyti yn gyfoethawc. Ac oed kam itti hynny!' 'Dioer,' heb y Lunet, 'ny thebygwn i na bei well dy synwyr di noc y mae. Oed well ytti geissaw goualu am ennill y gwrda hwnnw noc am peth arall ny ellych byth y gaffel.' 'Y rof i a Duw,' heb yr iarlles, 'ny allwn i vyth ennill vy arglwyd i o dyn arall (640) yn y byt.' 'Gallut,' heb y Lunet, 'gwrha gwr a vei gystal ac ef neu well noc ef.' 'Y rof i a Duw,' heb yr iarlles, 'pei na bei wrthmun gennyf peri dihenydyaw dyn a uackwn, mi a barwn dy dihenydyaw am gyffelybu wrthyf peth mor aghywir a hynny. A pheri dy dehol ditheu mi a'e gwnaf!' 'Da yw gennyf,' heb y Lunet, 'nat achaws itty hynny namyn am uenegi ohonaf i ytti dy les lle nys metrut dy hun. A mevyl idi ohonam y gyntaf a yrro att y gilyd, ae miui y adolwyn gwahawd itti, ae titheu y'm gwahawd inneu.' Ac ar hynny mynet a oruc Lunet ymeith.

A chyfodi a oruc yr iarlles hyt ar drws yr ystauell yn ol Lunet, a phessychu yn uchel. Ac edrych a oruc Lunet tu draechefyn, ac emneidaw a oruc yr iarlles ar Lunet. A dyuot drachefyn a oruc Lunet att yr iarlles. 'Y rof i a Duw,' hcb yr iarlles wrth

---

390 *arnaf i, ac a oed itti, ac ys gwneuthum i dy ti ȳ gyfoethawc, ac a oed kam itti na delut y edrych y gofut a uu arnaf i, ac oed kam itti hynny* R.   402 *a miui* R.

Lunet, 'drwc yw dy anyan. A chanys vy lles i yd oedut ti yn y uenegi im, manac pa fford vei hynny.' 'Mi a'e managaf,' heb hi. 'Ti a wdost na ellir kynnal dy gyfoeth di namyn o vilwryaeth ac arueu; ac am hynny keis yn ebrwyd a'e kynhalyo.' 'Pa fford y gallaf i hynny?' heb yr iarlles. 'Managaf,' heb y Lunet; 'ony elly di gynnal y ffynnawn ny elly gynnal dy gyuoeth. Ny eill kynnal y ffynnawn namyn vn o teulu Arthur, a minneu a af,' heb y Lunet, 'hyt yn llys Arthur, a mefyl im,' heb hi, 'o deuaf odyno heb uilwr a gattwo y ffynnawn yn gystal neu yn well no'r gwr a'e kedwis gynt.' 'Anhawd yw hynny,' heb yr iarlles; 'ac eissoes dos y brofi yr hynn a dywedy.'

Kychwyn a oruc Lunet ar uedwl mynet y lys Arthur, a dyuot a oruc y'r llofft att Owein. Ac yno y bu hi gyt ac Owein yny oed amser idi dyuot o lys Arthur.

Ac yna gwisgaw ymdanei a oruc hi a dyuot y ymwelet a'r iarlles. A llawen uu y iarlles wrthi. 'Chwedleu o lys Arthur gennyt?' heb yr iarlles. 'Goreu chwedyl gennyf, arglwydes,' heb hi, 'kaffel ohonaf vy neges. A pha bryt y mynny di dangos itt yr un(641)benn a doeth gyt a mi?' 'Dyret ti ac ef,' heb yr iarlles, 'am hanner dyd avory y ymwelet a mi, a minneu a baraf ysgyfalhau y dref erbyn hynny.' A dyuot a wnaeth hi adref.

Ac am hanner dyd trannoeth y gwisgwys Owein ymdanaw peis a swrcot a mantell o bali melyn, ac orffreis lydan yn y vantell o eurllin, a dwy wintas o gordwal brith am y draet a llun llew o eur yn eu kaeu. A dyuot a wnaethant hyt yn ystauell y iarlles, a llawen uu y iarlles wrthunt. Ac edrych ar Owein yn graff a oruc y iarlles. 'Lunet,' heb hi, 'nyt oes wed kerdetwr ar yr unben hwnn.' 'Py drwc yw hynny, arglwydes?' heb y Lunet. 'Y rof fi a Duw,' heb y iarlles, 'na duc dyn eneit vy arglwyd i o'e gorff namyn y gwr hwnn.' 'Handit gwell itt, arglwydes; pei na bei drech noc ef nys dygei ynteu y eneit ef. Ny ellir dim wrth hynny,' heb hi, 'kan deryw.' 'Ewch chwi drachefyn atref,' heb yr iarlles, 'a minneu a gymeraf gyghor.'

433 *wnaethnt* R.

CHWEDYL IARLLES Y FFYNNAWN

A pheri dyfynnu y holl gyuoeth y un lle drannoeth a oruc y iarlles, a menegi udunt uot y hiarllaeth yn wedu, ac na ellit y chynnal onyt o uarch ac arueu a milwryaeth: 'ac ys ef y rodaf inneu ar awch dewis chwi, ae un ohonawch chwi a'm kymero i, 445 ae vyg kannyadu ynneu y gymrut gwr a'e kanhalyo o le arall.' Sef a gawsant yn eu kyghor, kanhadu idi gwra o le arall. Ac yna y duc hitheu escyb ac archescyb o'e llys y wneuthur y phriodas hi ac Owein. A gwrhau a orugant gwyr y iarllaeth y Owein, ac Owein a gedwis y ffynnawn o waew a chledyf. Sef mal y kedwis: a 450 delei o varchawc yno, Owein a'e byryei ac a'e gwerthei yr y lawn werth. A'r da hwnnw a rannei Owein y varwnyeit a'e uarchogyon (642) hyt nat oed vwy gan y gyfoeth garyat dyn o'r byt oll no'r eidaw ef. A their blyned y bu ef uelly.

Ac ual yd oed Walchmei diwarnawt yn gorymdeith y gyt a'r 455 amherawdyr Arthur, edrych a oruc ar Arthur a'e welet yn trist gystudedic; a doluryaw a oruc Gwalchmei yn uawr o welet Arthur yn y drych hwnnw, a gofyn a oruc idaw. 'Arglwyd,' heb ef, 'py derw itti?' 'Y rof a Duw, Walchmei,' heb yr Arthur, 'hiraeth yssyd arnaf am Owein a golles y gennyf meint teir 460 blyned. Ac o bydaf y bedwared vlwydyn heb y welet, ny byd vy eneit y'm korff. A mi a wn yn hyspys panyw o ymdidan Kynon mab Clydno y kolles Owein y gennym.' 'Nyt reit itti,' heb y Gwalchmei, 'luydyaw dy gyfoeth yr hynny; namyn ti a gwyr dy ty a eill dial Owein or llas, neu y rydhau ot ydiw yg 465 karchar, ac os buw, y dwyn gyt a thi.' Ac ar a dywawt Gwalchmei y trigywyt.

Ac ymgyweiryaw a wnaeth Arthur a gwyr y dy gyt ac ef y geissaw Owein. Sef oed meint y nifer, teir mil heb amlawdynyon, a Chynon mab Clydno yn gyfarwyd udunt. A dyuot a oruc 470 Arthur hyt y gaer y buassei Gynon yndi, a phan deuthant yno yd oed y gweisson yn saethu yn yr un lle, a'r gwr melyn yn

459 *ef* omit R.   464 *heb y Gwalchmei* R, [*argl*]*wyd* W.
464 *hynny heb y* [*Gwalchmei*] W.   465 *ty* R, *lys* W.   465 *eill* R, *d*[*igawn*] W.   466 *ac* R, *neu* W.   470 *udunt* R, *idaw* W.

seuyll ach eu llaw. A phan welas y gwr melyn Arthur kyuarch
gwell a oruc idaw a'e wahawd; a chymryt gwahawd a oruc
Arthur, ac y'r gaer yd aethant. A chyt bei mawr eu niuer, ny
wydit eu hystyr yn y gaer. A chyuodi a oruc y morynyon y eu
gwassanaethu; a bei a welsant ar bop gwassanaeth eiryoet
eithyr gwassanaeth y gwraged. Ac nyt oed waeth gwassanaeth
gweisson y meirch y nos (643) honno noc vydei ar Arthur yn
y lys e hun.

A'r bore trannoeth y kychwynnwys Arthur, a Chynon yn
gyfarwyd idaw, odyno, ac wynt a deuthant hyt lle yd oed y gwr
du. A hoffach o lawer oed gan Arthur meint y gwr du noc y
dywedyssit idaw. Ac hyt ym penn yr allt y deuthant, ac y'r
dyffryn, hyt yn ymyl y prenn glas, ac yny welsant y ffynnawn
a'r kawc a'r llech. Ac yna y doeth Kei ar Arthur, a dywedut,
'Arglwyd,' heb ef, 'mi a wnn achaws y kerdet hwnn oll, ac
eruyn yw gennyf gadu y mi bwrw y dwfyr ar y llech ac erbynyeit y gofut kyntaf a del.' A'e ganhadu a oruc Arthur.

A bwrw kawgeit o'r dwfyr ar y llech a oruc Kei. Ac yn y lle
ar ol hynny y deuth y twryf, ac yn ol y twryf y gawat. Ac ny
chlywyssynt eiryoet twryf a chawat kyffelyb y rei hynny, a llawer
o amlawdynyon a oed yg kyweithas Arthur a ladawd y gawat.
A gwedy peidyaw y gawat y goleuhawys yr awyr, a phan edrychassant ar y pren nyt oed un dalen arnaw. A disgynnu a oruc yr
adar ar y prenn, a diheu oed gantunt na chlywyssynt eiryoet kerd
kystal a'r adar yn kanu. Ac ar hynny y gwelynt uarchawc y ar
varch purdu, a gwisc o bali purdu ymdanaw, a cherdet gwrd
gantaw. A'e erbynnyeit a oruc Kei, ac ymwan ac ef. Ac ny bu hir
yr ymwan; Kei a vyrywyt. Ac yna pebyllyaw a oruc y marchawc
a phebyllyaw a oruc Arthur a'e lu y nos honno.

A phan gyfodant y bore trannoeth y vynyd yd oed arwyd
ymwan ar waew y marchawc. A dyuot a oruc Kei ar Arthur, a
dywedut wrthaw, 'Arglwyd,' heb ef, 'kam y'm byrywyt i doe; ac
a edy ti y mi hediw vynet y ymwan a'r marchawc?' 'Ga(644)daf,'

505 *a edy ti*: *a oed da y ti* R, with *da* added above.

CHWEDYL IARLLES Y FFYNNAWN

heb yr Arthur. A mynet a oruc Kei y'r marchawc; ac yn y lle bwrw Kei a oruc ef, ac edrych arnaw, a'e wan ac arllost y waew yn y tal yny tyr y helym a'r penffestin a'r croen a'r kic hyt yr asgwrn kyflet a phenn y paladyr. Ac ymchoelut a oruc Kei ar y gedymdeithon drachefyn. Ac o hynny allan yd aeth 510 teulu Arthur bop eilwers y ymwan a'r marchawc hyt nat oed un heb y vwrw o'r marchawc namyn Arthur a Gwalchmei.

Ac Arthur a wisgawd ymdanaw y vynet y ymwan a'r marchawc. 'Och, arglwyd,' heb y Gwalchmei, 'gat y mi vynet y ymwan a'r marchawc yn gyntaf.' A'e adu a wnaeth Arthur. Ac 515 ynteu a aeth y ymwan a'r marchawc, a chwnsallt o bali ymdanaw a anuonassei uerch Iarll Rangyw ymdanaw ac am y varch; wrth hynny nys atwaenat neb o'r llu ef. Ac ymgyrchu a wnaethant, ac ymwan y dyd hwnnw hyt ucher, ac ny bu agos yr un onadunt a bwrw y gilyd y'r llawr. A thrannoeth yd aethant y ymwan a 520 pheleidyr godeuawc gantunt. Ac ny orfu yr un onadunt ar y gilyd. A'r trydyd dyd yd aethant y ymwan a pheleidyr kadarnuras godeuawc gan bob un onadunt. Ac ennynnv o lit a wnaethant, ac ymgyrchu a wnaethant am hanner dyd e hun, a hwrd a rodes pob un onadunt y gilyd yny torres holl gegleu 525 eu meirch, ac yny vyd pob un onadunt dros bedrein y varch y'r llawr. A chyuodi y vynyd a orugant yn gyflym, a thynnu clefydeu ac ymffust. A diheu oed gan y nifer a'e gwelei wynt uelly na welsynt eiryoet deu wr kyn wychet a'r rei hynny na chyn gryfet. A phei tywyll y nos hi a vydei oleu gan y tan o'e 530 harueu. Ac ar hynny dyrnawt a rodes y marchawc y Walchmei hyt pan troes yr helym y ar y wyneb (645) mal y hadnabu y marchawc panyw Gwalchmei oed. Ac yna y dywawt Owein, 'Arglwyd Walchmei, nyt atwaenwn i didi o achaws dy gwnsallt, a'm kefynderw wyt. Hwde di uyg kledyf i a'm harueu!' 'Tidi, 535 Owein, yssyd arglwyd,' heb y Gwalchmei, 'a thi a oruu; a chymer di vyg cledyf i!' Ac ar hynny yd arganuu Arthur (249)

532 *hyt pan troes* R, *yny droes* W. 532 *mal y* R, *ac yny* W.
537 *vyg cledyf* R, [*uy*] *arfeu* W.

hwynt, a dyfot a oruc attunt. 'Arglwyd,' heb y Gwalchmei, 'llyma Owein wedy goruot arnaf i, ac ny myn vy arveu y gen-
540 hyf.' 'Arglwyd,' heb yr Owein, 'efo a oruu arnaf i, ac ny myn vyg cledyf.' 'Moesswch attaf i,' heb yr Arthur, 'awch cledyfeu, ac ny oruu yr vn ohonawch ar y gilyd gan hynny.' A mynet dwylaw mynwgyl y'r amherawdyr Arthur a oruc Owein, ac ymgaru a orugant. A dyfot a oruc y lu attunt yna gan ymsang
545 a brys y geissyaw gwelet Owein y vynet dwylaw mynwgyl idaw; ac ef a uu agos bot caladen yn yr ymsag hwnnw. A'r nos honno yd aeth pawb y eu pebylleu.

A thrannoeth arouyn a oruc yr amherawdyr Arthur ymdeith. 'Arglwyd,' heb yr Owein, 'nyt velly y mae iawn yt. Teir blyned
550 y'r amser hwn y deuthum i y wrthyt ti, arglwyd, ac y mae meu i y lle hwn. Ac yr hynny hyt hediw yd wyf i yn darparu gwled ytti, can gwydywn i y dout ti y'm keissyaw i. A thi a deuy gyt a mi y vwrw dy ludet, ti a'th wyr, ac enneint a geffwch.' A dyfot a orugant y gyt oll hyt yg kaer iarlles y ffynhyawn. A'r
555 wled y buwyt teir blyned yn y darparu, yn vn trimis y treulwyt, ac ny bu esmwythyach udunt wled eiryoet no honno na gwell.

Ac yna arouun a oruc Arthur ymdeith, a gyrru kenhadeu a oruc Arthur ar yr iarlles y erchi idi ellwg Owein gyt ac ef y dangos y vyrda Ynys Prydein a'y gwragedda vn trimis. A'r
560 iarlles a'y canyhadawd, ac anawd uu genthi hynny. A dyfot a oruc Owein (250) gyt ac Arthur y Ynys Prydein. A gwedy y dyfot ym plith y genedyl a'y gytgyuedachwyr ef a drigywys teir blyned yg kyfeir y trimis.

Ac val yd oed Owein diwarnawt yn bwyta ar y bwrt yn llys yr

---

538 *dyuot attunt a oruc* R.   538 *Arglwyd Arthur* R.   541 *clefydeu* R.   543 *mynwgyl y Arthur* R.   544 *a orugant y llu* R.   545 *dwylaw* R, *dwylyw* W.   546 *agos a bot* R.   547 *yd aethant y* R.   548 *yr amherawdyr* omit R.   550 *hwnn yd euthum* R.   550 *y meu* R.   552 *i* omit R twice.   554 *y gyt* omit and add after *ffynhyawn* R.   556 *na gwell no honno* R.   558 *ar* W, *att* R.   558 *y gyt* R.   558–9 *o'e dangos* R.   564–5 *yn llys ... Arthur* omit R.

CHWEDYL IARLLES Y FFYNNAWN

amherawdyr Arthur yg Kaer Llion ar Wysc, nachaf vorwyn yn 565
dyfot ar varch gwineu myngrych a'e vwg a gaffei y llawr, a
gwisc o bali melyn ymdeni, a'r ffrwyn ac a welit o'r kyfrwy, eur
oll oed. A hyt rac bron Owein y doeth a chymryt y vodrwy a
oed ar y law; 'Val hyn,' heb hi, 'y gwneir y dwyllwr aghywir
bradwr yr meuyl ar dy varyf!' Ac ymchoelut pen y march ac 570
ymdeith. Ac yna y deuth cof y Owein y gerdet; a thristau a
oruc. A ffan daruu bwyta dyuot y'w letty a oruc, a goualu yn
vawr a wnaeth y nos honno.

A thrannoeth y bore y kyfodes ac nyt llys Arthur a gyrchwys
namyn eithaued byt a diffeith vynyded. Ac ef a vu y velly ar 575
dro hyny daruu y dillat oll, ac hyny daruu y gorff hayach, ac
yny dyuawd blew hir trwydyaw oll; a chytgerdet a bwystuilet
gwyllt a wnai, a chytymborth ac wynt yny oedynt gynefin ac ef.
Ac ar hynny gwanhau a oruc ef hyt na allei eu kanhymdeith. Ac
estwng o'r mynyd y'r dyffryn a oruc, a chyrchu parc teccaf o'r 580
byt. A iarlles wedw biewed y parc.

A diwarnawt mynet a oruc yr iarlles a'e llawvorynyon y
orymdeith gan ystlys llynn a oed yn y parc hyt ar gyfeir y chanawl. Ac hwynt a welynt (251) yn y parc eilun dyn a'y delw, ac
val dala ofyn racdaw a orugant. Ac eissyoes nessau a orugant 585
attaw, a'y deimlyaw, a'y edrych yn graff. Sef y gwelynt gwytheu
yn llamu arnaw, ac ynteu yn kwynaw wrth yr heul. A dyfot a
oruc y iarlles trachefyn y'r castell, a chymryt lloneit gorflwch

---

566 *vwg* W, *vygen* R.   566 *y llawr* omit R.   567 *ymdanei o bali melyn* R.   568 *oed oll* R.   568–9 *uotrwy oed ar law Owein a wnaeth* R.   569 *twyllwr bratwr aghywir* R.   570 *ymchoelut* R, *ymhoelu* W.   571 *gerdet honno* R.   572 *dyuot* R, omit W.   572 *y'w* W, *y* R.   572–3 *yn vawr a wnaeth* omit R.   574 *y bore* omit R.   574 *llys Arthur* W, *y llys* R.   575 *eithafoed bydoed* R.   575–6 *ar dro* omit R.   577 *oll* omit R.   577 *chytgerdet a wnaei* R, and omit *a wnai* 578.   579 *heb allu* R.   580 *a oruc* omit R.   581 *bioed* R.   583 *llynn a oed yn* R only.   584 *yn y parc* W, *yno* R.   586 *yn graff* omit R.   586 *gwytheu* W, *gwythi* R.   587 *llamu* W, *llawn* R.   587 *kwynaw* W, *gwywaw* R.

o iryeit gwerthwawr, a'y rodi yn llaw y morwyn. 'Dos,' heb hi,
'a hwn genhyt, a dwc y march racko a'r dillat genhyt, a dot
gyrllaw y dyn gynheu. Ac ir efo a'r ireit hwn ar gyfeir y gallon,
ac or byd eneit yndaw ef a gyuyt gan yr ireit hwn; a gwylya
ditheu beth a wnel.' A'r vorwyn a doeth racdi a chwbyl o'r ireit
a rodes arnaw, ac adaw y march a'r dillat gyr y law, a chilyaw
a mynet ruthyr y wrthaw ac ymgudyaw a discwyl arnaw.

Ac ymphen rynhyawd hi a'y gwelei ef yn cossi y vreicheu ac
yn kyfodi y vynyd, ac yn edrych ar y gnawt, a chymryt kewilyd
yndaw e hun a oruc mor hagyr y gwelei y delw ry oed arnaw.
Ac arganfot a oruc y march a'r dillat y wrthaw, ac ymlithraw a
oruc hyny gafas y dillat, ac eu tynnu attaw o'r kyfrwy, ac eu
gwiscaw a oruc ymdanaw, ac escynnu ar y march o abreid. Ac
yna ymdangos a oruc y vorwyn idaw, a chyfarch gwell idaw
a oruc. A llawen uu ynteu vrth y vorwyn, a gofyn a oruc efo y'r
vorwyn pa dir oed hwnnw a ffa le. 'Dioer,' heb y vorwyn,
'iarlles wedw pieu y castell racco, a ffan uu varw y (252)
harglwyd priawt efo a edewis genthi dwy iarllaeth, a heno nyt
oes ar y helw namyn yr vn ty racco nys ry dycco iarll ieuanc
yssyd yn gymodawc idi, am nat ai yn vreic idaw.' 'Truan yw
hynny,' heb yr Owein. A cherdet a oruc Owein a'r vorwyn y'r
castell, a discynnu a oruc Owein yn y castell, a'r uorwyn a'e duc
y ystauell esmwyth, a chynneu tan idaw a'y adaw yno. A dyfot
a oruc y vorwyn at y iarlles a rodi y gorflwch yn y llaw.
'Ha vorwyn,' heb y iarlles, 'mae yr ireit oll?' 'Neur golles,

589 *y morwyn* W, *un o'r llawuorwynyon* R.   591 *efo* W, *ef* R.
591–2 *ar gyfeir . . . eneit yndaw* R only.   593 *ditheu* omit R.
594 *gyr* W, *ach* R.   594 *a chilyaw* omit R.   596 *ef* omit R.
598 *yndaw e hun* omit R.   598 *y gwelei* W, *oed* R.   598 *ry*
W, *a* R.   600 *y dillat ac eu tynnu* W, *tynnu y dillat* R.   601 *a oruc
ymdanaw* omit R.   601 *a oruc* after *abreid* R.   603 (first) *a
oruc* omit R.   603–4 *efo y'r vorwyn* W, *idi* R.   606 *harglwyd
priawt efo* W, *gwr ef* R.   606 *heno* W, *hediw* R.   607 *racco* W,
hwnn R.   608 (first) *yn* omit R.   610 *oruc* W, *wnaeth* R.
610–11 *Owein yn . . . y ystauell* R, *hi a'y dwyn ef a wnaeth y vorwyn
y'r castell* W.   612 *llaw* R, *law* W.

CHWEDYL IARLLES Y FFYNNAWN

arglwydes,' heb hi. 'Ha vorwyn,' heb y iarlles, 'nyt hawd genhyf i dy atneiryaw di; oed diryeit hagen y minheu treulaw gwerth seith ugein punt o iryeit gwerthuawr wrth dyn heb wybot pwy yw. Ac eissyoes, vorwyn, gwassanaethya di efo yny uo diwall o gwbyl.' A hynny a oruc y vorwyn, y wassanaethu ar fwyt a diawt a than a gwely ac enneint hyny uu iach. A'r blew a aeth y ar Owein yn toruenneu kennoc. Sef y bu yn hynny trimis, a gwynnach oed y gnawt yna no chynt.

Ac ar hynny diwarnawt y clywei Owein kynhwryf yn y kastell, ac arlwy mawr, a dwyn arueu y mywn. A gofyn a oruc Owein y'r vorwyn, 'Pa gynhwryf yw hwn?' heb ef. 'Y iarll a dywedeis ytti,' heb hi, 'yssyd yn dyfot wrth y castell y geissyaw diua y vreic hon a llu mawr ganthaw.' Ac yna gofyn a oruc Owein y'r vorwyn, 'A oes varch ac arueu y'r iarlles?' 'Oes,' heb y vorwyn, 'y rei (253) goreu o'r byt.' 'A ey di y erchi benfic march ac arueu y mi at yr iarlles,' heb yr Owein, 'val y gallwn vynet yn edrychyat ar y llu?' 'Af yn llawen,' heb y vorwyn. A dyfot at y iarlles a oruc y vorwyn a dyuedut wrthi cwbyl o'y ymadrawd. Sef a oruc y iarlles yna chwerthin: 'Y rof a Duw,' heb hi, 'mi a rodaf idaw varch ac arueu vyth, ac ny bu ar y helw ef eiryoet varch ac arueu well noc wynt. A da yw genhyf i eu kymryt ohonaw rac eu caffel o'm gelynnyon avory o'm hanfod. Ac ny wn beth a vyn ac wynt.' A dyfot a wnaethpwyt a gwascwyn du telediw, a chyfrwy fawyd arnaw, ac a dogyn o arueu gwr a march. A gwiscaw a oruc ymdanaw, ac escynnu ar y

---

614 *arglwydes* W, *oll* R.   615 *di yr hynny;* R.   615 *hagen* R only.   617 *yw* omit R.   617 *vorwyn heb hi* R.   620 *dorwennu kenfo* W.   621 *noc y buassei gynt* R.   622 *diwarnawt* after *Owein* R.   623 *ac arlwy mawr* omit R.   624 *heb ef* omit R.   625 *heb hi* after *iarll* 624 R.   625 *dywedeis i* R.   626 *Ac yna* omit R.   627 *y'r vorwyn* omit R.   628 *y mi* after *erchi* R.   629 *at yr iarlles* omit R.   629 *val y* W, *pei* R.   630 *yn llawen* omit R.   631 *y vorwyn* omit R.   631-2 *y hymadrawd o gwbyl* R.   632 *yna* omit R.   634 *ef* omit R.   634 *well noc* W, *kystal ac* R.   637 *o ffawyd* R.   638 *oruc Owein ymdanaw* R.

march a mynet ymdeith, a deu vaccwyf gyt ac ef yn gyweir o
veirych ac aruéu.

A ffan doethant parth a llu yr iarll, ny welynt nac emyl nac
eithaf idaw. A gofyn a oruc Owein y'r mackwyeit pa vydin yd
oed yr iarll yndi. 'Yn y vydin', heb wynt, 'y mae y pedeir
ystondard melynyon racco yndi. Dwy yssyd o'e vlaen a dwy
yn y ol.' 'Ie,' heb yr Owein, 'ewchi drachefyn ac arowch vyvy
ym porth y kastell.' Ac ymhoelut a orugant hwy. A cherdet a
oruc Owein racdaw trwy y dwy vydin vlaenhaf hyny gyueruyd
a'r iarll. A'e dynnu a oruc Owein efo o'y gyfrwy yny vyd y rydaw
a choryf, ac ymhoelut pen y varch parth a'r castell a oruc. A ffa
ovit bynhac a gafas (254) ef a doeth a'r iarll ganthaw hyny doeth
y borth y castell lle yd oydynt y macwyeit yn y aros. Ac y mywn
y doethant, a'r iarll a rodes Owein yn anrec y'r iarlles, a dywedut wrthi val hyn: 'Wely di yma ytti pwyth yr ireit bendigedic
a gefeis i genhyt ti!' A'r llu a bebyllywys yg kylch y castell, ac
yr rodi bywyt y'r iarll y rodes ef y dwy iarllaeth idi trachefyn.
Ac yr rydit idaw ynteu y rodes hanher y gyfoeth e hun, a chwbyl
o'e heur a'y haryant a'y thlysseu, a gwystlyon ar hynny. Ac
ymdeith yd aeth Owein, a'y wahawd a oruc y iarlles ef a'y
gyfoeth oll, ac ny mynwys Owein namyn kerdet racdaw eith-
avoed y byt a diffeithwch.

Ac val yd oed y velly yn kerdet, ef a glywei discyr vawr y
mywn coet, a'r eil, a'r drydet. A dyfot yno a oruc. A ffan daw,

639 *uackwy* R.   641 *emyl* W, *ol* R.   643 *Yn* omit R.
643 *heb wynt* after *yndi* R.   644 *yndi racko* R.   644 *yn y vlaen*
R.   645 *ewch chwi* R.   646 *ym* W, *yn ymyl* R.   646 *ac*
omit R.   647 *Owein* W, *ynteu* R.   647 *trwy y . . . vlaenhaf*
omit R.   648 *efo* omit R.   649 *a oruc* omit R.   650 *ganthaw hyny doeth* omit R.   651 *lle yd . . . y aros* W, *at y mackwyeit* R.
651 *ac Owein a rodes y iarll* R.   653 *val hyn* omit R.   654 *a
gefeis i genhyt ti* omit R.   655 *bywyt* R, *bwyt* W.   655 *ef* W,
ynteu R.   656 *ynteu* omit R.   657 *a* W, *a'e* R.   658 *a wnaeth
yr iarlles idaw ef* R.   658-9 *a'e holl gyfoeth* R.   660 *y* omit R.
661 *y velly* omit R.   661 *disgrech uawr* R.   662 *aoruc Owein* R.
662 *daw* W, *doeth* R.

ef a welei clocuryn mawr yg kanawl y koet a charrec lwyt yn ystlys y bryn. A hollt a oed yn y garrec, a sarff a oed yn yr hollt, a llew purwyn a oed yn emyl y sarff. A ffan geissyei y llew vynet 665 odyno y neityei y sarff idaw, ac yna y dodei ynteu diskyr. Sef a oruc Owein yna, dispeilyaw cledyf a nessau ar y garrec. Ac val yd oed y ssarf yn dyfot o'r garrec y tharaw a oruc Owein a chledyf yny vyd yn deu hanher y'r llowr, a sychu y gledyf, a dyfot y fford val kynt. Sef y gwelei, y llew yn y ganlyn, ac yn 670 gware yn y gylch ual milgi (255) a uackei e hun. A cherdet a orugant ar hyt y dyd educher.

A ffan uu amser gan Owein orffowys, discynnu a oruc ac ellwg y varch y bori y mywn dol wastat goedawc. A llad tan a oruc Owein, a ffan uu barawt y tan gan Owein yd oed gan y 675 llew dogyn o gynnut hyt ymphen teir nos. A difflannu a oruc y llew y ganthaw, ac yn y lle nachaf y llew yn dyfot attaw a chaeriwrch mawr telediw ganthaw, a'y vwrw ger bron Owein, a mynet y orwed y am y tan ac ef. A chymryt a oruc Owein y kaeriwrch a'y vligyaw, a dodi golhwythyon ar vereu yg kylch 680 y tan, a rodi y iwrch oll namyn hynny y'r llew y yssu. Ac val y bydei Owein y velly ef a glywei och wawr, a'r eil, a'r trydet, ac yn agos attaw. A gofyn a oruc Owein ay dyn bydawl a'y gwnaei. 'Ie, ys gwir,' heb y dyn. 'Pwy wyt titheu?' heb yr Owein. 'Dioer' heb hi, 'Lunet wyf i, llawvorwyn Iarlles y Ffynyhawn.' 685 'Beth a wney di yna?' heb yr Owein. 'Vyg karcharu,' heb hi, 'o achaws gwraang a doeth o lys yr amherawdyr y uynny y iarlles

---

665 *purwyn* W, *purdu* R.   665 *yn ymyl y garrec* R.   666 *idaw o'e vrathu* R.   666 *ac yna ... diskyr* omit R.   667 *yna* omit R.   669 *y'r llowr* omit R.   669 *a sychu y gledyf* R only.   670 *y'r fford* R.   672 *educher* W, *hyt ucher* R.   673–4 *a gellwng* R.   674 *y bori* omit R.   674 *goedawc wastat* R.   675 (first) *Owein* omit R.   677 *y ganthaw* W, *y wrthaw* R.   679 *y orwed y* omit R.   681 *oll* omit R.   681 *o'e yssu* R.   681–2 *ual yd oed Owein uelly* R.   682–3 *a'r dryded, yn gyfagos idaw* R.   683 *dyn* R only.   683 *a'y gwnaei* omit R.   686 *yma* R.   686–7 *yd ydys o achaws marchawc* R.   687 *o lys Arthur* R.   687–8 *y uynny y iarlles yn priawt* R only.

yn priawt, ac a uu rynnawd gyt a hi. Ac yd aeth y dreiglyaw llys Arthur, ac ny doeth vyth drachefyn. A'r kedymdyeith oed ef genhyf i mwyhaf a garwn o'r holl vyt. Sef a oruc deu o weissyon ystauell y iarlles, y oganu ef y'm gwyd i, a'e alw yn dwyllwr bradwr. Sef y dywedeis inheu na allei eu deu gorff hwynt amrysson a'e vn gorff ef. Ac am hynny (256) vyg karcharu yn y llestyr maen hwn a orugant, a dywedut na bydei vy eneit y'm korff ony deuhei ef y'm hamdiffyn i yn oet y dyd. Ac nyt pellach yr oet no threnhyd, ac nyt oes y mi neb a'e keissyo ef. Sef oed ynteu, Owein vab Uryen.' 'A oed diheu genhyt titheu,' heb yr ynteu, 'pei gwyppei y gwreanc hwnnw hynny y deuhei efo y'th hamdiffyn di?' 'Diheu, y rof a Duw,' heb hi. A ffan uu digawn poeth y golwythyon, eu rannu a oruc Owein yn deu hanher y rydaw a'r vorwyn, a bwytta a orugant. A gwedy hynny ymdidan hyny uu dyd dranoeth.

A thrannoeth gowyn a oruc Owein y'r vorwyn a oed le y gallei ef caffel bwyt a llewenyd y nos honno. 'Oes, arglwyd,' heb hi; 'dos yna drwod,' heb hi, 'y'r ryt, a cherda y fford gan ystlys yr afon, ac ymphen rynnawd ti a wely gaer vawr a thyryeu amhyl arnei. A'r iarll pieu y gaer honno goreu gwr am vwyt yw, ac yno y gelly vot heno.' Ac ny wylywys gwylwr y arglwyd eiryoet yn gystal ac y gwylywys y llew Owein y nos gynt.

Ac yna kyweiryaw y varch a oruc Owein, a cherdet racdaw trwy y ryt hyny welas y gaer. Ac y'r gaer y doeth Owein, a'y

688 *llys* R, *lys* W.   689–90 *A chedymdeith y mi oed ef mwyaf a garwn o'r byt* R.   690 *o* omit R.   691 *y'm gwyd i* omit R. 692 *bradwr* omit R.   692 *inheu* W, *i* R.   692 *y deu* R. 694 *hwn a orugant* omit R.   695 *deuhei* W, *delei* R.   696–7 *Sef yw ynteu* R.   697–8 *heb yr ynteu* omit R.   698 *gwreanc* W, *marchawc* R.   698 *efo* omit R.   699 *di* omit R.   699 *y rof i a* R.   699–700 *dogyn poethet* R.   700–1 *y ryngtaw* R. 703 *Trannoeth* R.   705 *heb hi, y'r ryt* omit R.   707 *yn amyl* R.   708 *yw o'r byt, ac* R.   708 *y gelly di uot* R. 709–10 *y nos honno* R.   711 *Ac yna y kyweirywys Owein y uarch, ac y kerdawd racdaw* R.   712 *Ac y doeth y'r gaer*, R.

aruoll a wnaethpwyt idaw yno yn anrydedus, a chyweiryaw
y varch yn diwall, a dodi dogyn o vwyt ger y vron. A mynet a
oruc y llew y bresseb y march y orwed, hyt na leuassei neb 715
o'r gaer vynet yg kyfyl y march racdaw. A diheu oed gan Owein
na welas eiryoet lle kystal y wassanaeth (651) a hwnnw. A chyn
dristet oed bop dyn yno a chyn bei agheu ym pop dyn onadunt.
A mynet a orugant y vwyta, ac eisted a oruc yr iarll ar y neill
law y Owein, ac un verch oed idaw ar y tu arall y Owein; a 720
diheu oed gan Owein na welas eiryoet vn vorwyn delediwach
no honno. A dyuot a oruc y llew rwng deutroet Owein dan y
bwrd, ac Owein a'e porthes o bop bwyt o'r a oed idaw ynteu.
Ac ny welas Owein bei kymeint yno a thristyt y dynyon.

Ac am hanner bwytta gressawu Owein a oruc y iarll. 'Madws 725
oed itt bot yn llawen,' heb yr Owein. 'Duw a wyr y ni nat wrthyt
ti ydym drist ni, namyn dyuot deunyd tristit in a gofal.' 'Beth
yw hynny?' heb yr Owein. 'Deu uab oed im, a mynet uyn
deu uab y'r mynyd doe y hela. Sef y mae bwystuil yno, a llad
dynyon a wna, ac eu hyssu. A dala vy meibon a oruc, ac auory 730
y mae oet dyd y rof i ac ef y rodi y vorwyn honno idaw, neu
ynteu a ladho vy meibon y'm gwyd. Ac eillun dyn yssyd arnaw,
ac nyt llei ef no chawr.' 'Dioer,' heb yr Owein, 'truan yw hynny.
A phy un a wney dithau o hynny?' 'Duw a wyr arnaf,' heb yr
iarll, 'uot yn diweirach gennyf diuetha vy meibon a gafas o'm 735
hanuod, no rodi uy merch idaw o'm bod (652) o'e llygru a'e
diuetha.' Ac ymdidan a wnaethant am betheu ereill. Ac yno y
bu Owein y nos honno.

A'r bore trannoeth wynt a glywynt twryf anveitrawl y ueint.
Sef oed hynny, y gwr mawr yn dyuot a'r deu uab gantaw. A 740
mynnu kadw y gaer a oruc y iarll racdaw a dilyssu y deu vab.
Gwisgaw a oruc Owein y arueu ymdanaw a mynet allan ac
ymbrawf a'r gwr, a'r llew yn y ol. A phan welas y gwr Owein
yn aruawc, y gyrchu a oruc, ac ymlad ac ef. A gwell o lawer yd

714 *rac y uronn* R.   716 *racdaw* omit R.   717 At this point
W finally breaks off, and we return to R at col. 651.

ymladei y llew a'r gwr mawr noc Owein. 'Y rof i a Duw,' heb y gwr wrth Owein, 'nyt oed gyfyg gennyf ymlad a thidi bei na bei yr anifeil gyt a thi.' Ac yna y byryawd Owein y llew y'r gaer a chaeu y porth arnaw, a dyuot y ymlad ual kynt a'r gwr mawr. A disgrech a oruc y llew am glybot gofut ar Owein, a drigyaw yny vyd ar neuad yr iarll, ac y ar y neuad hyt ar y gaer, ac y ar y gaer y neidyawd yny uu gyt ac Owein. A phaluawt a trewis y llew ar benn ysgwyd y gwr mawr yny uyd y balaf trwy bleth y dwyclun ual y gwelit y holl amysgar yn llithraw ohonaw. Ac yna y dygwydwys y gwr mawr yn varw. Ac yna y rodes Owein y deu vab y'r iarll; a gwahawd Owein a oruc yr iarll, ac nys mynnawd Owein namyn dyuot racdaw y'r dol yd oed Lunet yndi.

Ac ef a welei yno kynneu uawr o tan, a deu was penngrych wineu delediw yn mynet a'r uorwyn o'e bwrw yn y tan. A gofyn a oruc Owein py beth a holynt y'r uorwyn. A datkanu eu kyfranc a orugant idaw mal y datkanassei y uorwyn y (653) nos gynt; 'ac Owein a pallwys idi, ac am hynny y llosgwn ninneu hi.' 'Dioer,' heb yr Owein, 'marchawc da oed hwnnw, a ryued oed gennyf i pei gwypei ef uot ar y uorwyn hynny na delei y hamdiffyn. A phei mynnewch chwi vyui drostaw ef, miui a awn y chwi.' 'Mynnwn,' heb y gweisson, 'mynn y gwr a'n gwnaeth.' A mynet a orugant y ymdiot ac Owein. A gofut a gafas Owein gan y deu was, ac ar hynny y llew a nerthwys Owein, ac a oruuant ar y gweisson. Ac yna y dywedassant wynteu, 'Ha unbenn, nyt oed amot ynni ymlad namyn a thydi dy hun, ac ys anhaws ynni ymlad a'r anifeil racko noc a thydi.' Ac yna y dodes Owein y llew yn y lle y buassei y uorwyn yg karchar, a gwneuthur mur maen ar y drws, a mynet y ymlad a'r gwyr mal kynt. Ac ny dothoed Owein y nerth ettwa, a hydyr oed y deu was arnaw. A'r llew vyth yn disgrechu am vot gouut ar Owein. A rwygaw y mur a oruc y llew yny gauas ffordd allan, ac yn gyflym y lladawd y neill o'r gweisson, ac yn y lle y lladawd y llall. Ac uelly y differassant hwy Lunet rac y llosgi. Ac yna yd aeth

775 *disgrethu* R.

Owein a Lunet gyt ac ef y gyfoeth Iarlles y Ffynnawn. A phan doeth odyno y duc y iarlles gantaw y lys Arthur; a hi a uu wreic [idaw] tra uu vyw hi.

Ac yna y deuth ef fford y lys y Du Traws, ac ymladawd ac ef, ac nyt ymedewis y llew ac Owein yny oruu ar y Du Traws. A phan doeth ef fford y lys y Du Traws y neuad a gyrchwys, ac yno y gwelas ef pedeir gwraged ar hugeint, telediwaf o'r a welas neb eiryoet, ac nyt oed dillat ymdannunt werth pedeir ar hugeint o aryant. A chyn tristet oedynt ac (654) agheu.

A gofyn a oruc Owein udunt ystyr eu tristit. Y dywedassant wynteu panyw merchet ieirll oedynt, ac ny dothoedynt yno namyn a'r gwr mwyhaf a garei bop un onadunt gyt a hi. 'A phan doetham ni yma ni a gawssam lewenyd a pharch ac an gwneuthur yn vedw. A gwedy y beym uedw y deuei y kythreul bieu y llys honn, ac y lladei an gwyr oll, ac y dygei an meirch ninneu ac an dillat ac an eur ac an aryant. A chorfforoed y gwyr yssyd yn yr un ty [a ni], a llawer o galaned y gyt ac wynt. A llyna itti, unben, ystyr an tristit ni. A drwc yw gennym ni, unben, dy dyuot titheu yma rac drwc itt.' A thruan uu gan Owein hynny, a mynet a oruc y orymdeith allan.

Ac ef a welei uarchawc yn dyuot attaw, ac yn y aruoll trwy lewenyd a charyat ual bei brawt idaw. Sef oed hwnnw, y Du Traws. 'Duw a wyr,' heb yr Owein, 'nat y gyrchu dy lewenyd y dodwyf i yma.' 'Duw a wyr,' heb ynteu, 'nas keffy ditheu.' Ac yn y lle ymgyrchu a wnaethant, ac ymadoydi yn drut, ac ymdihauarchu ac ef a oruc Owein, a'e rwymaw a'e dwylaw ar y gefyn. A nawd a erchis y Du Traws y Owein, a dywedut wrthaw, 'Arglwyd Owein', heb ef, 'darogan oed dy dyuot ti yma y'm darestwng i, a thitheu a deuthost ac a orugost hynny. Ac yspeilwr uum i yma, ac yspeilty uu uyn ty. A dyro im vy eneit, a mi a af yn yspyttywr, a mi a gynhalyaf y ty hwnn yn yspytty y wann ac y gadarn tra vwyf vyw, rac dy eneit ti.' Ac Owein a gymerth hynny gantaw, ac yno y bu Owein y nos honno.

804 *Owein ac ef, a'e* R.

A thrannoeth y kymerth y pedeir gwraged ar hugeint a'e meirch a'e dillat, ac a dathoed gantunt o da a thlysseu, ac y kerdwys ac wynt gyt ac ef hyt yn llys Arthur. A llawen uuassei Arthur wrthaw gynt pan y kollassei, a llawenach yna. A'r gwraged hynny, a'r honn a vynnei drigyaw yn llys Arthur, (655) hi a'e kaffei, a'r honn a vynnei vynet ymeith, elei. Ac Owein a trigywys yn llys Arthur o hynny allann yn pennteulu, ac yn annwyl idaw, yny aeth ar y gyfoeth e hun. Sef oed hynny trychant cledyf Kenuerchyn a'r vranhes. Ac y'r lle yd elei Owein a hynny gantaw, goruot a wnaei.

A'r chwedyl hwn a elwir Chwedyl Iarlles y Ffynnawn.

816 *vnnei* R.

NOTES

On the various titles of the story see Introduction, section II.

1 *yr amherawdyr Arthur*: the title of emperor is given to Arthur here and in BR, and the word itself is also found in BM (WBM 178. 34) and in a more archaic spelling in Peniarth MS. 16 (WBM p. 90, col. 1) as *amperauder*, a spelling which M. Watkin, CFM 335, misinterprets. An earlier example of its application to Arthur occurs in BBC 72. 8–10 *ameraudur llywiaudir llawur* i.e. commander and director of battle (cf. use of *gweith* in the same sense as *llawur* here). It should be noted that the word is derived directly from L. *imperator*, and not through French, and may therefore have still retained the more general sense of 'commander-in-chief', if that is what Nennius' *dux bellorum* (chap. 56) means. For the scanty references to Arthur before Geoffrey of Monmouth see E. K. Chambers, *Arthur of Britain* (London, 1927), *Y Bywgraffiadur Cymreig* (London, 1953) 14–15, R. S. Loomis, 'The Arthurian Legend before 1139' in *Wales and the Arthurian Legend* (Cardiff, 1956) 179–220, K. H. Jackson's two chapters on Arthur in Loomis's *Arthurian Literature in the Middle Ages* (Oxford, 1959) 1–19, Rachel Bromwich, TYP 274–7, and T. Jones, *Bulletin* 17. 235–52.

1 *oeḃ*: the omission of the direct relative particle is normal in R before *oeḃ*, in contrast to J (as here), and W (as in 37, 126, 129). Cf. IEW § 83 (*b*).

1 *yg Kaer Llion ar Wysc*: this localization of Arthur's court agrees with Geoffrey (cf. BD IX 12, according to which Arthur held court there one Whitsuntide at the climax of his power), and is paralleled in Per. 152. 3, 165. 27, and Ger. 385. 2, 409. 25. In older tradition, as recorded in K & O 495. 25, 497. 26, 505. 23 by implication, his court was at Kelli Wic in Cornwall, and there is a hint of the same tradition in Kei's summons at the end of BR (21. 1–3) *pwy bynnac a vynno kanlyn Arthur, bit heno y Ghernyw gyt ac ef*, though Rhonabwy had met him near Rhyd-y-groes on the Severn.

1 *sef yḃ oeḃ yn eisteḃ biwarnawt*: *sef*, i.e. the pres. copula *ys* + 3 sg. m. pron. *ef* (OW *issem*) and *ys ef* 444 below, anticipates some element in the sentence, and the following relative particle shows the relationship of *sef*, and therefore of the anticipated element, to the verb. Here the indirect relative particle indicates an adverbial relationship— 'it is thus that he was, sitting one day.' That the words *oeḃ yn eisteḃ* do not form a continuous construction 'was sitting' is shown by the reading of L and C, which place *biwarnawt* after *oeḃ*. The instances of *sef* in a number of medieval prose texts have been collected and classified by Emrys Evans in *Bulletin* 18. 38–54. In this text there are

five examples of *sef*+*oeb*+subject+complement (469, 696, 740, 800, 819), and three of *sef*+*a oruc*+verbnoun (632, 666, 690), and one (446) of *sef*+verb+verbnoun, all with direct relative particle (omitted before *oeb*). The examples in 240, 289, 444, 586, 670, 692, all with anticipation of a noun or noun clause, seem logically to demand *a* rather than the *y* which actually occurs. They are explained as mere opening formulae equivalent to English 'now', 'then', and this implies that the construction had come to be used without any sense of its original force remaining. A case like *sef y bu yn hynny trimis* 620, is like the present one in that *trimis* is adverbial, i.e. 'it is thus (long) that he was in that state, for three months'. The construction is in most cases altered or omitted in the later copies.

2 *ystauell*: on the significance of the spelling in J here and in 10, see Introduction, section IV.

2 *Owein*: on the name and historical connexions of Owein, see TYP 479–83, and for his father Uryen, TYP 516–20.

3 *Kynon*: for the name and historical connexions of Kynon, probably contemporary with Owein in the North (i.e. Southern Scotland) in the latter part of the sixth century, see TYP 323–4, and for his father Clydno, associated with Edinburgh, TYP 309–10.

3 *Kei*: for Kei and his father Kynyr see TYP 303–8. The suggestion of R. M. Jones (*Bulletin* 14. 119) that both names are Irish and synonymous (both meaning 'path') is open to objection on the grounds that so well-known a character is unlikely to have a foreign name, that neither occurs as a common noun in Welsh, and that while in the satire on the conventional epic catalogue in K & O several such names occur, they are not meant seriously, whereas Kei has an established place in tradition.

3 *Gwenhwyuar*: see TYP 380–5.

4 *ffenestyr*: the MS. has *ffenest^r*, but the expansion is confirmed by the similar passage in 59 below. L and C add *wydyr* 'of glass'.

5 *dywettit*: subjunctive, as shown by the unvoicing ('caledïad') of -*d*- to -*tt*- by an adjacent -*h*- (from -*s*-). Cf. *gwypom* 21, *gwypych* 29, *tebyccwn* 98, *atteppych* 388, *cattwo* 417, and see IEW § 110, GCC § 132 (137).

5 *uot*: whereas J has *bod*, possibly with lenition unexpressed, though there is some fluctuation in usage. T. J. Morgan, TC § 91, declares that it is wrong to argue that the vn. *bot* in such cases is a direct object and so unlenited after an impersonal verb-form; when it introduces an object noun clause the early evidence favours lenition in all positions.

5 *porthawr*: though not one of the twenty-four officers of the court according to the Welsh laws (cf. LlB 8. 17), some of his rights and duties are noted in them; cf. LlB 7. 18, 24. 21, and LlIor 10. 15, 19. 12, and especially § 35.

NOTES

5 *Glewlwyt Gauaeluawr*: see TYP 361–3. R has *Gauaelawr*, J the normal *-uawr*.

6 *ar ureint*: although *breint* is 'right', 'privilege', the meaning of this phrase is probably no more than 'as'; cf. *Branwen* 127 *ar ureint kyweirdeb y neuab*, and Ger. 423. 39 *ar ureint rybut* 'by way of warning', and the modernization *yn lle* in L and C. According to K & O (456. 4) Glewlwyt filled this office only on the first of January each year: according to Ger. (385. 35) he filled it only at one of the three chief festivals (Christmas, Easter, and Whitsuntide), leaving it to his deputies during the rest of the year.

6 *ysp a phellennigyon*: cf. K & O *ospeit a ffellennigyon* 459. 15, and sg. 486. 16.

7 *moes y llys a'e deuawt*: cf. *Pwyll* 74.

9 *y'r neb a bylyei letty*: for the lodgings assigned to the various officers of the court cf. LlB 9. 7–10. 14; the text here implies that others also might have such rights. On *o'e venegi* 'to tell it' for the commoner *y*, see WG 277, GCC § 51(56), note 2.

11 *ar demyl*: *temyl* usually represents L. *templum*, but here the sense is rather 'mound', 'heap'. One might think of an archaic spelling *temel for *tyuyl from L. *tumulus*, were it not that the word occurs in its present form with the same sense in two poems in *Gwaith Guto'r Glyn* (ed. J. Ll. Williams and I. Williams, Cardiff, 1939) 154, 242. The occurrence in Thomas Richards's dictionary of 1753 is copied from AB 238, which in turn derives from this present instance. With *irvrwyn* cf. Ir *urluachra*, TBC 889.

12 *gobennyb*: cf. LlB 10. 8 *a'r gobennyb yb eistebho y brenhin y dyb a vyb dan y benn ynteu y nos* with reference to the *brawdwr llys*.

13 *goganewch*: M. Watkin, CFM 269–70, suggests a French origin for this verb in view of its contrasting senses, 'make fun of' here and 'praise' elsewhere (see GBGG), but it seems preferable with L & P § 515 note, to treat it as a native derivative of *canu* 'sing' along with *dychanu* 'satirize' and *darogan* 'prophesy'. The cognate OIr *fo-cain* does not help with the semantic problem. For the noun *gogan*, cf. Ger. 416. 4.

15 *ysteneit*: the suffix *-eit* is attached to some, but not all, names of containers, and to the adjective *llawn* (to give *lloneit*, cf. *Pwyll* 341, and below *lloneit y bwrn* 23, and *lloneit gorflwch* 588), meaning the amount the container can hold.

15 *golwyth*: for the twelve *golwython kyfreithawl* see LlB 51. 24–, and rather differently LlIor § 136 and GMWL 158; for the word itself, K & O 456. 21, and Per. 120. 31.

19 *teckaf*: spv. with unvoicing similar to that in *dywettit* 5 above, and for the same phonetic reason; the superlative ends in *-haf* from *-samo-*.

22 *y'r gegin ac y'r vebgell*: for the association of the two cf. PKM

52. 8. Kei's status as steward is clearly implicit in this statement, for in the Laws we find *ac ef* [sc. *y distein*] *o gyureith a geiff mebyant ynn y gegin a'r vebgell* (LlB 11. 24). The status of the steward was high enough for him in some respects to act as the king's deputy: cf. LlB 12. 12 *Distein bieu tygu dros y brenhin pan vo reit*, and 12. 27 *Ef a gynneil breint llys yn awssen y brenhin*.

25 *weithon*: 'now'. Cf., with synonyms in place of *gweith*, *yr awrhon* and *y wershon* in Per. 119. 12, 128. 22.

25 *bieu*: on the rise and analysis of the form see IEW §§ 83, 161, WG § 192, and GCC §§ 83–84 (88–89). Here we have an instance of the less common sense of obligation: Kei has fulfilled his part of the bargain; now the others are in duty bound to do their share. The history of the senses of English *owe*, *ought*, and *own*, or *have* and *have to*, provide something of a semantic parallel.

25 *uy ymbiban*: i.e., as J puts it, *yr ymbiban a ebewit ym*. The objective genitive sense with possessive particles is far commoner in Celtic than in English, which prefers the subjective use.

29 *odidockaf*: for the unvoicing see note on *teckaf* 19. The diphthong *-aw-* remains only in what were stressed syllables in Old Welsh, i.e. in final syllables (and monosyllables), but becomes *-o-* in originally unstressed ones. Cf. sg. *marchawc*, pl. *marchogyon*. The stress moved back to the penult in Med. Welsh, probably in the eleventh century (LHEB § 207), whence Mod. Welsh sg. *marchog*, but *-aw-* continued to be written in final syllables for several centuries. With the added *g-* of Mod. Welsh *godidog* cf. the frequent prosthetic *f-*, likewise lost in lenition, attached to initial vowels in Irish.

31 *namyn*: usually 'except', 'but for', but here apparently reinforcing *vn*, 'the one and only son'.

32 *ryvic*: frequently referred to with disapproval in the romances as a fault of character, e.g. Per. 124. 12, Ger. 386. 39, and *camryuic* 399. 8.

32 *bot yn y byt a orffei*: *bot*, lacking in R, is supplied from J. The subjunctive in *a orffei* depends on the indefiniteness of the antecedent, which is only implied in the relative pronoun. Cf. *kaffel a ymbibanei a mi* 90, and *yn keisaw a orffei arnaf* 95.

33 *a gwedy daruot im goruot*: J has *ac wedy*, which is phonetically identical with R (except perhaps for the position of juncture): a parallel instance is *ac irat* for *a girat* in Ger. 441. 19. For *daruot* here cf. *kynn daruot ibaw ymgyweiraw* in *Pwyll* 239: when the vn. is used after a preposition as the equivalent of a subordinate clause the notion of past time is conveyed by the use of *daruot* 'happen', 'befall'. Without *daruot* such phrases have no specific time-reference.

33 *ar bob camhwri o'r a oeb*: cf. *Pwyll*, note on 19. After 'each, all, every, any, other' and any superlative adjective the partitive *o'r a* is

NOTES

the normal Med. Welsh form of the positive relative. *Camhwri* is a formation from *camp* 'feat' from L. *campus*.

34 *yn vn wlat a mi*: may be taken either as 'in (the) same country as I' or as 'homochthonous with me', reading *vnwlat*. Cf. *unllef, unlliw* in *Pwyll* 12, 20, and *unuam* in *Branwen* 7, and *vntwf ac vnpryt ac vnoet ac vnwisc* in Per. 133. 20, in all of which scribal habit separates the numeral from the noun (as it does in a case like *vnllygeityawc* 'one-eyed' (Per. 152. 35), where we should certainly join them, or in the three instances of *teirnossic* in K & O 490. 6, 27, 492. 19), but the absence of the article suggests that we are dealing with adjectives, and that *yn* here is the predicative particle, not the preposition.

38 *a'r parth arall y kerbeis*: 'and on the other side I traversed it'; the oblique relative *y* shows that *parth arall* is adverbial, and this is more explicit in C which has *ac ar y parth arall ir afon y cerddais i*. R and J have *a gerbeis*, making *parth* the object 'and I traversed the other part'. Kynon seems to have crossed the river at noon, but it is not clear whether he then continued in the same direction or was retracing his steps along the other bank after finding a ford. Since the castle was near the sea, this latter part of the journey must have been downstream, and since during the first part of the day's journey he had seen no sign of the castle, it seems most likely that he was following the river downstream from the moment he entered the valley. Cf. the parallel version in 237.

39 *pryt nawn*: 'the hour of nones', i.e. about 3 p.m. The elements are also used as a compound meaning 'afternoon', for which cf. 330.

40 *gwelwn*: the impft. is specially common with *gwelet* in narrative, meaning 'I could see', while the pret. *gweleis* is rather 'I caught sight of', as in 55. With the scene cf. K & O 472. 8 *hyt pan deuuant y uaestir mawr yny uyb kaer a welynt mwyaf ar keyryt y byt*.

40 *kaer vawr llywychedic*: on the possible significance of the apparent non-lenition of *llywychedic* here see Introduction, section IV. For a similar but more splendid description cf. BM 180. 35 *cant y neuab a tebygei y vot yn vaen llywychedic gwerthuawr*.

40 *gweilgi*: from its occurrence here and in *Branwen* 4. 253, this must be a quite ordinary prose word for 'sea', but the cognate MIr *fáelchú* 'wolf' suggests rather a kenning drawn from the language of poetry; cf. GBGG. The phrase *mor a gweilgi* occurs in BM 180. 14, 186. 28.

41 *deu was pengrych melyn*: R and J have *velyn* with lenition after a dual noun, though neither has it in the first adjective. This mutation loses ground after the Med. Welsh period (cf. TC § 21), but is still present in C. With the description cf. that in BM 181.

42 *ractal*: cf. BM 181. 7, Per. 120. 23.

43 *am bop vn*: so R; W repeats the preceding phrase *am ben pop vn* in error.

43 *cordwal*: the *-l*, in contrast to the expected *-n* (which occurs in J) is unexplained. C substitutes *mychuddliw* 'jet-black' for *newyð*.

47 *paun*: on this and the R form *pawin* see ELIG § 59.

48 *a chyllell* . . .: the text is not quite clear here. W, as it stands, mentions the knives with gilded blades and ivory hafts, and says that the young men were shooting them. R mentions the knives, saying that the ivory hafts were *nodeu* to them, and that they were shooting their knives. J mentions the knives, and their ivory hafts as being targets for them to shoot at. The translators, without the help of J, have not taken *not* as target, and have therefore assumed *saethu* must mean 'throw' instead of 'shoot at'. The text of W, with *ac eu carneu* added from R and J, will give the required meaning if for *ym pob* 'in each' we read *yn bob* 'as each', making *yn bob vn o'r ðeu not* the equivalent of *yn nodeu uðunt* (*yw saethu*) in R and J. It would be odd if the narrator were to give these youths such splendid bows and arrows if they were to engage only in knife-throwing. We are to understand rather that so great was their skill with the bow already that for practice their targets were now the ivory hafts of their daggers viewed end on, a small white circle. The later versions agree with this interpretation; combining L and C we get (in MW spelling) *a'r rei hynny gwedy roi eu blaeneu yn y ðayar oeð yn lle nodeu ganthunt yn eu saethu*, i.e. 'and those [their daggers], their blades being thrust into the ground, they had as targets in their shooting'. The less explicit reference in Per. 146. 17 confirms the probability of the practice. (I am glad to have this interpretation confirmed by the independent conclusions of E. Rowlands in *Llên Cymru* 6. 109–10.)

51 *yn y ðewreð*: cf. PKM 50. 8 *er amser y bu hitheu* [Riannon] *yn y dewreð* 'when she was in her prime', and Ger. 413. 20 *a thitheu gwas ieuanc vyt ac ymblodeu dy ðewreð a'th ieuengtit*, and GPC s.v. *dewredd*.

52 *yn newyð eillaw*: *newyð* plus a lenited vbn. has the force of an adverb, 'newly', with a passive participle; a commoner example is *newyð eni* 'new-born', cf. *Buched Dewi* 21. 7, and M. Richards, *Cystrawen y Frawddeg Gymraeg* (Cardiff, 1938) § 52.

53 *ac ysnoden*: *a chysnoden* W, in which *kysnoden* is not otherwise recorded, seems to imply an erroneous interpretation on the part of the scribe of a spelling in which *a* or *ac* was not separated from the following word, and perhaps a manuscript in which the spirant mutation was not regularly expressed. Cf. Introduction, section IV.

55 *a chyuarch gwell iðaw*: Loth, Mab. 2. 188, proposed to add *a uynnwn* since, in fact, it is the host who gives the first greeting, and to preserve the parallelism with 242 *yn mynnv kyuarch gwell y'r gwr melyn*, but Kynon for vividness' sake states the intention as a fact, and no change is really necessary.

56 *gwybot*: for the sense 'manners', 'courtesy', cf. Per. 129. 11, Ger. 390. 22, and the negative *anwybot* in *Pwyll* 33.

NOTES

58 *nyt oeb gyuanheb yn y gaer*: for lenition of the subject after some verbal forms see IEW § 16 (g), GCC § 17 (21), and, for a full discussion, TC chap. IX. The meaning is not quite clear: *kyuanheb* may mean the buildings themselves (as in *Pwyll* 71), or inhabited buildings (though there is no suggestion in what follows that the place was ruinous like that of Ynywl in *Gereint*), or signs of life; this last is the most appropriate in the context. Elsewhere in the romances it means an inhabited place, e.g. Per. 119. 20, Ger. 391. 36, or 'habitation', 'settlement', as Per. 149. 23, 25, but the most similar to the present instance is the passage in PKM 51, where it is clearly signs of life or living beings that is meant, for in this case the buildings remain *yn wac, diffeith, anghyuanheb, heb byn heb uil ynbunt*.

59 *pedeir morwyn ar ugeint*: for *hugeint* R and Mod. Welsh *hugain* see TC § 147 (iii) and *Orgraff yr Iaith Gymraeg* (Cardiff, 1928) § 94 (4), and for the arrangement of the elements in compound numerals see WG 258.

61 *haccraf*: cf. note on *teckaf* 19; the unvoicing affects not only an immediately preceding voiced stop, but also one followed by a liquid, e.g. *cwpplaf* in *Pwyll* 643, spv. of *cwbyl*, or a nasal, e.g. *dyckynet* 357, eqv. of *dygyn*. The unvoicing appears in the eqv. and spv. in MW, and in Mod. Welsh is extended to the cpv.

62 *harbach oeb no Gwenhwyvar*: it seems tactless to use this expression in the queen's presence, but the comparison is probably a conventional one, and the hearer or reader is not expected to remember that she is listening. Indeed, until she interposes to reprove Kei (222), we do not know for sure that she has been within earshot, or paying any attention to the story.

64 *kyfodi*: as a mark of respect; cf. Per. 129. 10, 153. 1, 155. 30.

67 *role*: *rol* R, *roly* J. The meaning is uncertain as the word is not found elsewhere in Welsh. The later manuscripts have 'oil'. We may compare MIr *roludh* vn. with a quotation *luirecha aga roludh 7 slega aca slibudh*, i.e. 'breastplates being polished and spears being sharpened', from ZCP 6. 29, line 3. The source is ME or OFr; cf. NED s.v. Roll. v.[3] 'polish, burnish' with a solitary example from Laȝamon's *Brut*, in the later manuscript written *c*. 1275, where it replaces 'rock' of the earlier manuscript (which continued in use, cf. *Sir Gawain and the Green Knight* 2018). *Y mywn role* implies some kind of polishing instrument, whence J & J's 'rocker'.

67 *kyn wynhet a'r dim gwynhaf*: this rather feeble type of comparison is not infrequent; cf. Per. 134. 1 *cochach oebynt no'r dim cochaf*, and 176. 5 *a chyn vlaenllymet a'r dim blaenllymaf*, though for the former Peniarth MS. 7 (WBM 615. 30) has *cochach oebynt no fion* (than a foxglove), like K & O 476. 12.

68 *a'r drydeb chwech ... a'r petweryb chwech*: numerals are normally treated as masculine nouns, but in the former of these two cases we

have a fem. adj. in W and J, and a masc. one in R. Perhaps the fact they are female has confused the issue. At the same time adjectives that do not distinguish gender but do distinguish number treat the numerals as plural nouns, hence *chwech ereill* 66, and *y pedwar hynny* GCC § 46 (51).

70 *crys*: J & J translate as 'girdle', like Ir *crios*, but as 'shirt' in Per. 139. 22, the more usual meaning. From Ger. 393. 27, 400. 33, where they render it 'shift', it appears that the *crys* was also a female garment.

71 *bliant*: cf. NED s.v. Bleaunt; the *-n-* in ME, MLG, and Welsh is peculiar, for the OFr forms, from which they must all derive, start with *blialt*, whence *bliaut*, and if the word was really current, its pronunciation cannot have depended on a misreading of *bliant* for *bliaut*. Originally the name of an article of dress, and often still so in ME, the word came also to indicate a rich fabric, and has exclusively this sense in MW.

71 *orffreis*: ME and OFr *orfreis* from Med. L. *auriphrygium* 'gold embroidery'; for the detail cf. ZCP 13. 373 § 6 *brat co srethaib di or impe*.

73 *y danaf ac y'm kylch*: similarly J, but R has the plural, i.e. not Kynon alone, but his host also sat down. On the possible palaeographic implications see the Introduction, section IV.

73 *eiste*: on the loss of final *ð* see WG 180–1.

74 *a'y gorugant yn ðiwall o'e holl ystarn*: *diwall* is often associated with abundance of food, as *Pwyll* 91, Ger. 393. 41 *diwallu o wellt ac yt*, and similarly 400. 14 *diwallu [y tei] o wellt a than*, i.e. 'supply', 'furnish'. The adjective is derived from *gwall* (cf. Ir *faill*, earlier *fall*) 'lack, defect, fault', and 'they made him faultless as regards all his harness' gives good sense and is confirmed by the paraphrase in C *ac velly y chwech cyntaf a gymerth fy march i ai cwairoedd ef yn ddiwall, ac a sychoedd harnais yn lana ag y gallai vod*, i.e. 'and so the first six, who took my horse, groomed him perfectly, and polished (his) harness as clean as could be'. I do not understand J & J's 'made its bedding without stint', for the derived verb *ystarnu* 209, below, must, from the context, mean 'to harness'; cf. LlB 24. 10. J's reading, with *prouant* for *ystarn*, means that they saw to it that Kynon's horse lacked nothing in the way of provisions. Cf. E. Rowlands, *Llên Cymru* 7. 118 for the interpretation 'relieved him of his harness'.

75 *ysweineit*: so R. W's *ysgweineit* is probably a slip—perhaps the scribe was expecting *ysgwier* (cf. WBM p. 209. 5)—but for the possibility of an archaic spelling see Introduction, section IV.

78 *y gwr gynheu*: the adverb is used adjectivally, i.e. 'the man [I mentioned] just now'. Cf. *y dyn gynheu* 591, 'the man [we saw] just now'.

81 *lieineu y bwrt*: so R, but W has *y llieinyeu*. The double article is probably only a slip, the scribe not having looked far enough ahead and

so thinking the clause was *a bliant oebynt y llieinyeu*, a perfectly possible reading. He then added *y bwrt*, but forgot to delete the first *y*. A less likely explanation is that the double article is a sign of French influence; cf. M. Watkin, YBH xvi.

82 *neu uuelyn*: lenition after *neu* 'or'. On *bual*, from which *buelyn* is derived, see ELIG §§ 38, 92. Cf. K & O 458. 16 *buelin goreureit*, and 456. 15 *llynn ymual*, and LlB 108. 5 *tri chorn buelyn*.

82 *an bwyt*: *an* may be one morpheme or two, according to whether it contains *a* 'and' as well as *an* 'our'. The contraction is not common in MW, which prefers *ac an*, but it may occur in *Pwyll* 58 (see note) and certainly occurs in PKM 83. 20. It is, however, so uncommon for a sentence in narrative not to begin with *a* 'and' that we should probably be justified in reading *a'n* 'and our' here.

83 *eirmoet*: lit. 'during my lifetime', and so appropriate only when the subject is 1st pers. sg.; the neutral form is *eirioet*, really 3rd sg. m., which J uses here.

83 *ac nas kigleu*: the sense may be either the restricted one 'heard of', or the extended one covering perception by any sense except sight, and so here 'tasted'. Note the anticipatory infixed obj. pron. -*s*, and cf. *mi a'e managwn* 99, in each case with an object to follow. On *kigleu*, see WG 338, 371–2, IEW § 133 (b), GCC § 128 (4) (133. c. 2), and for the analogical 1st sg. *kiglef*, cf. K & O 470. 18, Ger. 408. 6, 423. 20.

86 *hanher bwytta*: but *bwyt* in R and J. When the phrase is repeated 249, 725, it is in the same form as W has here.

89 *pa ryw gerðet*: the omission in R is a mechanical one, the scribe's eye having jumped from one occurrence of *ryw* to the next. The inquiry is the normal one made of a guest, and asks in effect who he is, where he has come from, where he is going, and what his business is. Though it is a formal opening gambit in conversation, it is not merely a formality, and an adequate answer is expected. Cf. Ger. 428. 24, 436. 39, 437. 33; the pejorative negative *agherðet* (405. 38) has the sense of 'misadventure'.

91 *bei kymeint ac eu drycket ymbiðanðynnyon*: lit. 'so great a fault as their badness of conversationalists', i.e. '. . . as that they were such poor conversationalists'. For the silence cf. OGL 127 note 25. With *ymbiðanðyn* cf. *ymbiðanwreic* WBM 62. 31.

92 *ymbiðanem . . . ony bei . . .*: 'we should have conversed if it had not been . . .'. The imperfect indicative and subjunctive are frequent in MW in conditional clauses where English uses the pluperfect.

96 *neu vinheu a orffei arnaw*: the construction is not parallel to the preceding clause, which would lead us to expect *neu y gorffwn inheu arnaw*. Instead, the subject is made emphatic, and the verb after a disjunctive pronoun subject is in the 3rd pers. sg. in W and R, though J has *a orffwn* (cf. *minneu a vynnaf* 18). The implication of the R

and J reading *ar bawp*, followed by L and C, is perhaps that this is for Kynon the final test, that he will either be overcome or will have overcome every opponent.

99 *a geissy*: the alternative in R, *yb wyt yn y geissaw* is more modern, and is adopted by L and C. Note that the preceding object must be resumed in pronominal form before the vn., or that if it is suppressed, as in J (perhaps only accidentally), the mutation remains.

99 *kymryt tristyt a goueileint ynof*: for the idiom cf. Per. 130. 20 *llefein a drycyruerth a gymerth pawb ynbunt*, and for similar phrases but with a different verb see *Pwyll* 450, 574, and Ger. 416. 25.

101 *arnaf*: cf. 367 below, and Per. 134. 13 *a Pheredur a adnabu ar y vorwyn mynnu robi ibaw ef . . . mwy noc y arall*; the meaning is 'sense, perceive, notice, something in or about someone'.

101 *kanys gwell genhyt ti*: 'since you prefer'; the addition of *yw* in R is superfluous, as *kanys* already contains the copula *ys*, but shows that, as with *os*, the sense of the presence of the copula was weakening, and *kanys* was on the way to being felt as conjunction only.

102 *dy afles no'th les*: for the contrast cf. Per. 139. 17 *o gallaf les mi a'e gwnaf: afles ny wnaf inheu*, and Ger. 410. 38 *yr a bel nac o les nac o afles y mi*; cf. too Ir *leas* and *aimhleas*.

103 *yn vore*: adv. 'early'; but *y bore* J, i.e. 'in the morning', and the adv. *yuory* 'tomorrow', which could easily be confused, are all possible readings.

104 *y dobwyt*: the older translators do what they can with R's *yb wyt*, but the reading of W is superior. On the formation of these tenses with *bot* in verbs which are not otherwise compounds of *bot* see GCC § 138 note 2 (143 note 3).

104 *vchot*: the adv. is etymologically connected with *uch* 'higher', but the sense 'up there' is not always clearly demanded by the context, and it seems more nearly synonymous with *racco* 'yonder'. One might compare OIr *ucut* 'yonder', which Thurneysen, GOI 300, associates with *ocut* 'near thee'; see also WG 403, and cf. 144, and *Pwyll* 339.

107 *llannerch vawr o vaes*: cf. *Pwyll* 13 *ef a welei lannerch yn y coet, o uaes guastat*, and Per. 120. 16.

108 *ym penn yr orsseb*: so R and J; the W reading repeats *ym perueb* from the preceding sentence. Cf. K & O 472. 19 where the giant herdsman is also found *ar benn gorsetua*.

108 *gwr du mawr*: there is no idiomatic reason for assuming a dark-skinned man, for adjectives of colour applied to human beings usually denote the colour of their hair or clothing. This is generally accepted when *melyn* is applied to the two youths and Kynon's host (42, 51). Loomis, indeed, calls the latter the 'Yellow Man' (AT 279), and justifies it on the ground that he was dressed in yellow as well as having yellow hair, but this is not in accord with modern English

usage. Cf. 194 below, where *y gwr du* refers to the knight dressed in black, and Per. 128. 7 *y gwas melyn*, where the colour of the hair is referred to.

109 *vn llygat yg knewillyn y tal*: cf. the *gwr du mawr vnllygeityawc* in Per. 152. 35. W's *yg gnewillin* involves the mechanical error of writing *-g g-* for *-g k-*.

111 *deuwr yn y byt ny chaffo . . .*: an indefinite or negatived antecedent plus reference to the future requires the subjunctive in the relative clause. The usual rule is that in direct relative clauses when the relative is positive the verb is 3rd pers. sg., but when it is negative the verb agrees in number with the antecedent; but this was not invariably the medieval practice, as Professor Thomas Jones shows in *Llên Cymru* 7. 112–15.

112 *anhygar . . . hagyr . . .*: cf. Ger. 443. 41 *nyt gwell y mi uot yn hegar vrthyt ti noc yn anhegar—a robi bonclust a oruc ibi*, PKM 88. 8 *a dodi garymleis anhygar*, BR 11. 9 *gwr garwgoch anhegar*. The persistence of the spelling *anhegar* in R is hard to explain as it is not an etymological vowel but merely an early spelling for *-y-*, the prefix *hy-* corresponding to Ir *so-*. The giant is not hostile but he is ugly, and Kynon is being warned that his bark will prove worse than his bite. The reading of J, *agyr*, is perhaps no more than an error, for it is not found elsewhere, and the absence of *h-* weakens the intended word-play; if genuine, it could be a loan-form of L. *acer*, and thus not inconsistent with the giant's *gwrthgrocheb*; cf. also OIr *acher*.

112 *coydwr*: 'forester'. R prefers the English loanword *wtwart*, which occurs also in *Gwaith Dafydd ap Gwilym* (ed. Thomas Parry, Cardiff, 1952) 27. 3; the later manuscripts have *ceidwad* 'keeper'. Loomis points out (AT 287) the semantic parallel with the Irish character Fer Caille in *Togail Bruidne Da Derga* (ed. Eleanor Knott, Dublin, 1936); among the points of similarity between the giant and Fer Caille, such as the one eye, the one foot, and the club, it may be noted that the description of him as *maeldub* (l. 345) supports the interpretation of *du* in note on 108 above.

114 *o'r llannerch*: so R, correctly, for f. sg. nouns are not lenited after the article if they begin with a consonant homorganic with the *-r* of the article, such as *ll-*. The spelling *lannerch* in W seems to preserve a spelling from a period when *ll-* and *l-* were not yet distinguished orthographically.

122 *ymphen*: the W spelling has the same phonetic intention as Mod. Welsh *ym mhen*, but preserves the radical *p-* in the same way as in its usual orthography *ym pen*; cf. *ympherueb* 146 below.

123 *mwy o lawer oeb ef*: so R; W perhaps omits *o* by accident, but cf. BM 180. 6 *mwy lawer a thegach oeb honno* (like J), and TC 252–3, where, on the analogy of L. *multo*, this is described as the 'ablative' use of *llawer*. For W's separation of *lawer* from the cpv. it qualifies,

cf. the parallel passage in BM from Peniarth MS. 16 (WBM p. 90 b 11) *mwy a thegach oeð honno lawer*, though loss of *o* would be very easy here. The phrase *o lawer* 'by a great deal' is frequent with the cpv., e.g. below 246, 265, 483, 744, all from R.

124 *a'r ffon hayarn a ðywedassei y gwr . . . ynði*: 'the iron club in which the man had said . . .'. In such cases MW fluctuates between direct and oblique relative particles, while modern literary Welsh prefers the oblique. The whole sentence is, of course, uncoordinated, and the phrase *y ffon hayarn* is never incorporated in it, but it will be plain, if we tidy it up grammatically into *Ac hyspys oeð genhyf i, Gei, vot yn y ffon hayarn y dywedassei y gwr vot llwyth deuwr ynði, lwyth petwar milwr*, that the resulting sentence is far less clear at first hearing. It is not that MW is incapable of the more complex sentence-types, but that other features of the structure of the language leave complex sentences always in danger of obscurity, and in a narrative orally delivered this cannot be allowed.

126 *yn llaw y gwr du*: Fer Caille (see note on 112) was also one-handed, and it may be that we should read here *yn vn llaw* 'in the one hand of . . .'. Even if this is not so, it would be a good point that he could wield with one hand a club too heavy for four warriors to lift.

130 *a chymryt . . . a tharaw . . . hyny ryð ynteu*: the vns are, as usual, equivalent to past tenses in narrative (cf. 21–23 above), but for vividness we have the present indicative in the subordinate clause. Such combinations of present and past are not unusual: cf. 179 below, and in Per. 136. 15 and 138. 36 *pan ðaw* followed by a past tense, and Ger. (WBM p. 216. 5, from Peniarth MS. 6) *a phan edrych*, against the parallel passage 431. 8 *a ffan edrychawð*. *Hyny* is primarily a temporal conjunction 'until', but in narrative it is often used with final sense 'so that', rather like the weakening of the sense of OIr *co* (GOI § 896); in this instance either interpretation is possible, and it is presumably on the basis of such ambiguous cases that the shift of meaning takes place.

134 *hyny o seirff*: the pl. demonstrative adjective used as a pl. pronoun 'those ones', cf. *Pwyll* 12 note, and 345 below; *o* is 'consisting of'. In Mod. Welsh the phrase would mean 'that of serpents', i.e. those serpents.

137 *val y gwnaei gwyr*: 'as men would do'. The subjunctive is used only in the protasis of conditional clauses, the indicative, as here, in the apodosis. In many verbs no formal distinction between past indicative and subjunctive exists but the rule may be deduced from examples containing irregular verbs or those in which in MW unvoicing occurs in the subjunctive. One instance, the 'modal' use of *oeð*, often with suppressed protasis, occurs frequently, e.g. 219, 746 below. Cf. IEW § 114 (d) *bei ys cuypun . . . nys gunaun* (not subj. *gunelun*), K & O 491. 9 *pei as gwypwn mi a'e ðywedwn* (not *dywettwn*), and *deuhei* 698, not *delei*, and *awn* 765, not *elwn*.

145 *ystrat megys dyffryn mawr*: the phrase is difficult to translate as both *ystrat* and *dyffryn* mean a broad valley as opposed to the narrower *cwm* and *glyn*. Loth's 'grande vallée arrosée' and J & J's 'vale like a great waterway' both allude to the etymology of *dyffryn* in *dwfyr* and *hynt*, i.e. watercourse.

146 *gwely*: so R and J, correctly. W has *gwelei*, perhaps merely a slip into the person and tense most common in narrative, but possibly a misinterpretation of an ambiguous older spelling such as *guele*.

148 *llech wawr*: but cf. *llech varmor* at 168. R has *varmor* in both places and is supported by L and C. With the description here cf. PKM 56. 10 *fynnawn a gueith marmor yn y chylch, ac ar lann y fynnawn cawg eur yn rwymedic urth bedeir cadwyn*.

151 *gorgrymhu*: the word is quite possible, *gor*+*crymu* (cf. Ir *cromadh*), but it is not recorded elsewhere, and R's *ergrynu* from *crynu* 'tremble' is to be preferred as supported by C's *yny dybygych di grynu'r nef ar llawr*.

152 *ef a ðaw cawat aboer*: *cawat* is f., but the introductory *ef a* formula does not vary for gender or number. Cf. *Pwyll* 77, with pl. subject following, and Per. 138. 8 for another f. sg. subject.

153 *ac a vyð abreið ytti y dioðef hi*: 'and which it will be difficult for you to endure'. The genitive of the relative fluctuates in MW, between being regarded as direct and oblique. The construction in R 'and it will be difficult for you to endure it' is smoother.

153 *a chynllysc vyð*: R adds *y gawat*, but it seems preferable to take *byð* absolutely, as in *hinon a vyð* below, where it would be difficult to supply a subject.

155 *nyr ðarffo y'r kawat y dwyn*: the effect of *daruot* together with the perfective *ry* in *nyr* is probably to give a future-perfect meaning 'that the shower will not have carried (it) off.' The objective pronoun *y* marks the relative as accusative with a phrasal verb. Cf. note on *daruot* 33, and cf. K & O 497. 33 *neur ðaroeð iðaw ðiffeithaw* 'he had laid waste'.

157 *digriffaf*: this may be an isolated example of the *-ff-* spelling for *-f-* (= [v]), but there is no good reason why other consonants than stops should not be unvoiced in the superlative and subjunctive (see notes on 5, 19 above); the change is attested in *dyffryn* (see note on 145 above), in the adjective *diwethaf* (spv. from n. *diweð*), and in verbal forms like *rotho* and *notho* beside indicative *roðaf*, *noðaf*, but was given up quite early in favour of analogical forms. See L & P § 203.

161 *yn gyntaf y gallo*: for *kyntaf* 'quickest' cf. *Pwyll* 232.

164 *tra vych vyw*: 'as long as you live'; cf. 781 below, and Ger. 396. 14.

170 *y twryf*: a regular accompaniment of supernatural events; cf.

Pwyll 523 and 527, PKM 51. 22, 57. 11, Per. 152. 34, Ger. 449. 37.

170 *yn wwy yn ba*: 'much greater'; the commoner *o lawer* is substituted by L and C.

173 *yn wyw*: goes with *diaghei*, i.e. 'would not escape alive'.

174 *hyny attalei yr ascwrn*: an infixed object pron. *y* is concealed in *hyny*, i.e. 'until the bone stopped it'. Cf., with 1st sg. pron., *hyny'm* 191.

176 *baryflen*: lit. 'beard-cover'; Kynon seems to have closed his visor, though the wording suggests rather that he put some object over his whole head.

179 *edrychaf*: but *edrycheis* R. For the vivid present see note 130 above, and cf. 182, 647-8, 669, below.

180 *y discynnu*: the equivalent of the present participle *yn d.* On *yn* and *y* in such contexts see Arwyn Watkins in *Bulletin* 18. 362 ff; in view of the extreme rarity of *y*+vn., ibid. 369, we may be justified in emending to *yn*, with R.

186 *pan wnelut*: 'seeing that you did', rather than the temporal 'when'. For a similar use of the synonymous *pryt* cf. 388-9.

191 *a chyn bei*: cf. 718 below; on *kyn* beside *kyt* see WG 446-7.

192 *arllost y vayw*: cf. Per. 124. 27, and Ger. 437. 10. In each case the use of the butt-end seems to be a sign of contempt.

194 *ny wnaeth . . . o vawreb ymdanaf i*: the use of *mawreb* here seems not to be paralleled. The Black Knight did not take Kynon seriously enough even to hold him to ransom or despoil him of his weapons. L and C have the same reading; S has *ny wnaeth ef kyn fychaned o honof am rhoi yng-harchar*, which implies just the opposite attitude. J & J translate 'out of pride', which may be right, but *o vawreb* is oddly placed if this is the intention.

197 *tra'm kefyn*: cf. Per. 124. 19 *tra'th gefyn*, and *tu draechefyn* 406 below.

209 The sentence has no main verb as it stands in R, for though *gwedy* is not repeated, the use of the conjunction *a(c)* implies that all three verbnouns are parallel. The most probable correction is to omit *a* and add *a orugum* after *dyuot* so as to make it the main verb. Alternatively, with E. Rowlands, *Llên Cymru* 7. 118, we may read *ac wedyn* for *a gweby*. With *adaw vy mendyth* cf. Ir *co farcbad bennachtain ocai ria n-écaib*, i.e. 'to take leave of him before he died', ZCP 3. 2, § 2.

211 *ystauell*: presumably for *ystabyl* 'stable'. The mistake is probably due to *ystauell* being much the commoner word in tales of this kind, but it might also be the result of an over-eagerness to modernize the spelling, resulting in *-b-* (= [b]) being taken as the archaic *-b-* (= [v])—*ystauell* would probably be **stabell* in OW—and therefore changed into *-u-*. Such an expectation (on the part of the RB scribe

NOTES

or one of his predecessors) of archaic spellings would imply considerable antiquity for the manuscript they were copying.

212 *nas robwn*: 'that I would not give it (in exchange)'. There is no verb of saying to require the conjunct negation, but the asseveration of *y rof a Duw* has the same effect. Cf. *na buc* 437 below, and *Pwyll* 289–90, *pei caffwn bewis . . . y mae ti a bewisswn* 'if I had a choice . . . (I assure you) that it is yourself that I should choose'.

214 *chwedyl vethedigach no hwnn*: 'a tale of greater failure than this'; the noun is m., as appears from the demonstrative pron. The mutation is normal in a cpv. adjective in a negative or interrogative clause. Cf. TC §§ 24, 127 (iii), *Pwyll* 35, 224, *Branwen* 21, and *was well* 297 below, and a further example at 634.

214–18 Like 209–10 this also lacks a main verb as it stands in R. An antithesis with 213–14 is required: no one has ever told a tale of such failure against himself, but Kynon has related it now because no one he has met has ever been able to tell him more of the adventure than he knows already, and because, although the site of it is not too remote, no one but himself has come on it. To get this required sense we need to add *y bywedeis* 'that I have related it', after *hynny*, though the length of the stressed element is unwieldy. The fragmentary remains of W here (*ny y dywede*) show that this was its reading. The translators all appear to have emended to *ac eissoes odidocket yw gennyf i . . .* 'and yet I think it so remarkable that . . .'.

220 *mynn llaw vyg kyfeillt*: Kei's own oath. Cf. 224 below, and K & O 458. 22.

221 *yr hynny peth*: the translators all take this as if it were merely 'that which', but this is impossible. Either the interpretation or the text is wrong. *Yr hynny* would normally be construed as 'nevertheless', 'despite that'; this is weak in sense as there is no obvious point of contrast, as there might be if *yr hynny* were placed after *weithret* or after *gwnelut*. We have the alternative, following the translators, of omitting *peth*, or else omitting *hynny* and reading *y peth*; L has *yr hwn* (as often for *yr hyn*), and S *yr hyn*. Note the resumptive objective pronoun in *nys gwnelut*.

222 *oeb gwell*: modal *oeb*, cf. note on 137. R has *ys oeb*, which J. G. Evans transferred to WBM, but the remaining fragment of W clearly has *yfar o*, i.e. the end of *Gwenhwyfar* and the beginning of *oeb*. *Ys* occurs elsewhere before a verb, see note on 390 below. Probably the scribe of R hesitated between two forms of the copula without deleting whichever he favoured least.

225 *nyt mwy o volyant . . .*: Kei's answer seems equivocal, and it is not certain whether he means that he has always been as ready to praise Owein as she has, or that she has not always spoken well of him any more than Kei has. The translators preserve the ambiguity, except E & L who come down on the unfavourable side. The original

may, however, not be intentionally ambiguous. An exact rendering can sometimes give the wrong impression in English; for example, 'he was no worse a guide in the land he had never seen than in his own land' (K & O 471. 29) does not inspire much confidence in Kyndylic as a guide, for English idiom demands 'as good' in place of 'no worse'. Similarly here 'no more praise' should perhaps be understood as 'as much praise'. L and S omit Kei's reply.

227 *do, arglwyð*: when the question is put in the preterite the usual practice of repeating the verb in the shortest possible form as the equivalent of 'yes' gives way to the use of *do* for an affirmative, and *na ðo* for a negative reply.

228 *amser, arglwyð*: when the question is asked with the copula preceding the complement, the positive answer is simply the repetition of the complement.

230 *difflan*: 'vanish', 'slip away unnoticed'; also *difflannu* 313, 676 below. The usual Mod. Welsh form is *diflannu*, and though GPC notes *difflan(nu)* it treats the examples merely as variants. Cf. Per. 156. 21 *diflannu*, 157. 4 *difflannwys*.

234 *kerðet racðaw*: for the idiom cf. *Pwyll* 140 note, and below *kychwyn racði* 314.

236 *panyw hwnnw oeð*: 'that it was *that* one'; for *panyw* cf. WG 448, and 462 below.

249 *no chan Gynon*: the preposition *gan* normally occurs in a permanently lenited form, but where the original radical *c-* would be subject to the spirant mutation, *ch-* is found, as here, after *no* and elsewhere after *a*.

272 *ymgyfogi*: cf. GPC s.v. *cyfogaf*[1]. The reciprocal sense is recorded earlier than that of the simplex. S has *yn ol hir ymffyst*, for which see 528 below. L and C have *ymolchi*!

273 *trwy y helym ...*: 'through his helmet, headpiece, and visor' Lady Guest, 'le heaume, la cervelière et la ventaille' Loth, 'through his helmet, mail-cap, bonnet, and ventail' E & L, 'through his helm, both mail-cap and bourgoyne coif' J & J. Loth, in his footnote (Mab. 2. 18) and critical notes (2. 191), defines the cervelière (= *pennffestin*) as a mailed cap for the upper part of the head, and the ventaille (= *penguwch*) as a protector for the lower part of the face. Later *pennffestin* seems to have replaced *helym* in ordinary usage for the helmet. *Pwrqwin* might be 'of Burgundy', but Loth rejects Gaidoz's suggestion (ZCP 1. 37) that it could represent bourguignotte, a lightweight Burgundian helmet. *Penguch* occurs also in YBH 545, where Professor Watkin translates it 'the first layer of the head-armour', and where it is again linked with *bwrkwin*, rendered 'of Burgundy'; see also his notes, p. 91. For *pengwch* cf. LlB 28. 15, 62. 14. It is clear that the sword penetrates three layers before reaching the skin, flesh, and bone beneath: these are the helmet itself (*helym*), the mail-cap

sewn with rings or metal plates (*pennffestin*), and finally a woollen, linen, or silken cap, in this case of Burgundian cloth (*penngwch pwrqwin*). *Pennffestin* may, however, be synonymous with *paylet*, in which case it covers not only the top of the head but the whole head and shoulders, a sort of extensive mailed Balaclava, for which the French term is 'camail'. Cf. Per. 139. 28, Ger. 435. 3, 16. Had the blow split the Black Knight's head as far down as Loth's ventaille, it seems unlikely that he would have survived even so long as he did.

276 *duawc*: as he is usually called *y marchawc du* (but cf. 281) the adj. *duawc* at first sight looks like a mere dittography of the last syllable of *marchawc*. Cf. GPC s.v. *duog*; the citation from AB 234 simply reflects this passage, and that from Walters's dictionary is either from AB or a new formation on *du* 'ink', as the definition suggests. The quotation from Gruffudd Llwyd, fl. 1380–1420, however, of a passage referring to this story (*Cywyddau Iolo Goch ac Eraill*, ed. H. Lewis, T. Roberts and I Williams, Cardiff, 1937, 123. 9) with the form *y marchog duog*, suggests that this is not just a copyist's slip, but a genuine alternative form. It is not clear whether it is simply synonymous with *du*, or whether it has anything of the sense of its Irish cognate *dubhach* 'gloomy', 'mournful'. L, C, and S omit.

276 *ry gaffel*: perfective *ry*+vn., equivalent to a perfect infinitive.

276 *dyrnawt agheuawl*: cf. *Pwyll* 116, *angheuawl byrnawt*.

277 *ffo*: for the vn. *ffo*, against Mod. Welsh *ffoi*, cf. Per. 117. 16, 178. 25.

282 *obis y pardwgyl y kyfrwy*: GCC §§ 222, 237 has no examples of the prep. *y* after *obis* or *obuch*, and this appears to be another example of the double article (cf. note on 81), or double possessive. As in the former case the mistake is a natural one, since *y kyfrwy* is not strictly necessary to the sense, and the copyist was not expecting it. The simplest correction is to follow L in omitting the first *y*, but alternatively we could convert the second into *y'r* like C.

284 *gan y sodleu Owein*: the name is in apposition to the possessive particle and clarifies it. Cf. *Pwyll* 474, *y hwyneb hitheu Riannon*.

285 *troelleu yr ysparduneu*: *yspardun* 'spur' obviously has its origin in OFr, but the source of the -*d*- is unexplained (cf. YBH 544 note). The word is found in the oldest manuscript of the Laws, about 1200; cf. GMWL 303. *Troell*, from its connexion with *troi* 'turn' must be 'rowel'; for the implications, see Introduction, section VIII.

290 *ystret*: if this is *ýstret*, with initial stress, it is cognate with Ir *sreath* and means 'row'; cf. *ýstrat* and *srath*. If it represents OE *stræt* it will have initial stress if borrowed before the eleventh-century accent-shift (cf. note on 29), final stress if after that date. In prose texts there can be no certainty about the stress, and the etymology remains uncertain: the sense-development 'street' to 'row' or vice

versa, is equally unhelpful, and so is the question of the quality of the final consonant, for English -*t* could be replaced by Welsh -*d* at any period. Mod. Welsh has (*y*)*stryd* for 'street', apparently from the fourteenth century (EEW 127), though this seems very early in view of the history of the English vowel.

293 *erchi agori*: presumably she made the request aloud for the gatekeeper to hear, but he had gone on with everyone else into the town to see what would happen to his lord, with the result that Owein is the only person to hear and answer her.

295 *obyna*: presumably for *obyno* 'from there', i.e. from her side of the gate. The text as it stands means 'any more than you can release me after that', but then we should expect *gallut* not *gelly*, since he is speaking of an impossible condition. Occasional scribal confusion of *yma*, *yna*, *yno* is more or less inevitable, though allowance must also be made for differences of idiom. Correction to *obyno*, as in S, is indicated.

295 *oeb dyheb mawr*: cf. K & O 475. 2 *oed dyheb kelu y ryw was hwnn*.

298 *gorberch*: the parallelism with *cares* : *kar* in the preceding phrase shows that *gorberch* can refer both to male and female. In the romances the word is used of a lover and his mistress. Cf. Per. 120. 5, *gorbercha hi* 'make love to her'. This strong affection for Owein is referred to again 689 below.

300 *hwde*: quasi-imperative, also at 535 below, and Per. 168. 30. *Moesswch* 541 below (sg. *moes* in *Pwyll* 264) is a similar case. Cf. WG § 200.

301 *y maen*: the omission of R's *hwnn* makes *maen* the jewel of the ring, not a separate talisman, at first sight a more probable situation. However below, when Owein has overstayed his leave, a ring is taken from his finger by his wife's messenger, the ring which is, according to Crestien, not Lunet's, but his wife's parting gift. Of Lunet's ring no more is heard in any version.

302 *euo a'th gub ditheu*: for other examples of invisibility conferred by magic cf. K & O 472. 5, *Branwen* 420, BR 11. 20.

303 *hambwyllont hwy o'r lleon*: for the verb cf. K & O 485. 26, *Pwyll* 18; *o'r lleon* 'from here' is *o'r lle hon*. For the feminine gender of *lle*, against *y lle hwn* 551 below, cf. PKM 102–3.

319 *ystyllen heb belw eureit arnei*: cf. BM 180. 8, *y neill ystyllen a welei yn eureit a'r llall yn aryaneit*, of one of the ships he saw in his dream. See also Introduction, section VIII.

327 *lle kyn amlet anrec odidawc*: 'a place with so many rare dishes' J & J; but the text lacks any formal connexion between *lle* and *anrec*, and, at the risk of repetition, it might be better to read *yn vn lle* 'anywhere' (as E & L translate), or *yn lle arall* 'elsewhere'.

330 *prytnawn hir*: cf. 39 note, and see PKM 56. 21 *prynhawn byrr*

and note ibid. 239; Sir Ifor notes that the phrase follows close on a reference to the end of the day, and concludes that this must mean that only a little of the afternoon was left. It will be seen, on the other hand, that a good deal of time must elapse before nightfall, for Manawydan has to return home and Riannon come out to the magic *kaer* before we read *gyt ac y bu nos* 'as soon as it was dark'. One is half inclined to think that PKM should have *hanner dyb* instead of *diweb y dyb* to allow time for all this; otherwise, the difference between *prytnawn hir* and *prynhawn byrr*—assuming there is a difference— disappears. *Hir bylgeint* PKM 82. 5 would then mean 'late in the period between cock-crow and dawn' though J & J have 'at early cock-crow'. The examples are too few for a reliable interpretation. Dr. Mac Cana draws my attention to the Donegal Irish phrases *árd-tráthnóna* 'early afternoon', and *tráthnóna beag* 'late afternoon' (Seán Mac Maoláin, *Cora Cainnte as Tír Chonaill*, 309). Another possible parallel is OFr *none basse* (*Yvain* 5890), apparently 'late afternoon'. For the idea that *hir* might be 'late', cf. Skeat's note on Langland's *hei3 prime* (A text, passus VII, line 105) in his edition, vol. 2, p. 110. On the phonology of *nawn*, cf. ELIG § 33, LHEB 307–8.

335 *ysgarlat a gra a phali a syndal a bliant*: all are kinds of material, though the first subsequently becomes a colour-name. A similar change occurs generally, cf. NED s.v. Scarlet sb. and a.; 'clothed in purple and fine linen' (Luke xvi. 19) provides a well-known instance of the same kind.

344 *nac ymyl nac eithaf*: cf. 641 below, Ger. 422. 35, and K & O 472. 17 *heb or a heb eithaf*.

354 *y dwy ysgwyb*: 'her (two) shoulders'; the dual is common where items naturally occur in pairs. Cf. *ar bwy ysgwyb yr ehawc* K & O 492. 28, *deuglust* 497. 29, and *deudroet* in *Pwyll* 346.

356 *ryueb oeb . . .*: cf. *Chwedleu Seith Doethon Rufein* (ed. H. Lewis, Wrexham, 1925) 86, *a ryueb nat oeb yssic penneu y bysseb, rac ffestet y maebei benneu y bysseb a'e dwylaw y gyt*.

358 *kymryt*: eqv. adjective from noun *pryt* 'beauty'; similarly K & O 458. 9, 471. 18, and Per. 133. 29. For other examples of compared adjectives formed from nouns, see *Pwyll* 145 *amserach*, 273 *llessach*, and GCC § 36 note 3 (41 note 4), and WG § 149.

358 *beyt uei*: 'if (only) she had been'; for *pei yt uei*, cf. WG 349. For the pluperfect sense, cf. note on 92 above, and below 439 and 530.

360 *yny oeb gyflawn pop lle ynbaw*: cf. BM 182. 22 *kygwn vn ascwrn ynbaw na mynwes vn ewin anoethach lle a wei uwy no hwnnw nyt oeb, ny bei gyflawn o garyat y vorwyn*; and K & O 454. 19 *lliuaw a oruc y mab a mynet a oruc serch y uorwyn ym pob aelawt itaw kyn nys rywelhei erioet*.

367 *mwyhaf gwreic a garaf*: cf. *Pwyll* 271, *y gwr mwyhaf a gery* and

note, and 320. The construction is common in the older period, cf. K & O 491. 3 *aniueil gynt a rithwys Duw no mi* '. . . that God formed earlier than me', and 491. 20 *yr anniueil hynaf . . . a mwyaf a dreigyl* '. . . and that gets about most'.

377 *dyrchafel*: the verb requires an object, and the parallel passage at 323, which has *dodi bwrð*, suggests the addition of the same word here.

380 *gwedy daruot iðaw y ginyaw*: if the construction is parallel to that at 33, we should add *uwytta* after *iðaw*, 'when he had eaten his dinner'; but there is a variety of ways of expressing the same idea. Cf. *Pwyll* 605 *guedy daruot bwyta*, 256 *a phan ðaruu uðunt y bwyd*, 437 *a phan ðaruu y wleð*, the first of which is non-personal, and the others have *daruot* in the sense of 'come to an end'.

381 *dos yma*: presumably 'come here', though *dos* is the imperative of *mynet*, not of *dyuot*. L has *dos di y gysgy*, and B adds *yth wely*. Cf. GCC § 138 note 5 (143 note 6).

385 *dyn*: 'human being' (cf. *Pwyll* 488 and note), here 'anyone'; with reference to a female, see below 397, 683–4.

386 *Lunet*: see TYP 241. S invariably has spellings with initial *E*- as *Elined*, cf. *Bulletin* 10. 44. For a similar abrupt introduction of the name of a character who has been known to us for some time but not named, cf. *Elen* in BM 187. 40.

387 *py ðerw*: on *pa*, *py* as interrogative pronouns see GCC § 78 (83). *Derw* for *deryw* (440) is not uncommon; see below 459 and *Pwyll* 328.

388 *pryt nat atteppych*: 'seeing that you do not answer'; cf. K & O 489. 17 *pryt na'm gedy* 'seeing that you will not leave me alone'.

389 *py wyneb yssyð arnat ti*: Guest has 'what change hath befallen thee', Loth gives 'quel honneur est le tien', E & L 'where is your respect', and J & J 'what a face hast thou'. Loth points out that *wyneb* often means 'honour', but his unusually literal rendering suggests he was not quite sure what the meaning was. One's natural inclination to render it 'how can you have the face (to come now) seeing that you didn't come . . .' probably need not be resisted for it conveys the notion that she ought to be ashamed of herself or has dishonoured herself by showing disloyalty and ingratitude.

390 The text in R is rather confused unless it is meant to give an impression of incoherence, but that is unlikely. The emendation is that suggested by J & J 282. The inclusion of *ys* is somewhat doubtful, assuming it is the syllabic form of the 3rd sg. infixed pronoun object (for which see *Bulletin* 2. 284), since the supporting pronoun is *dydi*, 2nd sg. The spelling *dyti* is peculiar, and *tydi*, with unexpressed lenition, would be more normal. If *ys* is correct we must assume it anticipates the noun object *dy dy* 'thy house', where again the spelling *ti* for *ty* is unusual. B has *paham na ddoi ti i edrych y govud a vy*

NOTES

arnaf j, a minnav gwedy dy wnaethur di yn gywoethog, with which L agrees.

391 *ny thebygwn i na bei well dy synnwyr*: the two negatives give a strongly positive effect, 'I really did think you would have more sense'.

393 *ennill*: as is clear from 394, the sense is 'make good the loss of', 'replace'. *Y gwrda hwnnw* is the lady's late husband.

393 *peth arall ny ellych byth y gaffel*: 'something else thou mayest never obtain' J & J, 'anything else. You cannot get him back' E & L. Both punctuations are at first sight possible, and E & L were probably led to adopt the reading they did because the negative relative is *ny* not *na*. But the construction is normal for MW, and the subjunctive in *gellych* would not be possible in a principal clause.

395 *gallut gwrha gwr*: the translators take the text as *gallut wrha gwr* 'you could marry a man', but the failure of lenition in *gwrha* leaves open an alternative, perhaps preferable, 'Yes, you could;' said Lunet, 'marry (impv.) someone as good or better than he.'

395 *gwr a vei gystal*: the use of the relative with compared adjectives is a sporadic feature of MW prose. Some examples in PKM are *llathen aryant a uo kyuref a'e uys bychan* 33. 19, *tebygach ganthunt cael kywilyb a uei uwy no chael iawn a uei uwy* 34. 1, *llessach ubunt uynet y gysgu noc eisteb a wei hwy* 37. 3, *kyweira attep a uo gwell* 41. 22; the concentration of examples in *Branwen* is interesting. In Irish the comparative-superlative is always predicative in a relative clause, and the same may once have been true of Welsh. Cf. L & P § 324. For an even hastier marriage between a widow and her husband's slayer, cf. Per. 131–2, where it is imposed by Peredur as a condition of granting quarter to the latter.

398 *kyffelybu*: vn. from adj. *kyffelyb*; the usual sense is therefore 'compare', 'liken', as in Per. 140. 22 *kyffelybu duhet y vran . . . y wallt y wreic uwyhaf a garei*, or reflexively, as at 155. 22 *ymgyffelybet pawb ohonawch a'e gilyb*, i.e. 'match yourselves with', 'pair yourselves off'. The sense required here, 'mention', 'propose', is not paralleled in any of the early examples in GPC s.v. *cyffelybaf*, and these examples are followed by *y* not *wrth*. On both grounds correction to *kyrbwyll* (cf. 204) is possible.

402 *att y gilyb*: the reciprocal pronoun is fossilized in the 3rd sg. m. form; cf. L & P § 385 (4).

409 *drwc yw dy anyan*: such an opening is hardly calculated to conciliate Lunet, and it will imply greater tact in her mistress if *anyan* is understood as 'temper' rather than 'nature', so that she is reproached merely with bridling up without sufficient cause. On the other hand Lunet cannot afford to take offence again or she may lose all opportunity of getting her own way. Cf. the compound *drycanyan*, LlB 113. 17, where it is obviously considered a serious failing.

412 *pa fforð y gallaf i hynny*: the omission of a main verb after *gallu* in such cases is normal. Cf. 440 below, and *Pwyll* 48, 51, 516.

420 *ar ueðwl mynet*: one would expect this to mean 'with the intention of going', but it is clearly equivalent to *yn rith mynet* 'under pretence of going'.

424 *chwedleu o lys Arthur gennyt*: for a similar verbless formula cf. K & O 457. 23, 487. 1.

426 *kaffel ohonaf*: 'that I have obtained', i.e. that she has been successful in her mission. For *o* expressing the agent with a vn., cf. *Pwyll* 180.

429 *yscyfalhau*: cf. the noun *yscaualwch* in *Pwyll* 576, and the note in PKM 155 where Sir Ifor collects examples of the adj. *ysgyualaf* 'private', the noun *yscyfalwch* 'privacy', and this one instance of the verb; we may add three from Ger. 415. 32, 417. 11, 30. In view of the noun *yscyfalawch*, beside the form *yscaualwch* from a stem *yscaual-*, it seems that *-af* simply represents *-a*, as in C.Ch. 119 (for loss of *-f* see WG 180). The verb, like most examples of the noun, is based on this short stem. The variation may suggest that the word is not of native origin, and Watkin (YBH 34 note, CFM 185–6) suggests an OFr etymology. The most likely sense for the verb is 'empty', 'clear', so as to create privacy. Although the word *ysgafala* survived in the Welsh Bible (1588), as Sir Ifor notes, the later manuscripts misunderstood this passage; C has *a mi a baraf wnaethur ysgaffyllde o pop parth yr dre megis y Caffo pawb olwc arno ef*, with which L, B, and S are in agreement. Here it has suggested the idea of scaffolding, as if Owein was to make a triumphal entry into the town. This seems to be exactly the opposite of the old meaning. The translators have taken *tref* to mean 'town', except for Loth, who renders it 'maison', and *erbyn hynny* ('by that time') rather improbably as 'en vue d'un entretien particulier'.

432 *llun llew*: it is curious to find these lion clasps at this stage of the story. If they are not an anticipation of the title 'Knight of the Lion' that Crestien bestows on Owein, they may imply that for some quite other reason Owein was traditionally associated with the lion. The later manuscripts, which, except for S, omit the lion episodes entirely, nevertheless all include this detail here.

438 *handit gwell itt*: 'it is the better for you'; pres. impers. of *hanuot* 'be', see GCC § 153 (156).

442 *y iarlles*: hitherto *yr iarlles*, as in Mod. Welsh, but both forms of the article are found in MW before consonantal *i-*; cf. GCC § 23 (27), WG § 114 (ii).

444 *ys ef y roðaf*: cf. note on 1 above. If we do not translate 'now I give you the choice' (*Bulletin* 18. 53), we may make sense of *y* by taking it as 'it is thus that I give you your choice in the matter', lit.

'... that I put it at your choice'. For a local use, cf. K & O 452. 13 *sef y dyuu* 'this is where it came (to her)'.

446 *o le arall*: goes with *gwr* or *kymrut*; if the former, it cannot follow immediately as the relative clause takes precedence, as below 517 with *ac am y varch*.

450 *a belei o varchawc*: 'whatever knight came'; *a* is antecedent and relative, and the indefinite relative requires the subjunctive. For the idiomatic sg. in a partitive construction representing 'all the', cf. K & O 499. 7–12 *ac yna y kynnullwys Arthur a oeb o gynifywr ... ac a oeb a gicwr dethol a march clotuawr*, and *Branwen* 179 *a oeb o of yn Iwerbon yno, o'r a oeb o perchen geuel a mwrthwl*; and see further Dr. Mac Cana in *Ériu* 20, 212.

452 *a'r da hwnnw a rannei Owein*: cf. Ger. 415. 23, *yny gyuoethoges y lys a'e gydymdeithon a'e vyrda o'r meirch goreu a'r arueu goreu ac o'r eurdlysseu arbenniccaf a goreu*.

453 *hyt nat oeb vwy gan y gyfoeth garyat dyn o'r byt oll no'r eibaw ef*: the usual copula order, complement before subject; lit. 'so that the love of no man in the whole world by his subjects was greater than his', i.e. 'so that no one in the whole world was more beloved by his subjects than he.' Cf. *caredic gan y gyuoeth* in *Pwyll* 647. *Eibaw* is 3rd sg. m. possessive pronoun 'his', like Fr *le sien*, usually with the article and often with supporting pronouns as well. Cf. GCC § 58 (57), WG § 161, *Branwen* 35 *by ryw neges yw yr eibaw ef?*, and the 1st sg. *meu* 550 below.

455 *Gwalchmei*: see TYP 369–75, and cf. *Llên Cymru* 6. 241–3.

462 *ymbiban Kynon*: although Kynon's story is not retailed immediately to Arthur (as in F), he has come to hear of it since, presumably in consequence of Owein's disappearance.

465 *or llas*: 'if he has been killed'; an isolated form of the past passive, formed in much the same way as the corresponding OIr one, with a *-to-* suffix which forms verbal adjectives in Greek, Latin, and Germanic. As in Latin and Germanic the bringing together of two dental stops produced *-s(s)*. For other instances cf. K & O 503. 2, 5, 8, 26, 34, but *llabwyt* 4.

469 *amlawbynyon*: cf. GPC s.v. *amlaw*[1], with examples only from this passage and 493 below. The meaning is given as 'camp followers, ignoble crowd', but it is difficult to see why such an explanation is necessary in this context, without any other evidence for the meanings 'ignoble, mean, common' being adduced, and why the word should not be referred to *amlaw*[2] to give the meaning 'additional personnel, supernumeraries', a more direct route to the required sense 'camp followers'.

474 *gwahawb*: the act of inviting to stay; cf. 658, 755, and Ger. 399. 40.

475 *ny wybit eu hystyr yn y gaer*: 'their presence was scarcely

observed in the castle' Guest, 'on ne s'apercevait pas de leur présence dans le château' Loth, 'it [their number] was not noticed in the fort' or 'their purpose in the court was not known' E & L, 'their presence was not felt in the castle' J & J. It is difficult to know what sense attaches to *ystyr* here with any precision; E & L, remembering that it can mean 'reason, cause, account, story, explanation', give alternatively in a footnote the not unreasonable interpretation that their hosts did not know the reason for their journey, but this does not follow very cogently on *kyt bei mawr eu niuer*. The usual interpretation, explicit in Lady Guest's 'so vast was its extent', is that the castle was so huge that even three thousand plus camp followers did not make it seem crowded, but the sense-development in *ystyr* is not clear in this instance. B, the only late manuscript available at this point, has *a chyd bei vawr yr eniver, nid oedd gyvyngach y gaer erddynt* (and similarly S), which suggests that this interpretation is correct.

479 *noc vybei*: probably for *noc a vybei* 'than what was usual'. The *gweisson y meirch* are taken as the very bottom of the social scale.

492 *kyffelyb y rei hynny*: probably for *y'r rei*, i.e. 'like to those ones'; otherwise perhaps 'the like of those', but GPC does not encourage that interpretation.

502 *arwyb ymwan*: cf. Per. 136. 17, 150. 32, a token of his readiness to take on all comers.

505 *a edy ti*: R has *a oeb ba y ti* 'would it be good for you'. In view of the answer *gadaf* 'I allow', the question must have contained *a edy ti* 'will you allow?'. *Da* is written above in the manuscript and may therefore be an attempt at mending the text. With it removed, the emendation adopted here becomes both easier and more necessary.

511 *bop eilwers*: 'alternately'; cf. Ger. 421. 37.

516 *cwnsallt*: a loose garment worn over his armour and covering the horse as well. Sometimes apparently it had one's arms on it, but in this case clearly not, as its effect was to serve as a disguise. GPC gives no etymology; cf. BR 15. 17 note, where Dr. Richards rejects Watkin's suggestion of OFr *corselet*. D. Silvan Evans's Latin *consolida* is hardly better, and should have given *kysswllt*. Professor Watkin revises his opinion in YBH 541 note, and CFM 77, proposing OFr *ca(i)nsil* as the starting-point. He also suggests, CFM 406, OFr *cainse* as the origin of *chamse* (K & O 475. 36, which he would read *chainse*), but the apparently different treatment of two similar or identical syllables makes it hard to accept both of these suggestions. Other examples occur in Per. 173. 11, 39, and Ger. 450. 5. Cf. too KB 241.

517 *Rangyw*: see Introduction, section VIII, p. lxii.

517 *ymdanaw*: apparently a dittography of *ymdanaw* 516, so that we should read *ibaw* with all the later manuscripts.

521 *godeuawc*: the form of this adjective is uncertain; -*d*- may be

d or *ḃ*, *-u-* may be the vowel *u* or the consonant *v*. The later manuscripts have *gobenawg* (L), *gobenawc* (C), *gobennawg* (B) here (S omits), and *goddefawg* (L, S), *goddefawc* (C), *goddevawg* (B) in 523 below. *Gobennawc* looks a perfectly possible word, but I do not find it in the dictionaries, and it may be only a misreading (*b* for *d*, and *n* for *u*) of *godeuawc*. Despite the unanimity of the later manuscripts that this represents *goḃevawc*, as well as the spelling *godhefawc* in T. Wiliems's dictionary (MS. Peniarth 228) s.v. *aggressio*, Anwyl modernizes it as *godeuog*, and glosses it 'keen, sharp'.

528 *clefyḃeu*: cf. *cleḃyfeu* 541, the normal form; for a similar metathesis cf. K & O 471. 2 *cleuyḃawd Kei* 'a blow from Kei's sword', and L & P § 257.

528 *ymffust*: *ffust* (cf. Ir *súiste*, both from L. *fustis*, see LHEB 126, 130) is 'flail', here with reciprocal-reflexive *ym-*. Cf. Ger. 398. 18, 434. 41.

532 *helym*: all the later manuscripts have 'visor'.

532 *mal y hadnabu y marchawc*: the prefixed *h-* implies an infixed object pron. 3rd sg. m. (as well as f. and pl., see TC § 62 (ii) and 63 (vii)), i.e. 'so that the knight recognised him'.

535 *kefynderw*: 'first cousin'; see GPC s.v. *caifn* (MW *keifyn*) and *derw*², a cognate of OIr *derb* 'sure, genuine', a type of compound found also in OIr *derbbráthir*.

539 *ny myn*: lenition after *ny* does not always affect *m-* in MW. Cf. TC § 131, 659 below, *Pwyll* 286, 640, and Per. 168. 6, against *cany uynhy dy wahawḃ* Ger. 400. 1.

542 *mynet dwylaw mynwgyl y*: 'embrace', i.e. put one's arms round someone's neck. Cf. Per. 134. 3, 144. 7, and TBC 2947–8.

544 *ymgaru*: cf. Per. 168. 10, where it has the sense of 'love each other'; here rather 'show affection for each other'.

548 *arouyn ymdeith*: lit. 'ask away', i.e. ask leave to depart. Similarly below 557, and Per. 170. 36, Ger. 414. 28.

550 *y mae meu i y lle hwn*: cf. note on 453. The order is copula, complement, subject. Following on *teir blyned*, 'and this place has been mine'; cf. note on 551.

551 *yḃ wyf i yn darparu*: 'I have been preparing'; note the present tense here, and cf. *Pwyll* 457.

553 *enneint*: despite the connexion with anointing implicit in the Mod. Welsh vn. *eneinio*, the noun in MW usually means 'bath', as is made clear in some contexts, e.g. PKM 86. 26, where it is associated with *kerwyn* 'cauldron' or 'vat', and similarly in Per. 155. 36 *ac a'e heneinawḃ y mywn kerwyn oeḃ is law y drws a dwfyr twym ynḃi*, and Ger. 400. 15 *ac ar oet byrr y barawt yr enneint, ac yḃ ayth Gereint iḃaw a golchi y benn a wnaythpwyt*, though sometimes the etymological sense is possible, as in 619 below, and *Pwyll* 419. The exact form of the source is not certain: the word, like the custom, is likely to date

back to Roman times in Britain, and one thinks of L. *inunctio*, but the correspondence is by no means exact, and M. Watkin in CFM 176 proposes a borrowing through OFr.

563 *yg kyfeir y trimis*: 'instead of the three months'. The literal meaning 'in the direction of' (cf. *Pwyll* 4) splits into two extended meanings: (*a*) 'opposite, corresponding to, as opposed to, instead of' as here and at Ger. 449. 18 *ac yuallen a oeb ynghyueir drws y pebyll*, and, since what is put opposite someone may be intended for them, there is also (*b*) 'for (the benefit of)', as at Per. 121. 3 *a'r neill hanner y'r bwyt a'r llyn a gymerth Peredur ibaw e hun, a'r llall a adawb yghyfeir y uorwyn*.

568 *y vodrwy*: cf. 301 above and note. Although the text is not explicit, it may be that the stone (or jewel) of invisibility was a separate item from the ring and that our correction above is unjustified. For a *maen* with magic properties cf. Per. 154. 16–19.

569 *twyllwr, bradwr*: for the combination cf. Per. 167. 39 *na thwyllwr na bradwr*, and 167. 34 *o'th twyll a'th vrat*. The phrase *yr meuyl ar dy varyf* was apparently a deadly insult, for the use of it by a wife to her husband was one of the three occasions on which the Laws gave him the right to strike her without reparation; cf. LlIor § 51.

572 *y'w letty*: on *y'w* beside the more usual *y* see WG 277, GCC § 51 (56) note 2.

583 *llynn a oeb yn y parc hyt ar gyfeir y chanawl*: *llynn*, though generally m. in Mod. Welsh (see *Rhestr o Enwau Lleoedd*, Cardiff, 1957, pp. 72–75, for examples of both genders) was also f. in MW (cf. PKM 181); *parc*, from the absence of mutation here and in the adj. in 580, appears to be m., but *páirc* is f. in Ir. The mutation in *y chanawl* implies reference to a f. noun, and the sense is best if we take it that the noun is *llynn*, and translate, with J & J, 'a lake that was in the park, until level with its [the lake's] centre'.

586 *a'y edrych*: for *edrych* with direct object meaning 'examine', 'search', cf. *Pwyll* 467, *Branwen* 474.

586 *gwytheu*: there is some variety in the forms of this word in Mod. Welsh: *gwythïen*, pl. *gwythi* (as R here), and *gwythen*, pl. *gwythennau*. While correction to *gwythen* is easy, we cannot exclude the possibility of a genuine pl. *gwytheu*.

587 *kwynaw wrth yr heul*: 'moaning because of the sun' J & J. The sense 'complain of', i.e. be suffering from, recorded by GPC, is probably imitative of English, where it is first recorded about 1600; the use of *wrth* is odd, cf. *Chwedleu Odo* (ed. Ifor Williams, Wrexham, 1926) 1. 10, *dyuot y gwynaw wrth yr eryr rac y vran*, i.e. 'to complain to the eagle about the crow', and similarly PKM 83. 18 *rac Aranrot*. We may perhaps compare the misreading in K & O *ny chwynei*, 455. 36, emended in J & J 278 and GPC s.v. *chwifiaf*, to *chwyuei*.

A reading *chwyuaw* would imply that Owein was tossing and turning in a delirium or fever.

607 *namyn yr vn ty racco*: for a similar situation, cf. Per. 135. 20.

608 *kymodawc*: 'neighbour'; Mod. Welsh *cymydog*, a derivative of *cwmwd* 'commote'. GPC regards *cymodog* as a variant under the influence of *cymod* 'agreement', though such a connotation is hardly appropriate here. We might think rather of a *cymod* from *kom-butā 'joint dwelling', and so *cymodog* 'one who shares a dwelling': cf. Gothic *garazna* 'neighbour', *razn* 'house'. For the spelling cf. Per. 152. 30 *kymodogyon*.

608 *truan yw hynny*: cf. his reticence again below, 733. The point may be that after breaking faith with his wife he is unwilling to make any sort of promise.

613 *mae*: 'where is?'; cf. *Pwyll* 256, and Per. 122. 25.

613 *Neur golles*: perhaps 'it is gone' rather than 'it is lost'.

620 *toruenneu kennoc*: for a fanciful attempt to interpret the obscure *dorwennu* of W (but not its *kenfo*) see E. Rowlands in *Llên Cymru* 7. 119–20.

628 *benfic*: from L. *beneficium*, cf. ELIG §§ 7, 48b, 96, here without the Mod. Welsh assimilation of *-nf-* to *-nth-*.

630 *edrychyat*: presumably 'observer', 'onlooker', as all the translators agree and the later manuscripts explicitly state, but H. M. Evans and W. O. Thomas, *Y Geiriadur Mawr* (3rd edn., Llandybie, 1963), give the obsolete sense as 'supervisor, overseer'. This suits some contexts (e.g. in LlB 9. 23 we have *kannys ef* [the steward] *a byly gwassannaethu y'r llys ac edrych ar y gegin*, i.e. supervise the kitchen), but is inappropriate here. Owein's hostess has no reason to place such confidence in him, and her words *ny wn beth a vyn ac wynt* 636 below, make it clear that he has not asked for the command of her forces.

639 *deu vaccwyf*: on the spelling with *-f*, see Introduction, section IV.

639 *kyweir o veirych ac arueu*: cf. Per. 167. 26, Ger. 397. 8 and 420. 32. For the pl. *meirych* as well as *meirch*, cf. *Pwyll* 555, and WG 17.

645 *ewchi*: i.e. *ewch chwi*, but the final consonant of the verb and the initial of the pronoun are the same, and are not articulated separately; cf. *Pwyll* 208 *ohonawchi*, and a similar instance in 2 sg. *noc a weleisti* in *Pwyll* 249.

648 *y ryδaw a choryf*: for the phrase cf. Per. 176. 33 and Ger. 444. 39.

649 *a ffa ovit bynhac a gafas*: for a similar formula for passing over some details, cf. *Branwen* 458, *pa hyt bynnac y byδynt ar y forδ*.

653 *pwyth yr ireit bendigedic*: for *pwyth* see ELIG § 83. There is a reference to the idiom *talu'r pwyth* 'repay'; cf. Per. 150. 23 *mi a talaf y bwyth it*. GPC does not include this example of *bendigedic*, and gives only meanings in the range 'blessed, sacred'; a more appropriate

sense is found ibid. s.v. *bendigaid*—(c) 'curative' (of herbs). So here perhaps 'the healing ointment'.

655 *bywyt*: this reading from R is more probable than W's *bwyt*. In exchange for his life the earl restored her lands, and in exchange for his freedom gave half his own domain and restored all her other property. If *bwyt* were correct we should have to assume that he was starved until he agreed to these conditions.

658 *a'y gyfoeth oll*: 'and the Countess and all her subjects besought him to remain' (Guest, as if *a'y chyfoeth oll*, a natural correction if one is needed), Loth omits altogether, 'and the Countess offered him herself and all her dominions' E & L (which gives an unusual sense to *gwahawð*), 'and the countess offered him a welcome, him and the whole of his dominions' J & J, which is exactly what the text says. The other translators, however, have avoided this rendering because it seems so inappropriate that she should refer to his lands when she found him naked and delirious in her park, and, in 632–6 above, clearly had no high opinion of him. Mr. Rowlands (*Llên Cymru* (September 1965) 7. 120–3) suggests keeping the text unaltered, taking *ef* as a rhagenw ategol, and *a'y gyfoeth oll* as 'and all (to be) his domain', but apart from S *ar Jarlles a gennigawdd y kyffoeth hynny oll . . . y Owain* there is no clear sign that she intended him to stay permanently, any more than the hosts at 474 and 755 did.

665 *purwyn*: so W, but R has *purðu*. The colour of the lion is not mentioned again, so that there is no means of discovering which reading is to be preferred.

672 *educher*: cf. *hyt ucher* 519, and for this older form, K & O 486. 6, 499. 27.

676 *hyt ymphen teir nos*: *teir nos* may be taken either as 'three nights' or as *teirnos* 'a period of three nights'; cf. *trimis* above 555, 563, where the prefixing of *vn* shows that it is a single unit, though scribal practice is generally to separate the numeral element from the rest. See note on 34 above.

678 *kaeriwrch*: cf. GPC s.v. *caeriwrch* for the first element.

679 *y am y tan ac ef*: 'on the other side of the fire from him'. Cf. K & O 492. 31 *am y uagwyr a'r karcharawr*.

687 *y uynny y iarlles yn priawt*: a curious misrepresentation, coming from Lunet, who must surely have known Owein's intention in undertaking the adventure better than this.

689 *ny ðoeth vyth drachefyn*: the modern usage whereby *vyth* goes with present and future tenses and *eiryoet* with past ones, is not yet established in MW. GPC cites only one example, from *Chwedleu Odo*, *sef y canei ynteu vyth*.

689 *a'r kedymdyeith oeð ef . . .*: 'and he was the friend I loved best in the world' Guest, 'c'était pour moi un ami, celui que j'aimais le plus au monde' Loth, 'and my companion was he, whom I loved best

in the whole world' E & L, 'and such a friend was he to me, I loved him best of the whole world' J & J. These are for the most part translations of the R version, but *y mi* and *genhyf i* should have very different values, and the W version means 'and he was the companion whom I think I loved best in the whole world'.

694 *y llestyr maen hwn*: on this phrase see Introduction, section VIII.

695 *oet y dyb*: cf. *oet dyb* 731 below; *oet* is the regular term for 'appointment', as well as for the time that elapses between making and keeping the appointment, cf. for examples *Pwyll* 61, 461, and the vn. *oedi* 'postpone' 458. With *dyb* the phrase is equivalent to 'appointed day'. Cf. Ger. 396. 11.

706 *gaer vawr a thyryeu amhyl arnei*: for the description cf. Per. 133. 5, and BM 180. 1.

708 *ac ny wylwys* . . .: this is inconsistent with 701 above, where Owein and Lunet are said to have talked until dawn. Even if they had been asleep and the lion on guard, we should have expected this sentence to occur earlier.

715 *na leuassei*: the vowel of the first syllable varies; cf. Per. 117. 23 *ny lywassei*, and 176. 18 *ny lafasswys*.

726 *Duw a wyr y ni*: cf. 101 note, and below 734 *Duw a wyr arnaf*, where the two prepositions seem equivalent.

732 *eillun*: the word is divided over a line (651. 39–40) in the manuscript, *eil/lun*. An apparently similar case is *gallon* (647. 2–3), which Evans does not mark (RBM 184. 10) other than by omitting the link between the tops of the two ascenders, but in this case the *-ll-* is not uncommon; cf. most of the earliest examples in GPC s.v. *calon*. Cf. too *ymdan/nunt* 786.

741 *dilyssu*: 'abandon'; vn. from adj. *dilys*, cognate with OIr *díles*, whence the Irish verbs *dílsid* and *dílsigid*, cf. GPC s.v. *dilysaf* for the semantics. The two meanings of the Welsh verb are so nearly opposite that it is not surprising to find that they hardly co-existed, the sense here being current until the fourteenth century, the other 'accept as genuine, guarantee' since the fifteenth.

743 *ymbrawf*: clearly a vn. here, and either a vn. or noun in Ger. 391. 38. The etymological meaning is 'test oneself against', and so 'contend with'. On the analogical *-aw-* in *prawf* beside the regular *-o-* in *profi*, L. *probare*, cf. ELIG 45–46.

767 *ymbiot*: cf. GPC s.v. *diodaf*²; the etymological sense is 'cut each other down'.

774 *ny bothoeb Owein y nerth ettwa*: the meaning may be that Owein has not yet fully recovered from the effects of his privations, but it is also possible that there is an allusion to waxing and waning strength like that of Gawain, or that his full might lies still in the future, as with Peredur, when his uncle says to him, '*deu parth de bewreb ar*

gefeist, a'r trayan yssyb heb gahel; a gwedy keffych gwbyl, ny byby wrth neb' (Per. 130. 7–10).

774 *hydyr oeb y beu was arnaw*: they were pressing him hard or getting the better of him. Cf. cpv. *hytrach* 'rather', i.e. 'more strongly'.

781 *tra uu vyw hi*: note the copula order, verb–complement–subject; cf. K & O 507. 11, and, for a similar expression, *Tochmarc Emire* § 90, *niro scarsat íar suidiu co fúaratar bás dib línaib*.

782 The Du Traws story at first sight appears somewhat detached from what has gone before (and in R its beginning is marked by the same large capital as marks the beginning of *Peredur*), but 814–15 suggest that it is supposed to take place as Owein is on his way back to Arthur's court. With the Du Traws we may compare in Per. 154. 21 *y Du Trahawc*, who explains his title as reflecting the fact that he is an unjust oppressor of all his neighbours.

795 [*a ni*]: the addition seems probable, as there is nothing particularly atrocious in the bodies of the dead paramours being in the same building as many other corpses.

803 *ymaboydi*: cf. GPC s.v. *addoedaf*, from *addoed* m. (cf. K & O 479. 19), 'wound', 'seek to kill', here reciprocal, and another of the numerous variations on 'fight' to be found in this text. *Ymbihauarchu*: cf. GPC s.v. *dihafarch* a. 'bold, active'; the sense here is 'get the upper hand of', as the later manuscripts confirm.

806 *darogan*: for the same idea cf. K & O 453. 37, Per. 144. 36, 158. 27, and the roughly synonymous *tyghetuen a gweledigaeth* of Per. 139. 32.

809 *yspyttywr . . . yspytty*: on the Hospitallers (the Order of St. John of Jerusalem), see William Rees, *A History of the Order of St. John of Jerusalem in Wales and on the Welsh border* (Cardiff, 1947), 19: 'In general, the Order of St. John found its earlier and chief donors in Wales among the Norman Lords of the March rather than among the Welsh magnates. In due course, however, the avowed objects of the organisation could not fail to win the sympathy of the Welsh and, in the latter half of the twelfth century, Welsh rulers came to be included among the patrons of the Order, possibly as a result of the appeal made by Archbishop Baldwin and Giraldus Cambrensis in 1188 when they conducted a preaching tour through Wales on behalf of the Crusade. It was to the Lord Rhys of Deheubarth that the Hospitallers owed their estates of Ystrad Meurig and Llanrhystyd in Ceredigion, acquired in the latter half of the twelfth century, while they obtained their first footing in Gwynedd probably in the time of Llywelyn the Great.' Of their activities he writes, p. 22: 'The brethren placed hospitality high among the virtues, for we read in the Statutes of the Order that "hospitality is one of the most eminent acts of piety and humanity". On the great pilgrim routes to the East, as we have seen, the brethren were concerned not only with

the welfare of the pilgrim but also with the healing of the sick, whereas in the provincial houses of the Order, it was the provision of hospitality which was the main concern and the care of the sick was but incidental.' On the term *yspyttywr* he has this to say, p. 24: 'They [the Hospitallers] appear to have exercised rights of justice not only over the tenants on their own estates but also over certain "outsiders" or "foreigners" (*forinseci*). These were known as *expedores*, but the exact meaning of this term, current only in Wales, particularly at Slebech and Halston, is obscure. It would seem, however, that it is the mediaeval Latin equivalent of the Welsh term *ysbytŷwyr*, meaning Hospitallers. The term *expedores* is undoubtedly used on occasion in reference to certain tenants of the Hospitallers, but it appears to be more strictly applicable to particular persons who were tenants of other lords and resided outside the lands of the Order.' E & L 2. 66 footnote, comment: 'There is here a dig at the Knights Hospitallers, whose hospices in Wales were simply centres of brigandage, in whose jurisdiction the King's writ did not run.' Professor Rees's only reference to anything of the kind is on p. 67: 'During the turbulent times of the *fifteenth century* [my italics], Yspytty Ifan had so far departed from its original high function that it harboured a nest of depredators and outlaws who, taking advantage of the privilege of sanctuary and profiting from the remoteness of the site, made the lands of the hospice their base of operations. Thus protected from the hands of the law, they could with impunity sally forth to rob and kill, becoming a terror to the countryside for twenty miles around. . . . More than a hundred of these marauders, well-mounted and well-armed, had their home in the sacred precincts of the old *Yspytty*.' Cf. also Glanmor Williams, *The Welsh Church from Conquest to Reformation* (Cardiff, 1962) 241. While there is undoubtedly a pun on *yspeilty* and *yspytty*, E & L's interpretation is anachronistic. Moreover, it is not certain that MW *yspytty* is in any way dependent on the existence of the Order; it occurs already in K & O 456. 23, *bwyt . . . a ḋaw attat y'r yspytty; yno y bwyta pellenigyon a mabyon gwladoeḋ ereill . . . ny byḋ gwaeth it yno nocet y Arthur yn y llys*, and the first element *yspyt* (L. *hospitium*, or *hospit-em*) may occur in *yspydawt* in *Branwen* 448 (cf. PKM 220).

818 *pennteulu*: for the *penteulu* see the Laws, e.g. LlB 10. 15–11. 9, and especially 11. 1, *mab y'r brenhin neu ney ibaw a ḋyly bot yn bennteulu*.

819 *yny aeth ar y gyfoeth e hun*: perhaps under similar circumstances to Gereint 409–10, because his father Erbin was *yn amdrymmu, ac yn llescu, ac yn denessau ar heneint, a'r gyttirogyon . . . yn camderuynu arnaw ac yn chwynychu y dir a'y gyuoyth*.

820 *trychant*: '300'; cf. Per. 155. 8 for the composite numeral.

820 *Kenuerchyn*: Owein's grandfather was Kynuarch, and the

derivative means collectively 'descendants of K.'. See GPC s.v. Cynferching; the assumption of the suffix *-ing* seems a little doubtful when we notice that the *-g* has had to be supplied in all the three examples, though in one case (see GBGG) the emendation is suggested by rhyme. The use of *g* for *ng* is the normal MW convention, but the loss of *g* from *ng* is rare.

820 *branhes*: for the formation of this collective cf. *dauates* 'flock of sheep' in K & O 472. 17. For the activity of Owein's ravens see BR 14. 24–15. 10. On the punctuation, *a'r* versus *ar*, cf. Eurys I. Rowlands in a review of TYP (*Llên Cymru* 6. 246), who prefers the preposition, interpreting it as 'as a Flight of Ravens', but here there is neither a possessive nor an ordinal numeral, the two marks of his proposed analogous construction.

VOCABULARY

The arrangement of words in this vocabulary follows the order of the roman alphabet, and the words themselves appear in the same spelling as in the text, with the following exceptions:
  (i) C and K are treated as one letter and placed under C.
  (ii) where MS. D represents the voiced spirant, ƀ is printed both in the head-words and in the quotations.
  (iii) CHW- is treated as a separate initial after C.
  (iv) initial U- is distinguished according as it represents U-, V-, or W-.
  (v) mutated initial consonants are restored to their radicals, except where the mutation has become permanent; variable initials, e.g. *trannoeth/drannoeth, tros/dros*, are entered under whichever occurs first in the text.
  (vi) certain words having Y prefixed (*y am, y ar, y dan, y gan, y gyt, y mywyn, y rof* (see under (*y*) *rwng*), *y velly, y uynyd, y wrth*) are entered under the second element.
  (vii) parts of verbs are entered under the verbal noun, but cross-references are provided for the parts of the irregular verbs.
  (viii) the personal forms of prepositions are entered under the simple preposition.

In the identification of the parts of verbs the label 'pres.' is understood to include future meaning (except with *bot*), and the imperfect indicative and subjunctive are distinguished only where formal grounds exist for doing so. The composite nature of the text means that the spelling of some words is at variance as between the parts drawn from W and those drawn from R. In these cases the form of the head-word is determined by the first occurrence of the word; where the difference is between double and single letters brackets are used, as in *pen(n)*, to show that both spellings occur. In a few cases where the spelling may be misleading a more normal form appears at the end of the article.

1. a (len.) vocative particle 184R; cf. *ha*.
2. a (len.) direct relative particle 14, 16, 18; relative pronoun 17, 18, 21; antecedent and relative 32, 58, 90; with object pronouns, 1 sg. *a'm* 65, 306, 445; 2 sg. *a'th* 162, 163; 3 sg. m. *a'e* 21, 99, 102, *a'y* 74; f. *a'y* 683; 3 pl. *a'e* 66.
3. a (len.) interrogative particle 138, 505, 627; in indirect question, whether 226.

VOCABULARY

4. a (asp.) conj. and 3, 4, 6; before vowels and some consonants **ac**, 2, 7, 10, *ac ny(t)* 32, 57, 81, *ac nat* 91, *ac nachaf* 41, *ac rac* 56, *ac weithon* 93, *ac hwynteu* 49, *ac hwynt* 584. With art. *a'r* 38, 384; with pronouns (poss. and obj.) 1 sg. *a'm* 194, 198; 2 sg. *a'th* 161; 3 sg. m. *a'e* 230, 231, 691; *a'y* 611, 658, 678; f. *a'e* 4, 8, *a'y* 657; 1 pl. *ac an* 791, 794; 3 pl. *a'e* 559R, *a'y* 559, *ac eu* 246, 600.

5. a (asp.) prep. and conj. with, as 22, 72; before vowels **ac**, 2, 22, 47. With pers. prons. 1 sg. *a mi* 89, 91; 2 sg. *a thi* 93, 94, 106; 3 sg. f. *a hi* 131, 315; with art. *a'r* 41, 57, 67; with pronouns (poss. and obj.) 1 sg. *a'm* 195; 3 sg. m. *a'e* 324, 693.

abreið a. difficult 153; *o a.* with difficulty 601.

ac, see 4. *a* and 5. *a*.

ach prep. only in *ach y law* near him 594R, *ach eu llaw* near them 473.

achaws m. cause, reason 400, 487; *o a.* because of 534, 687. (L. occasio.)

adaneð pl. feathers 47; sg. *adein*.

adar pl. birds 155, 180, 268; sg. *ederyn*.

adaw vn. leave 210, 594, 611; pres. 3 sg. *edeu* 163; pret. 3 sg. *edewis* 187, 606.

aðaw vn. promise; plupft. 3 sg. *abawssei* 17; impers. impft. *ebewit* 18.

aðef vn. admit, confess; pret. 3 sg. *aðeuawð* 213.

adnabot vn. recognize, perceive 100, 275; impft. 1 sg. *atwaenwn* 534; 3 sg. *atwaenat* 518; pret. 3 sg. *adnabu* 532.

aðoer a. chill, cold 153.

aðoli (y) vn. do homage to, reverence, honour 137.

adolwyn (y) vn. beg, beseech 402; stem *adolyg-*.

adref adv. home(wards) 429, *atref* 441.

ae interrogative particle with copula 227; in indirect question, whether it is *ay* 683; *ae ... ae ...* either ... or ... 402–3, 445–6.

a'e, see 2. *a*, 4. *a*, 5. *a*.

aeth, af, see *mynet*.

afles m. disadvantage, what is not for one's good 102. (Ir aimhleas.)

agheu m. death 718, 787. (*angheu*.) (Ir éag.)

agheuawl a. deadly, mortal 276. (*angheuawl*.)

aghywir a. faithless, fickle 399, 569 (*anghywir*). (Ir éagcóir.)

agori vn. open 293, 374, unlock 316; with *-i* marked for deletion, i.e. **agor** 343.

agos (at) a. near 519, 546, 683.

ai, see *mynet*.

allan adv. outside, out of doors; (rest) 188, **allann** 798; (motion) 742, 776; *o hynny allann* thenceforth 818.

allt f. slope (of a hill) 144, 165, 484. (Ir alt.)

am prep. on (of footwear, clothing, etc.) 44, 301, about 204, on account of 304, at (of time) 86; *am pen* about, on (of something worn) 42, 43; *am nat* conj. because ... not 608: *y am ... ac ...*

VOCABULARY

prep. on the other side of . . . from . . . 679. With personal pronouns: 1 sg. *ymdanaf* 70, 118, 195; 3 sg. m. *ymdanaw* 53, 160, 190; f. *ymdanei* 291, 355, 423, *ymdeni* 567; 3 pl. *ymdannunt* 786.

a'm, see 2. *a*, 4. *a*, 5. *a*.

amdiffin vn. defend 695, **amdiffyn** 699, 765.

amgen adv. otherwise; *nyt a.* namely, to wit 70.

amherawdyr m. emperor 1, 10, 16. (L. imperator.)

amhyl a. numerous, frequent 72, 707, **amyl** 350, 354; eqv. *kyn hamlet* 133, *kyn amlet* 327. (L. amplus.)

amlawdynyon pl. camp-followers 469, 493; see note 469.

amot m. condition, stipulation 770.

amowyn (a) vn. enquire, ask, seek 89, **amouyn** 164, **amofyn** 250.

amrysson vn. contend 693.

amryual a. various, diverse 135, 320, **amryuael** 135R.

amser m. time 227, 422, 550. (Ir aimsear.)

amysgar m. entrails, guts 753.

an poss. part. our 82, 793.

anfod m. unwillingness, displeasure; *o'm hanfod* against my will 635, *o'm hanuod* 736.

anhard a. not beautiful; spv. *anharbaf* least beautiful 62.

anhawd a. difficult 418, **anawd** 560; *oed yn a. gantaw* he was reluctant 253; cpv. *anhaws* 771.

anhygar, anhegar a. unamiable, unpleasant, discourteous 112.

aniueil, anifeil m. animal, beast 747, 771; pl. *aniueileit* 113, 132, *aniweileit* 121, 129, *aniveileit* 139. (L. animalium.)

annwyl a. beloved, dear 819.

anrec f. (1) dish, course 328; (2) gift 652.

anrydedu vn. honour 7.

anrydedus a. honourable 713.

anueitrawl a. immeasurable 340, **anveitrawl** 739.

anuon vn. send; plpft. 3 sg. *anuonassei* 517.

anyan f. nature, disposition, temperament 409.

ar prep. on 5, 11, 36; *dyuot ar* come to 486, 503, *ymchoelut ar* return to 510, *mynet ar* go to 819; *y ar* (mounted) on 159, 497, off, from 532, 620, 750. With personal pronouns: 1 sg. *arnaf* 32, 89, 95; 2 sg. *arnat* 389; 3 sg. m. *arnaw* 96, 179, 213; f. *arnei* 320, 350, 707, *erni* 263; 3 pl. *arnunt* 313, *arnadunt* 23, 46, 135.

a'r, see 4. *a*, 5. *a*.

arall a. and pron. other 38, 70, 238; pl. *ereill* 66, 737.

archescyb pl. archbishops 448; sg. *archescob*.

arganfot vn. perceive 599; pret. 3 sg. *arganuu* 537.

arglwyd m. lord, feudal superior 137, 227, 394.

arglwydes f. lady 365, 425, 436.

arhoy, see *aros*.

arllost f. butt-end (of spear), shaft 192, 507.

arlwy m. preparation 623.
arlwyaw vn. prepare; pret. 3 pl. *arlwyassant* 69.
arnaƀunt, arnaf, arnat, arnaw, arnei, arnunt, see *ar*.
aros vn. await, wait for 14, 305; pres. 2 sg. *arhoy* 162; impv. 2 pl. *arowch* 645.
arouyn vn. ask leave (to go) 548, **arouun** 557.
aruawc a. armed 744.
arueu pl. weapons, arms, armour 66, 210, 232; sg. *aryf* (L. arma).
aruoll vn. receive, greet 6, 713, 799.
arwyƀ m. sign, flag 190, 502.
aryant m. silver 657, 787, 794; as a. 76, 80, 149. (Ir airgead.)
askellu vn. feather (an arrow) 47.
ascwrn m. bone 174, **asgwrn** 275, 375, 509; a. *eliffant* ivory 45, a. *eliphant* 373, 375, a. *morwil* walrus ivory 46, 48.
a'th, see 2. *a*, 4. *a*.
atneiryaw vn. reproach, blame 615.
att prep. to (motion in space), towards 314, 402, 408, **at** 612, 629. With personal pronouns: 1 sg. *attaf* 184, 308, 541; 2 sg. *attat* 159; 3 sg. m. *attaw* 55, 586, 683; f. *attei* 386; 3 pl. *attunt* 544.
attal vn. stop, restrain; impft. 3 sg. *attalei* 174.
att-at, -aw, -unt, see *att*.
atteb (y) vn. answer; pret. 3 sg. *attebawƀ* 386; subj. pres. 2 sg. *atteppych* 388.
attei, see *att*.
atwaen-at, -wn, see *adnabot*.
avon f. river 37, **auon** 237, **afon** 706. (Ir abhainn.)
avory adv. tomorrow 428, 635, **auory** 730.
awwyneu pl. reins 193; sg. *avwyn* ibid. R. (L. habena.)
awch poss. part. your 445, 541.
awn, see *mynet*.
awr f. hour, time 337. (L. hora.)
awyr f. sky, firmament 133, 267, 347. (L. aer.)
ay, see *ae*.
a'y, see 2. *a*, 4. *a*.

barwn m. baron 351; pl. *barwnyeit* 452. (OFr, ME barun.)
baryf f. beard 52, 570, **baraf** 376. (L. barba.)
baryflen f. visor 176.
bei m. (1) fault, failing 91, 477, 724; (2) see *bot*, and *pei*.
bendigedic a. blessed (see note) 653.
bendyth f. blessing 210. (L. benedictio.)
benfic m. loan 628. (L. beneficium.)
ber m. spit; pl. *bereu* 23, 680. (Cog. L. ueru, Ir. bior.)
beth interrog. pron. what 185, 593, 636; len. form of *peth*, q.v.
bewn, beym, see *bot*.

beyt, see *pei.*
blaen m. front, tip; *yn y vlaen* in front of him 243, *o'e vlaen* before him 644; as spv. adj. *blaenhaf* foremost 647.
blew m. hair, fur 577, 619.
bliant m. name of a material, fine linen, cambric, lawn 71, 77, 80. (OFr bliaut, ME blihant.)
bligyaw vn. flay, skin 680. (blingyaw.)
blwyðyn f. year 461. (Ir. bliadhain.)
blyghau vn. grow angry 387. (blynghau.)
blyneð f. year (with numerals) 454, 461, 549.
bo, see *bot.*
boð m. will, pleasure; *o'm boð* willingly, voluntarily 736.
bonheðic a. noble, well-born; spv. *bonheðickaf* 365.
bore m. morning 117, 207, 481; a. early 103, see note.
bot vn. be 5, 60; pres. 1 sg. *wyf* 551, 685; 2 sg. *wyt* 27, 535, 684; 3 sg. *yw* 19, 112, 181, *ydiw* 465, *mae* 147, 149, 211, *may* 199, *mae* where is? 613, *yssyð* 109, 139, 252, *oes* 111, 435, 627; 1 pl. *ydym* 727; impers. *ydys* 686R; impft. 1 sg. *oeðwn* 31, 90, 142; 2 sg. *oeðut* 298, 409; 3 sg. *oeð* 1, 5, 34, (modally) 83, 219, 295; 3 pl. *oeðynt* 67, 80, 266, *oyðynt* 651; fut. and hab. pres. 1 sg. *bybaf* 305, 461; 3 sg. *byð* 115, 153, 305; hab. impft. and cond. 3 sg. *bybei* 479, 682, 694; pret. 1 sg. *bum* 205, 808; 3 sg. *bu* 63, 87, 117; 1 pl. *buassam* 201; impers. *buwyt* 202, 555; plpft. 1 sg. *buasswn* 201R; 3 sg. *buassei* 471, 772, 814; pres. subj. 1 sg. *bwyf* 810; 2 sg. *bych* 164; 3 sg. *bo* 108, 157, 617; past subj. 1 sg. *bewn* 14; 3 sg. *bei* 93, 191, 298; 1 pl. *beym* 792.
bradwr m. traitor, betrayer 570, 692.
branhes f. flight of ravens 820, see note.
brathu vn. bite, sting 666R.
brawt m. brother 800.
breich f. arm; pl. *breicheu* 596. (L. bracchium.)
breint f. right, privilege; *ar ureint* (acting) as 6, see note.
breiuat m. belling (of a stag), roaring, bellowing 131, also **breuarat, brefarat** ibid. R. (Cf. *Arch. Brit.* 142 s.v. Rugio, Rhŷo vel lhêu, brevy [*Dimet.* breivad] breverad.)
bric m. tree-top, tip (of a branch) 147; pl. *brigeu* hair (of the head) 354.
brith a. speckled, variegated, of more than one colour 54, 292, 356.
briw m. wound 354.
bron(n) f. breast; *rac bron(n)* before 377, 568, *rac y vronn* (3 sg. m.) 323, *ger bron* before 678, *ger y vron* (3 sg. m.) 714.
bryn m. hill 664.
brys m. haste 545.
bu, see *bot.*
bual m. buffalo 82J, = *buelyn, bueli,* q.v. (L. bubalus.)
buass-am, -ei, -wn, see *bot.*

VOCABULARY

buelyn m. buffalo-horn; as a. 82, **bueli** ibid. R.
bum, buwyt, see *bot*.
bwa m. bow 45. (OE boga, ME bowe.)
bwrð m. table 78, 80, 323, *bwrt* 81, 564; pl. *byrðeu* 68, 228. (OE bord.)
bwrw vn. cast throw, overthrow 169, 488, 507, rid oneself of, recover from 553; impft. 3 sg. *byryei* 451; pret. 3 sg. *byryawð* 747; impers. *byrywyt* 192, 500; impv. 2 sg. *bwrw* 150.
bwyf, see *bot*.
bwystuil m. beast, monster, animal 729; pl. *-et* 577, *-eit* ibid. R.
bwyt m. food, meal 14, 69, 82.
bwyta vn. eat 86, **bwytta** 86, 88, 93.
bychan a. little, small 130, 138.
bychydic m. a little, a small amount 368.
byð, -af, see *bot*.
bydawl a. mortal, of this world 683.
byðei, see *bot*.
byðin f. troop, division of an army 642, 647. (Ir buidhean.)
bynhac; *pa ovit b.* whatever trouble 650.
byry-awð, -ei, -wyt, see *bwrw*.
bys m. finger 301; pl. *bysseð* 357.
byt m. world, inhabited world 32, 35, 109; pl. *bydoeð* 575R. (Ir bioth.)
byth adv. ever (pres. & fut.) 393, 775, (past) 689, for ever, to keep 633.
byw a. alive 153, 173, **buw** 466; *tra vych vyw* as long as you live 164. (Ir beo.)
bywyt m. life 655.

kadarn a. strong 810.
kadarnuras a. strong and stout 522. (k.+bras.)
kadeir f. chair; pl. *kadeireu* 246. (L. cathedra.)
kadw vn. keep, guard 741; pret. 3 sg. *kedwis* 418, 450; pres. subj. 3 sg. *cattwo* 417.
kadwyn f. chain 149, 168. (L. catena.)
cae, caeu, caewyt, see *kau*.
kaer f. castle, fortress, keep 40, 57, 200.
kaeriwrch m. roebuck 678, 680.
kaffel (gan) vn. get, find, obtain (from) 90, 393, **caffel** 704, **kaffael** 276W, reach 566; pres. 2 sg. *keffy* 163, 802; 2 pl. *keffwch* 553; impft. 1 sg. *caffwnn* 203; 3 sg. *caffei* 566, 817; pret. 1 sg. *kefeis* 200, 654; 3 sg. *cafas* 188, 378, 600, *cauas* 776; 1 pl. *cawssam* 791; 3 pl. *cawsant* 447; pres. subj. 2 sg. *keffych* 116; 3 sg. *caffo* 111.
calaneð pl. dead men, corpses 546, 795; sg. *kelein*.
cam m. wrong 391; a. 504. (Ir cam.)
camhwri m. feat of arms 33.

VOCABULARY 69

kan conj. since, seeing that 440, **can** for 552; (with copula) *kanys* since it is 101, 409; (with negative) *kany* since . . . not 173.

canawl m. groove 375, middle, midst, centre 583; *yg kanawl* in the middle of 663. (L. canalis.)

kanhymdeith vn. accompany, keep up with 579.

canlyn vn. follow 670.

kannyadu vn. allow, permit 446, **kanhadu (y)** 447, 489; pret. 3 sg. *canyhadawð* 560.

canu vn. sing 181, 183, **kanu** sound (a horn) 229, chant 346; pres. 3 pl. *canant* 157. (Ir canadh.)

kany (1), see *kan*; (2), see *kyt*.

kanys, see *kan*.

kar m. lover 298. (Ir cara.)

karchar m. prison 466, 772. (L. carcer.)

karcharu vn. take prisoner, imprison 195, 686, 693.

kares f. lover 298.

carn f. hilt, handle 375; pl. *carneu* 48. (Cf. Ir carn.)

carrec f. rock 663.

karu vn. love; pres. 1 sg. *karaf* 367; 3 sg. *kar* 368; impft. 1 sg. *karwn* 690; 3 sg. *karei* 790. (Ir caradh.)

karw m. stag 131.

karyat m. love 360, 453, affection, friendliness 800.

castell m. castle 588, 605, 610, **kastell** 623, 646. (L. castellum.)

cattwo, see *kadw*.

kau vn. fasten, close, shut 45, 54, **kaeu** 317, 382, 433; pret. impers. *caewyt* 287; impv. 2 sg. *cae* 301.

cawat f. shower (of rain) 152, 171, 175, **kawat** 154; flock (of birds) 155.

kawc m. basin, bowl 149, 168; pl. *kawgeu* 76.

kawgeit m. basinful 150, **cawgeit** 169.

cawr m. giant 733.

cawsant, cawssam, see *caffel*.

kedwis, see *kadw*.

kedymdyeith m. companion 689; pl. *kedymdeithon* 510.

kefeis, keff-wch, -y, -ych, see *caffel*.

kefyn m. back; *ar y gefyn* behind his back 805.

kefynderw m. (first) cousin 535.

kegin f. kitchen 22. (L. coquina.)

kegyl f. saddle-girth, surcingle; pl. *kegleu* 525. (L. cingula, i.e. kengyl.)

keisaw vn. seek, try 95, 219, 311, **keissaw** 312; pres. 2 sg. *keissy* 99, 116; impft. 1 sg. *keisswn* 143; 3 sg. *keissyei* 665; pres. subj. 3 sg. *keissyo* 696; impv. 2 sg. *keis* 412.

kenedyl f. race, people, kindred 562. (Ir. cinéal.)

kenhadeu pl. messengers 557; sg. *kennat*.

VOCABULARY

kenn m. lichen 208.
kennoc a. scaly 620.
kerð f. song, music 157, 182, 269. (Cf. Ir ceárd.)
kerðet vn. travel, traverse 35, 38, 118; as n. m. quest, adventure, expedition 89, 95, 487; pres. 3 sg. *kerða* 284; pret. 1 sg. *kerðeis* 39; 3 sg. *kerðawð* 238, 711R, *kerðwys* 814; impv. 2 sg. *kerða* 106, 144, 705.
kerðetwr m. traveller, one who has been on a journey 435.
kic m. flesh 174, 508, *kig* 274. (Cf. Ir cíoch.)
kiglef, kigleu, see *clybot*.
kilyaw, vn. withdraw, retreat 594.
kinyaw f. dinner 324, 378.
kleðyf m. sword 272, 450, **cleðyf** 279, 541; pl. *clefyðeu* 528, *clebyfeu* 541. (Ir claidheamh.)
clocuryn m. cliff 663. (c.+bryn.)
klwyfaw vn. wound; pret. 3 sg. *klwyfawð* 275.
clybot vn. hear (of) 749; pres. 2 sg. *klywy* 151, 158; impft. 3 sg. *clywei* 622, 661; 3 pl. *clywynt* 331, 336, 739; pft. 1 sg. *kiglef* 182R, 215, *kigleu* 83 note, 182; pret. 2 sg. *klyweist* 156; plpft. 3 pl. *klywyssynt* 492, 496.
klyw-ei, -eist, -y, -ynt, -yssynt, see *clybot*.
knap m. button 54. (OE cnæpp.)
knawt m. flesh 597, 621.
knewillyn m. centre 110 note.
coch a. red 12, 73; eqv. *kyn gochet* 208.
coedawc a. wooded 674.
koet m. wood, forest 105, 112, 119.
cof m. memory, recollection 571.
colli vn. lose, be lost; pret. 3 sg. *colles* 460, 463, 613; plpft. 3 sg. *kollassei* 815.
cordwal m. leather, cordwain 43, 54, 292, **cordwan** in J. (Cf. ME cordewan.)
corff m. body (alive or dead) 178, 341, 438, **korff** 462. (L. corpus.)
corfforoeð pl. (dead) bodies, corpses 794; sg. *corffor*. (L. corpor-.)
korn m. horn 229, 359. (Cog. L. cornu.)
coryf f. saddle-bow, pommel 649. (? L. corbis.)
cossi vn. scratch 596.
coydwr m. forester, woodward 112. (Cf. koet.)
craff a. keen 435, 586.
crefyðwr m. cleric; pl. *crefyðwyr* 346, 348.
crochan m. pot 371. (Ir crocán.)
croen m. skin 173, 508, **kroen** 274.
crogi vn. hang 223. (Ir crochadh.)
cryf a. strong; eqv. *kyn gryfet* 530.
crys m. shirt, under body-garment 70.

VOCABULARY

kuḃyaw vn. cover, hide; pres. 3 sg. *kuḃ* 302; pres. subj. 2 sg. *kuḃyych* 302.

kwbyl m. the whole (usually without art.) 251, 255, 593, **cwbyl** 631, everything 618.

cwnsallt m. an all-enveloping garment 516 note, 534.

kwsc, see *kysgu*.

kwynaw vn. complain 587 note. (Ir caoineadh.)

kwynuan m. groaning 158.

kwyr m. wax; as a. 350. (L. cera.)

kychwyn vn. start, set off 314, 420; pret. 3 sg. *kychwynnwys* 481.

kyfagos (y) a. near (to) 41, 683R. (Cf. agos.)

kyfarwyḋ m. guide 470, 482.

kyfarwyneb (a) a. opposite 289.

kyfeillt m. friend 220, 224. (Ir. cómhalta.)

kyfeir m. direction, part; *ar g.* round about, over, in the direction of 583, 591R, *yg k.* instead of 563. (Ir. cómhair.)

kyffelyb (y) a. similar, like 492, **kyffelyp** 84R, **kyffelip** ibid. J.

kyffelybu vn. allude to, hint at 398 note.

kyffes f. confession 199. (L. confessio.)

kyflawn a. full, completely full 361. (Cf. llawn.)

kyflet eqv. a. as wide, broad 509; pos. *llydan*.

kyflym a. swift, quick 527, 776.

kyfodi vn. rise, get up 64, 117, 247, **kyuodi** 342; pres. 3 sg. *kyuyt* 592; 3 pl. *kyfodant* 502; pret. 3 sg. *kyfodeis* 207; 3 sg. *kyfodes* 574; impv. 2 sg. *kyfot* 103.

kyfoeth m. kingdom, domain 186, 217, 411, **kyuoeth** 414. (Ir cumhacht.)

kyfranc f. story, account 760. (Ir comhrac.)

kyfrwy m. saddle 283, 567, 600.

kyfryw m. equal, like 84.

kyfyl m. border, proximity; *yg k.* near 716.

kyghor m. counsel 441, *kyfyg gyghor* quandary, perplexity 288. (kynghor.)

kylch m. circuit; *yg k.* (round) about 654, 680; *y'm k.* (1 sg.) 73; *yn y gylch* (3 sg. m.) 114, 671; *yn y chylch* (3 sg. f.) 350; *y'n k.* (1 pl.) 73R. (L. circulus.)

kyllell f. knife; pl. *kyllell* 48, *kyllyll* 50, *kylleill* 48R, 50R, 240. (L. cultellus.)

kymeint eqv. a. so great 91, 724; m. an equal quantity; *tri chymeint* three times as much 121. (Cf. meint.)

kymer, -af, -o, -th, see *kymryt*.

kymodawc m. neighbour 608 note.

1. **kymryt (gan)** vn. take, get, accept (from) 15, 24, 321, **kymrut** 446; pres. 1 sg. *kymeraf* 441; pret. 3 sg. *kymerth* 65, 74, 811; pres. subj. 3 sg. *kymero* 445; impv. 2 sg. *kymer* 104, 150, 537, *kymher* 143.

VOCABULARY

2. kymryt a. of similar form, of equal beauty 358. (Cf. pryt, *Pwyll* 55.)
1. kyn eqv. part. as 67, 530, 717, **gyn** 133.
2. kyn, see *kyt*.
kynefin (a) a. familiar with, used to 578.
kynhal-yaf, -yo, see *kynnal*.
kynhwryf m. disturbance, bustle 622, 624. (Cf. twrwf.)
kynllyskyn m. hailstone 173, *kenllysgen* f. ibid. R.; pl. *kynllysc* 153, *ken-* ibid. R.
kynnal vn. maintain, keep, guard 411, 414, 444; pres. 1 sg. *kynhalyaf* 809; pres. subj. 3 sg. *kynhalyo* 412, 446.
kynnu vn. kindle 320, **kynneu** 370, 611; *kynneu* f. blaze 758.
kynnut m. firewood, fuel 676.
kynt adv. earlier, sooner, before 56, 621, 670, *gynt* 198, 418, *na chynt na gwedy* neither before nor since 181; cpv. a. previous 710.
kyntaf spv. a. first 20, 402, 489, quickest, swiftest 161.
kyrbwyll vn. mention, refer to; impft. 3 sg. *kyrbwyllei* 204; pret. 1 sg. *kyrbwylleis* 205.
kyrch m. journey, visit, quest 204.
kyrchu vn. approach, attack, make for 161, 744, fetch 303; pret. 3 sg. *kyrchwys* 574, 784.
kysku vn. sleep, fall asleep 16, 381, **kysgu** 382; impft. 1 sg. *kyskwn* 14; plpft. 3 sg. *kysgassei* 226; impv. 2 sg. *kwsc* 103.
kysnoden, see *ysnoden*.
kysswllt m. join, point of junction, crack at the join 289. (L. consolido.)
kystal eqv. a. as good 75, 157, 182.
kystuðedic a. afflicted, distressed 457.
kyt conj. though 4, 475, **kyn** 191, 718; *kany* (leg. *kyny*) although . . . not 306.
kytgerðet vn. go about with, keep company with 577.
kytgyueðachwyr pl. fellow carousers, drinking companions 562; sg. *-wr*.
kythreul m. devil 792. (L. contrarius.)
kytymborth vn. feed together 578.
kyuanheð m. 58 note.
kyuarch gwell (y) vn. greet 55, 127, 242, **kyfarch** 602; pret. 3 sg. *kyuarchawð* 56.
kyuodi, see *kyfodi*.
kyuoethawc a. landed, powerful, wealthy 351, *-f-* 390. (Ir cumhachtach.)
kyuyg a. confined 131, **kyfyg** difficult 746. See also *kyghor*. (kyfyng, Ir cumhang.)
kyveruyð, fut. 3 sg. of *kyuaruot (a)* meet 105, **kyueruyð** 647.
kyuyt, see *kyfodi*.
kyweir a. proper, complete 209, fully equipped 639.

kyweirdeb m. preparation, serving (of food) 84, 326.
kyweiryaw vn. make (a bed) 380, groom (a horse) 713; pret. 3 sg. *kyweirywys* saddle (a horse) 711.
kyweithas m. company, train 493.
kywilyb m. shame 200, **kewilyb** ibid. R.; *kymryt k. ynbaw e hun a oruc* he was ashamed 597.

chwech num. six 64, 68 note, 74.
chwedyl m. story, account, news 214, 425, 822; pl. *chwedleu* news 424. (Ir scéal.)
chwerthin vn. laugh 632.
chwi pers. pron. 2 pl. you 440, 445, *ewchi* 645 note; **chwitheu** disjunct. pron. 2 pl. you for your part, you on the other hand 15, 25.

da a. good 18, 219, as n. 296; m. goods, income, revenue 452, 813; *yn ba* adv. well, used as an intensive 170; *da yw gennyf* I am glad 399, 634.
daet eqv. a. and n. excellence 56, **dahet** ibid. R., 334.
dala vn. hold, seize 730; *d. ofyn rac* be afraid of 585.
dalen f. leaf 154, 179, 267.
dan prep. under 12, 722, carrying 351; **y dan** 147. With pers. pron. 1 sg. *y danaf* 73; 3 sg. m. *y danaw* 11; 1 pl. *y danam* 73R.
dangos (y) vn. show 426, 559; pres. 1 sg. *dangossaf* 130.
darestwng vn. lay low, vanquish 807.
darffo, see *daruot*.
darogan f. prophecy 806.
darparu vn. prepare, make provision for 551, 555.
daruot vn. happen, come to an end, perish 33, 230, 380; pret. 3 sg. *daruu* 572, 576; pft. 3 sg. *derw* 388, 459, *deryw* 440; pres. subj. 3 sg. *darffo* 155.
dathoeb, see *dyuot*.
datkanu vn. declare, disclose 760; plpft. 3 sg. *datkanassei* 761.
daw, see *dyuot*.
dayar f. earth 152.
dechreu vn. begin 7, 24, 181; impv. 2 sg. *dechreu* 28.
deffroi vn. wake up, awake 226.
defnyb m. matter, material, subject 217. (Cf. *deunyb*.)
deheu a. right 106.
dehol vn. banish, exile 399.
delw f. design, figure 320, appearance 584, 598. (Ir dealbh.)
del, -ei, -ut, -ych, see *dyuot*.
derw, deryw, see *daruot*.
deu num. m. (len.) two 41, 49, 54.
deu-af, -ant, -(h)ei, see *dyuot*.
deunyb m. source, cause, matter 727.
deuth, -ant, -ost, -um, see *dyuot*.

deuwr m. two (men), pair 109, 111, 125.
deuy, see *dyuot.*
deuawt f. usage, custom 8.
dewis m. choice 445.
dewreḋ m.; *yn y ḋ.* in the prime of life 52 note.
di pers. pron. 2 sg. thou 28, 162, 225, **dy** 138.
dianc vn. escape; impft. 3 sg. *diaghei* 172, *dihangei* ibid. R. (Stem dihang-.)
dial vn. avenge 465. (Ir díoghail.)
diarchenu vn. disarm, help to change; pret. 3 sg. *diarchenwys* 65.
diaspat f. cry, wail, lament 359.
diaspedein m. outcry, clamour 331, 336.
diawt f. drink 619.
diben m. end 40.
diffeith a. desolate, waste 235, 575.
diffeithwch m. desert, uninhabited region 35, 660.
differassant, pret. 3 pl. 778; vn. *diffryt (rac)* save, rescue (from).
difflan vn. slip away, disappear 230, **difflannu** 313, 676.
digawn (o) m. sufficient, enough 326; adv. 699.
digoni vn. do; pret. 1 sg. *digoneis* 185.
digrif a. delightful; spv. *digriffaf* 157, *digrifhaf* 183, *digrifaf* 269, 157R.
dihennyḋyaw vn. execute 304, **dihenyḋyaw** 397, **dihenyḋu** 311.
diheu a. certain, undoubted 697; *d. oeḋ* (or *yw) ytti* I do assure you 83, 110; *d. oeḋ genhyf i* I was certain 171, 324.
dillat coll. m. clothes 576, 590, 599.
dilyssu vn. abandon 741.
dim pron. anything, something 67, 204, 312, at all 369; *o ḋim* at all, by any amount 108R.
dinas m. city 346.
diod- take off; pret. 3 pl. *diodassant* 69.
dioḋef vn. suffer, bear 153, 385.
dioer interj. surely 26, 391, 604. (Duw a wyr, i.e. God knows.)
diryeit a. unlucky, unfortunate 615.
discwyl (ar) vn. watch, spy 595.
discynnu vn. perch, alight 156, 180, **disgynnu** 268, 495, dismount 610, 673. (L. descendo.)
discyr f. shriek, squeal, noise of distress 661, **diskyr** 666.
disgrech vn. howl, screech, roar 749, n.f. scream, howl 661R; **disgrechu** vn. id. 775.
dispeilaw vn. draw, unsheath (a sword) 272, **-yaw** 667. (L. despolio.)
ditheu disjunctive pron. 2 sg. 162, 294, 734. (Cf. titheu.)
diua vn. destroy 626.
diuetha vn. destroy 735, 737.
diwall a. abundant, unstinting 74 note, 714, plentifully supplied 617; cpv. *diwallach* 379.

VOCABULARY

diwarnawt m. day; as adv. one day 2, 455, 564. (L. diurnata.)
diweḋ m. end 35, 235.
diweir a. faithful, loyal, honourable; cpv. *diweirach* 735; spv. *diweiraf* 364.
do affirm. part. to question in pret., yes 227.
dodi vn. put, place 70, 175, 192; impft. 3 sg. *dodei* utter 666; pret. 3 sg. *dodes* 771; 3 pl. *dodassant* 68; impv. 2 sg. *dot* 300, 306.
doḋ-wyf, -(h)wyt, see *dyuot*.
ḋoe adv. yesterday 366, 504, 729.
doeth a. wise, prudent; spv. *doethaf* 364. (L. doctus.)
doeth, -am, -ost, -um, see *dyuot*.
dogyn m. a set 637; amount, quantity 676, 714.
dol f. meadow 674, 756.
doluryaw vn. grieve, be distressed 457. (Cf. dolur, L. dolor.)
dos, see *dyuot*, and *mynet*.
dothoeḋ, -ynt, see *dyuot*.
dout, see *dyuot*.
dor f. door 285, 286; *d. ḋyrchauat* portcullis 281.
drachefyn adv. back, again 407, 441, 510, **drachefen** 197R, **trachefyn** 588, 655; ref. to 1 sg. *tra'm kefyn* 197, 3 sg. f. *tu draechefyn* 406.
drannoeth adv. on the following day 117, 233, **dranoeth** 702, **trannoeth** 207, 430, 481.
drigyaw vn. climb 750. (dringyaw.)
dros prep. (hanging) over 354, 526; with pers. pron. 3 sg. m. *drostaw* in his place 765.
drut a. fierce 191, 271, 803.
drwc m. evil, harm, injury 185, 436, 797; a. evil, bad 409; *d. vyḋ gantunt* they will be upset 304, *d. yḋ aeth arnunt hynny* that upset them 313, *d. yw gennym ni* we are grieved at 796. (Ir droch-.)
drwoḋ adv. through; *drwoḋ y* prep. on to 705. (Cf. trwy.)
drws m. door, doorway, entrance 316, 382, 773.
drycket eqv. (of *drwc*) and n. badness 91.
drych m. form, shape, state 458. (Ir dreach.)
dryll m. severed portion, fragment 285.
drythyll a. high-spirited 31.
du a. black, black-haired 108, 122, 195. (Ir dubh.)
duawc a. black 276 note, 281.
duc, see *dwyn*
1. Duw m. God 212, 222, 297. (Ir Dia.)
2. duw m. day; *d. Nadolic* Christmas Day 63, *d. Pasc* Easter Day 64. (L. natalicius, pascha; Ir dia.)
dwc, see *dwyn*.
dwfyr m. water 76, 150, 169. (Ir dobhar.)
dwrn m. hand, (closed) fist 23, 301. (Ir dorn.)
dwy num. f. (len.) two 286, 354, 644, a pair of 43, 53.

VOCABULARY

dwyclun du. thighs 753; sg. *clun*.

dwylaw du. & pl. hands 357, 804; sg. *llaw*, q.v.

dwyn vn. bear, bring, carry off, take away 155, 466; pres. 1 sg. *dygaf* 199; impft. 3 sg. *dygei* 439, 793; pret. 3 sg. *duc* 437, 447, 780; perfective pres. subj. 3 sg. *ry bycco* 607; impv. 2 sg. *dwc* take 590. (Cog. L. duco.)

dy poss. part. 2 sg. thy 102, 221, *dy . . . dy hun* thine own . . . 156.

dycco, dygaf, see *dwyn*.

dyckynet eqv. a. (of *dygyn* vehement) 357.

dyð m. daylight, dawn 233, 702, day 519, 695.

dyffryn m. vale, broad valley 104, 119, 145 note, **dyffrynn** 238.

dyfynnu vn. summon 442.

dygwyð vn. fall; pret. 3 sg. *dygwyðwys* 754.

dyheð m. a pity 295.

dylyu vn. be entitled to; impft. 3 sg. *dylyei* 8. (Ir dligheadh.)

dyn m. human being, creature, man 130, 138, 172, as pron. anyone 385, 437; pl. *dynyon* people 724, 730. (Ir duine.)

dynessau (at) vn. approach 55.

dyrchafel vn. set up 377 note.

dyrchauat m. raising; see *dor*.

dyret, see *dyuot*.

dyrnawt m. blow 131, 273, 531. (Cf. dwrn.)

dyro, see *robi*.

dyuot vn. come, *d. a* bring 22, 324, **dyfot** 57, 98, 158; pres. 1 sg. *deuaf* 416; 2 sg. *deuy* 552; 3 sg. *daw* 152, 155, 662; 3 pl. *deuant* 303; impft. 2 sg. *dout* 552; 3 sg. *deuhei* 695, 698, *deuei* 792; pret. 1 sg. *deuthum* 39, 41, 120, *doethum* 167; 2 sg. *deuthost* 807, *doethost* 105R; 3 sg. *deuth* 239, 244, 258, *doeth* 82, 132, 238; 1 pl. *doetham* 791; 3 pl. *deuthant* 280, 312, 315; pft. 1 sg. *doðwyf* 802; 2 sg. *doðwyt* 104, *doðhwyt* 105; plpft. 3 sg. *dathoeb* 813, *dothoeb* 774; 3 pl. *dothoebynt* 789; pres. subj. 2 sg. *delych* 107, 145, 104R; 3 sg. *del* 489; past subj. 2 sg. *delut* 389; 3 sg. *delei* 451, 764; impv. 2 sg. *dyret* 306, 308, 427, *dos* 381 note.

dywanu (ar) vn. hit upon, come on by chance 35, 218, 220; pret. 3 sg. *dywanawð* 235.

dywawt, see *dywedut*.

dywedut (y) vn. say, tell 90, 95; pres. 1 sg. *dywedaf* 60; 2 sg. *dywedy* 419; 1 pl. *dywedwn* 21; impft. 2 sg. *dywedut* 221; 3 sg. *dywedei* 127; pret. 1 sg. *dywedeis* 216, 625, 692; 2 sg. *dywedeist* 225; 3 sg. *dywawt* 13, 86, 122; 3 pl. *dywedassant* 688, 769; plpft. 3 sg. *dywedassei* 124, 170, 266; impers. *dywedyssit* 484; past subj. impers. *dywettit* 5.

e, see *eu*.

ebrwyð a. quick, immediate 412.

edeu, edewis, see *adaw*.

VOCABULARY

1. **ebewit** m. promise 20.
2. **ebewit**, see *abaw*.
edrinaw vn. ring, resound 347.
edrych (ar) vn. look (at) 97, 135, 318; pres. 1 sg. *edrychaf* 179; pret. 1 sg. **edrycheis** 179R; 3 sg. *edrychawb* 267; 3 pl. *edrychassant* 494.
edrychyat m. observer, spectator 630.
educher adv. till evening 672. (Cf. *ucher*.)
ef pers. pron. 3 sg. m. he, him 2, 14, 56; **efo** 55, 112, 162, **euo** 212.
eibaw poss. pron. 3 sg. m.; *no'r eibaw ef* than his 454. WG § 161, GCC § 58 (57).
eil a. (len.) second 662, 682.
eilwers adv. a second time; *bop e.* each in turn 511.
eillaw vn. shave 52, 376.
eilun m. image, likeness 584, **eil/lun** (over line-division) 732.
eiroet adv. ever (of time past) 61, **eiryoet** 63, 85, 156; ref. to 1 sg. *eirmoet* 83, 182, 215.
eissyoes adv. nevertheless 115, 585, 617, **eissoes** 141, 214, 419.
eisteb vn. sit (down) 2, 11, **eiste** 73, 78.
eithaf spv. a. furthest out; as n. m. end, limit 344, 642; pl. *eithauoeb* outlying parts, remote regions 35, *eithafoeb* 234, *eithaueb* 575.
eithyr prep. except (for) 79, 478; conj. except (that) 84.
elei, see *mynet*.
eliffant, eliphant m. elephant, see *ascwrn*. (L. *elephantus*.)
ellwng vn. let go, let down, let drop 281, **ellwg** 558, 674; *ellwng y mywn* let in, admit 280.
ellyn f. razor 374, 375.
elor f. bier 349, 351.
el-wyf, -ych, see *mynet*.
emennyb m. brains 275.
emhyl m. side 166, **emyl** 641; *yn em(h)yl* beside 148, 168, 665. (Cf. *ymyl*.)
emneidaw (ar) vn. nod, beckon (to) 407.
eneit m. life, soul 178, 437, 462.
enneint m. bath 553, 619.
ennill vn. make good (the loss of) 393, 394.
ennynu vn. kindle, blaze, go on fire 360, 523.
er prep. since (of time); *er meitin* some time ago 93. (Cf. 2 *yr*.)
erbyn prep.; *yn erbyn* against 144; *erbyn hynny* by then 429.
erbynnyeit vn. go to meet, encounter 270, 499, **erbynyeit** 488.
erchi (y) vn. command, bid, ask 135, 293, 558; pret. 3 sg. *erchis* 310, 805.
ereill, see *arall*.
ergrynu vn. tremble, quake 151R.
erlit vn. pursue 278W.
erni, see *ar*.

VOCABULARY

eruyn m. request 488.

escyb pl. bishops 448; sg. *escob*. (L. episcopus.)

eskynnu (ar) vn. mount (horse) 118, **ysgynnu** 234, **escynnu** 601, 638. (L. ascendo.)

esgynuaen m. mounting-block 305.

esmwyth a. pleasant, comfortable 611; cpv. *esmwythyach* 556.

estwng vn. bow, bend, lower 136, descend, come down 580.

etto adv. yet, still 211, **ettwa** 212, 774.

eu poss. and obj. part. 3 pl. them, their 7, 44, 91, 111; *e* 246.

eur m. gold 433, 567, 657; as a. 23, 42, 44. (L. aurum.)

eureit a. gilded 48, 246, 375.

eurllin m. gold thread 53, 432.

euthum, ewch, ey, see *mynet*.

fawyð coll. beech trees; as a. of beech wood 637.

ffenestyr f. window 4, 343, **fenestyr** 59. (L. fenestra.)

fenitwyð coll. fir trees 147, **ffenytwyð** ibid. R.

fi pers. pron. 1 sg. me 308, 437, **vi** 196.

ffo (rac) vn. flee (from) 277; pres. 2 sg. *ffoy* 161. (L. fuga.)

ffon f. staff 110, 124, 130.

fforð f. road 37, 104, 115; *pa fforð* how 410, 412. (OE ford.)

ffrwyn f. bridle 193, 567. (L. frenum.)

ffuryf f. form, shape, guise 359. (L. forma.)

fynhawn f. spring, well 148, **ffynhyawn** 167, 554, **ffynnawn** 205, 262, 366, **ffynnawnn** 252, **ffynyhawn** 685. (L. fontana.)

gadu (y) vn. allow, let, permit 488, 515; pres. 1 sg. *gadaf* 505; 2 sg. *gedy* 505 note; impv. 2 sg. *gat* 515.

gallu vn. be able; pres. 1 sg. *gallaf* 300, 413; 2 sg. *gelly* 294, 414, 708; 3 sg. *geill* 415, 465; 2 pl. *gellwch* 15; impers. *gellir* 149, 294, 363; impft. 1 sg. *gallwn* 394, 629; 2 sg. *gallut* 395; 3 sg. *gallei* 287, 579, 692; impers. *gellit* 296, 443; pres. subj. 2 sg. *gellych* 393; 3 sg. *gallo* 161.

galw vn. call, name, entitle 691; pres. impers. *gelwir* 366, 822.

gan prep. (len.) in the opinion of 88, at, with 200, from, by 203; orig. *can*, hence *a chan* 203, *no chan* 249, 260. With pers. pron. 1 sg. *genhyf* 60, 88, 117, *gennyf* 211, 215, 425; 2 sg. *genhyt* 101, *gennyt* 425; 3 sg. m. *gantaw* 22, 253, *ganthaw* 194, 626, 678; f. *genthi* 560, 606; 3 pl. *gantunt* 305, 496. *Y gan* prep. from (with) 15; with pers. pron. 1 sg. *y gennyf* 460, 539; 3 sg. m. *y ganthaw* 677; 1 pl. *y gennym* 463.

garw a. rough, uncivil 140. (Ir garbh.)

geill, gell-ir, -it, -wch, -ych, see *gallu*.

geir m. word 89.

gelwir, see *galw*.

VOCABULARY

gelyn m. enemy, foe; pl. *gelynnyon* 635.
genh-yf, -yt, genn-yf, -yt, genthi, see *gan*.
ger prep.; *ger eu llaw* near them, beside them 241, *gyr llaw* 591, *gyr y law* (3 sg. m.) 594.
gieu coll. sinews 46.
gilyb (i.e. *kilyb* m. companion, with 3 sg. m. poss. part., as reciprocal pron.) each other 402, 522, 525. (Ir céile.)
girat a. terrible, dreadful 336.
glas a. green, fresh; cpv. *glassach* 146; spv. *glassaf* 147. (Ir glas.)
glo m. coal, charcoal 320, 370.
glyn m. valley 36, 37, *glynn* 235, 237. (Ir gleann.)
gnewillin m. centre 110 note.
gobennyb m. bolster, pillow, cushion 12; pl. *-eu* 72.
godeuawc a. keen, sharp 521, 523.
gofal, see *goual*.
gofyn (y) vn. ask 17, 226, 603, **gowyn** 128, **gouyn** 140, 141; impv. 2 sg. *gouyn* 114.
goganu vn. make fun of 691; impft. 2 pl. *goganewch* 13.
gogyfuch a. equally high, of even height 36.
golchi vn. clean, wash 374; pret. 3 pl. *golchassant* 66.
goleu a. light, bright 530.
goleuhau vn. lighten, grow brighter 266; pret. 3 sg. *goleuhawys* 494.
golwyth m. chop, collop; pl. *-on* 15, 23, *golhwythyon* 680, *golwythyon* 700.
gorberch mf. mistress, lover 298, 299.
gorberchu vn. woo, make love to 381.
gorbiwes vn. overtake, catch; pres. 3 sg. *gorbiweb* 163; impft. 3 sg. *gorbiwebei* 172.
goreu spv. a. best 20, 75, 212.
goreureit a. gilded; *aryant g.* silver gilt 323. (Cf. eureit.)
gorffei, see *goruot*.
gorffowys vn. rest 673.
gorflwch, see *gorvlwch*.
gorgrymhu vn. 151 note.
gormod (o) m. too much, excess 98.
gorssau-, stem of *gorsseuyll* vn. stop, halt; impft. 3 sg. *gorssauei* 173.
gorsseb f. mound, hillock 107, 108, 123.
goruc, gorug-am, -ant, -ost, -um, see *gwneuthur*.
gorvlwch m. goblet, cup 23, **gorflwch** bowl 372, jar 588, 612.
goruot (ar) vn. overcome 33, 539, 821; pret. 3 sg. *goruu* 536, 540, *-fu* 521; 3 pl. *goruuant* 769; past subj. 3 sg. *gorffei* 32, 95.
gorweb vn. lie (down) 679, 715.
gorymdeith vn. walk 455, 583, 798.
goual m. care, anxiety 384, **gofal** 727; pl. *goueileint*, *kymryt g.* be anxious 100.

goualu (am) vn. care (for), provide (for), concern oneself (about) 392, grieve 572.

gouut m. trouble, distress, harm, grief 98, 164, **gofut** 389, 489, 749, govit 650.

gouyn, gowyn, see *gofyn*.

gowenu vn. smile 97, 253.

gra m. a material or fur 335 note.

gressawu vn. welcome 725.

gwaec f. clasp, fastening; pl. *gwaegeu* 44.

gwaet m. blood 354.

gwaeth cpv. a. worse 478.

gwahanfforð f. side-road 106, 119.

gwahanu vn. separate 150.

gwahawð vn. invite 403, 474, 658; n. m. invitation 402, 474.

gwallt coll. hair 354. (Ir folt.)

gwan vn. thrust at, stab 507.

gwanhau vn. grow weak, weaken 579.

gwann a. weak 810. (Ir fann.)

gwarandaw (ar) vn. listen (to), hear 183.

gwarchadw vn. guard 252. (Cf. kadw.)

gware vn. play, frolic, gambol 671.

gwareðawc a. obedient, submissive, dutiful 137.

gwaret (y) vn. deliver 294, 296; n. m. deliverance 300. (OIr 3 sg. fo-reith.)

gwarthaedic a. slanderous, injurious 223.

gwas m. young man 42, 297, 758; pl. *gweison* 240, *gweisson* 472, 766; *gweissyon ystauell* chamberlains 690, *gweisson y meirch* grooms 479.

gwascwyn m. gascon (horse) 636.

gwasanaeth m. service 379, **-ss-** 477.

gwassanaethu (ar) vn. serve, wait on 80, 248, 477; plpft. 3 pl. *gwassanaethassynt* 248; impv. 2 sg. *gwassanaethya* 617.

gwastat a. level, smooth 674. (OIr fossad.)

gwatwar m. mockery, ridicule 200.

gwayw f. spear, lance 161, 190, 193, **gwaew** 450, 503. (OIr gae, L & P § 34 (3).)

gwðost, see *gwybot*.

gweð f. appearance 435.

gweðw a. widowed 581, 605, **gweðu** vacant 443. (OIr fedb.)

gwedy prep. after 33, 230, 266; adv. afterwards 182; *gwedy y* conj. after, when 792, neg. *gwedy na* 304; with vn. as pft. participle act. 209, or pass. 47, 209.

gweiði m. cry 332, 341, 347.

gweilgi f. sea 40.

gweiss(y)on, see *gwas*.

gweithret f. act, action 222.

VOCABULARY

gwelet vn. see 385, 456; pres. 2 sg. *gwely* 108, 113, 138; impfct. 1 sg. *gwelwn* 40, 51, 84; 3 sg. *gwelei* 239, 262, 325; 3 pl. *gwelynt* 497, 584; impers. *gwelit* 567, 753; pret. 1 sg. *gweleis* 55, 85, 297; 2 sg. *gweleist* 28, 61; 3 sg. *gwelas* 233, 327, 360; 3 pl. *gwelsant* 312, 477, 485; plpft. 3 sg. *gwelsei* 240, 325, 352; 3 pl. *gwelsynt* 529; pres. subj. 1 sg. *gwelwyf* 306; 3 pl. *gwelont* 304.

gwell cpv. a. better 27, 84, 88.

gwely m. bed 334, 381, 619.

gwerth m. value 452, 615; ? a. worth 786.

gwerthu vn. sell, ransom; impfct. 3 sg. *gwerthei* 451.

gwerthuawr a. precious, costly 319, 589, 616.

gwiber f. viper; pl. *-ot* 134. (L. uipera.)

gwineu a. brown, auburn (-haired) 566, 759.

gwineuðu a. dark brown 208. (gwineu+du.)

gwintas f. footwear, ankle-length boot 43, 53, 292.

gwir a. true 684. (Ir fíor.)

gwisc f. clothing, garments 70, 160, 189.

gwiscaw (am) vn. put on (clothes or armour), dress or arm oneself 118, **gwisgaw** 209, 233, 342; pret. 3 sg. *gwisgwys* 430, *gwisgawð* 513.

gwiw (y) a. worthy of, fit for 334. (Ir fiú.)

gwlat f. land 156. (Cf. Ir flaith.)

gwleð f. feast 551, 556. (Ir fleadh.)

gwn(n), see *gwybot*.

gwneuthur vn. do, make, perform 20, 296, 792; pres. 1 sg. *gwnaf* 30, 300, 399; 2 sg. *gwney* 686, 734; 3 sg. *gwna* 161, 730; impers. *gwneir* 569; impfct. 3 sg. *gwnaei* 137, 683, 821, *gwnai* 578; pret. 1 sg. *gwneuthum* 34, 36, 38; 2 sg. *gwnaethost* 186; 3 sg. *gwnaeth* 194, 229, 310; 1 pl. *gwnaetham* 78J; 3 pl. *gwnaethant* 24, 247; impers. *gwnaethpwyt* 229, 281, 636; pft. 1 sg. *gorugum* 73, 90, 118; 2 sg. *gorugost* 807; 3 sg. *goruc* 16, 21, 89; 1 pl. *gorugam* 78, 86; 3 pl. *gorugant* 64, 74, 136; pres. subj. 3 sg. *gwnel* 593; past subj. 2 sg. *gwnelut* 186, 221.

gwniaw vn. sew, embroider 4, 59, **gwnyaw** 245.

gwr m. man, husband 19, 27, 51; pl. *gwyr* 13, 109, 137; *mynn y gwr a'n gwnaeth* by Him that made us! (Ir fear.)

gwrð a. brisk, vehement 498.

gwrda m. nobleman, gentleman 337, 341, 393; pl. *gwyrda* 559.

gwreanc m. youth, young man 698, **gwraang** 687.

gwreic f. woman, wife 63, 296, 353; pl. *gwrageð* 79, 203, 345.

gwreicða f. lady 224; pl. *gwragebda* 559.

gwrha vn. marry (of a woman) 395, **gwra** 447.

gwrhau vn. pay homage 449.

gwrthgroch (wrth) a. gruff, surly 115.

gwrthgrocheð m. surliness, rudeness 128.

gwrthmun a. repugnant 397.

VOCABULARY

1. gwybot m. good manners, courtesy 56.
2. gwybot vn. know, find out 616; pres. 1 sg. *gwn* 462, 636, *gwnn* 487; 2 sg. *gwbost* 411; 3 sg. *gwyr* 213, 222, 293; fut. 1 sg. *gwybybaf* 307; impft. 1 sg. *gwybywn* 552; 2 sg. *gwybut* 187; 3 sg. *gwybyat* 236; impers. *gwybit* 476; pres. subj. 2 sg. *gwypych* 29; 1 pl. *gwypom* 21; impft. subj. 3 sg. *gwypei* 216, 764, *gwyppei* 698.
gwych a. valiant; eqv. *kyn wychet* 529.
1. gwyð m. presence 691, 732. (Ir *fiadh*.)
2. gwyð coll. trees, woodland 36. (Ir *fiodh*.)
gwyð-it, -ut, -yat, -ywn, see *gwybot*.
gwyllt a. wild 113, 121, 578.
gwylwr m. watchman 708.
gwylyaw vn. watch, observe, guard; pret. 3 sg. *gwylywys* 708, 709; impv. 2 sg. *gwylya* 592.
gwyn a. white, clean, bright 77, **gwynn** 322, 350; pl. *gwynnyon* 77R; eqv. *kyn wynhet* 67; cpv. *gwynnach* 621; spv. *gwynhaf* 67. (Ir *fionn*.)
gwyp(p)-ei, -om, -ych, see *gwybot*.
gwyr, see (1) *gwr*, (2) *gwybot*.
gwyrð a. green 77. (L. *uiridis*.)
gwystyl m. hostage, pledge; pl. *gwystlyon* 657. (Ir *giall*.)
gwytheu n. 586 note.
gwywaw vn. flag, become exhausted 587R.
gyn, see 1. *kyn*.
gynheu adv. just now (of time past); *y gwr g.* the man just mentioned 78, *y dyn g.* the man (we saw) just now 591.
gynt, see *kynt*.
gyr, see *ger*.
gyrru (att, ar) vn. send (to) 557; pres. subj. 3 sg. *gyrro* 402.
gyt adv. together; *gyt a(c)* prep. with 57, 134, 747; *y gyt* adv. together 357, with *a(c)* 2, 345.

ha vocative part. 13, 19, 92.
haccraf, see *hagyr*.
hael a. generous; spv. *haelaf* 364.
hagen adv. however, nevertheless 6.
hagyr a. ugly, hideous 112 note, 598; spv. *haccraf* 61.
hambwyllaw vn. think of, turn one's attention to; pres. subj. 3 pl. *hambwyllont* 303.
handit (pres. impers. of *hanuot*, GCC § 153 (156)) is 438.
hanner m. half 283, *hanher* 669; *h. dyð* midday 38, 428, 524; *h. nos* midnight 335; *h. bwytta* half-way through the meal 86, 249, 725.
harð a. beautiful, handsome; eqv. n. *harðet* beauty 247, a. *kyharbet* 352; cpv. *harðach* 62; spv. *harðaf* 63.
hawð a. easy 614.

VOCABULARY

hayach adv. any time, for long 227, a good deal 576.

hayarn m. iron 110; as a. 124.

1. heb vb. said (in quoting direct speech) 14, 103, **heb y** 19, 25, 26.

2. heb (len.) prep. without 218, 319, 385.

heðiw adv. today 186, 388, 505.

hela vn. hunt 729. (Ir sealg.)

helw m. possession; *ar y helw* in her possession 607, his 633. (Ir sealbh.)

helym f. helmet 273, 508, 532. (OE helm.)

heno adv. tonight 103, 606, 708.

heol f. street 289, 290; pl. -*yb* 344.

heul m. sun 587.

hi pers. pron. 3 sg. f. she, her 153, 299, 321.

hinon f. fine weather 154.

hinoni vn. become fine (of weather); pret. 3 sg. *hinones* 180.

hir a. long, tedious 117, 191, 499. (Ir síor.)

hiraeth (am) m. longing, nostalgia 460.

hitheu disjunctive pers. pron. 3 sg. f. 315.

hoel f. nail, peg 319.

hoff a. well thought of, esteemed; cpv. *hoffach oeb genhyf* I thought greater, I thought more highly of 120, 246, 483.

holl a. (before n.) whole 75, 690, all 525.

hollt f. cleft 664.

holy (y) vn. claim (from), want (of); impft. 2 sg. *holut* 185; 3 pl. *holynt* 760.

honn, honno, see *hwn, hwnnw*.

hun self, with preceding poss. part. 2 sg. *dy hun* 401, 770, 3 sg. m. *e hun* 214, f. *e hun* 385, and in apposition to a n., pron. or name; after n. itself preceded by a poss. part., own 156, 210, 656.

hwde interj. take hold, here 300, 535.

hwn dem. a. sg. m., this 109, **hwnn** 301R, 336, 436, pron. 214; **honn** dem. a. sg. f., this 300, pron. 365, *yr honn a* the one (f.) that, whoever 816; **hyn** dem. a. pl., these 139, pron. (= neut. sg. this) 60, *yr hynn a* that which 99, 116, *o'r hynn odidockaf a* from the most remarkable thing that 29; *val hyn* thus 569.

hwnnw dem. a. sg. m., that 113, 147, 211; **honno** dem. a. sg. f., that 117, 704, 731, pron. 106, 126, 182; **hynny** dem. a. pl. pron. 134, 345, (= neut. sg. that) 101, 124; *ar hynny* thereupon, at that 13, 75, 159; *wrth hynny* therefore 299; *am hynny* therefore 412; *yr hynny* on that account 464; *o hynny allan* thenceforth, after that 510; *gan hynny* thereby, in that way 542; *yn hynny* in that, thus 620.

hwrð m. thrust 525.

hwy pers. pron. 3 pl., they, them 61, 135, 157; **hwynt** 538, 692; **hwynteu** disjunctive pron. 3 pl. 49, 137. (Cf. *wy, wynt, -eu.*)

hyḋ m. deer 46.
hydwf a. well-grown 36J.
hydyr a. strong, overpowering 774 note.
1. **hyn** cpv. a. older 27; pos. *hen*.
2. **hyn**, see *hwn*.
hynny, see *hwnnw*.
hyny conj. (len.) until 67, 104, 107, with infixed pron. 1 sg. *hyny'm* 191; **yny** 238, 258, 577; so that 131.
hyspys a. clear, obvious, certain 125, 181, 236.
1. **hyt** m. length; *ar hyt* along 37, 104, 106.
2. **hyt** prep. (a) space: as far as, to 120, 210, 285; *hyt ar* to, on to 405, 750; *hyt yn* (in)to 416, 433, 484; *hyt lle yḋ oeḋ y gwr* to where the man was 482; (b) time: until 38, 86, 519; conj. *hyt pan* so that, until 532, 165R; *hyt na(t)* so that . . . not, until . . . not 453, 511, 579.

i pers. pron. 1 sg. I, me 31, 55, 87.
iach a. in good health, healthy 619.
iarll m. earl, count 517, 607, 624; pl. *ieirll* 789. (ON jarl.)
iarllaeth f. earldom 443, 449, 606.
iarlles f. countess, lady 365, 385, 554.
iawn a. right, proper 296, 359, 549; adv. very 112 J, 117 J.
iḋaw, iḋi, see *2. y*.
ie affirmative part., yes, well 645, 684.
ieuanc a. young 607.
im, see *2. y*.
inheu disjunctive pron. 1 sg. 79, 90, 194, **ynneu** 205, 446, **inneu** 403.
iraw vn. smear, anoint; impv. 2 sg. *ir* 591.
irvrwyn coll. fresh, green rushes 11. (ir+brwyn.)
iryeit m. ointment 589, 616, **ireit** 591, 592.
is prep.; *is vy llaw* (1 sg.) below me (in order of precedence) 79.
itt, itti, see *2. y*.
iwrch m. buck 681.

llaḋ vn. slay 729, strike (fire) 674; impft. 3 sg. *llaḋei* 793; pret. 2 sg. *lleḋeist* 366; 3 sg. *llaḋawḋ* 493, 777; pret. pass. *llas* 465 note; pres. subj. 3 sg. *llaḋho* 732. (Cf. OIr slaide.)
llafyn m. blade (of a knife); pl. *llafneu* 48. (L. lamina.)
llall pron. the other (in contrast to *neill*, q.v.) 777.
llamu vn. pulsate, beat 587. (Cf. OIr léimm, L & P § 8 (2).)
llann f. church, churchyard 342.
llannerch f. clearing, open space in a wood 107, 114, 120.
llanw vn. fill 371, 373.
llas, see *llaḋ*.

VOCABULARY

llaw f. hand 45, 126, 131; du. and pl. *dwylaw*, q.v. (Ir lámh.)
llawdyr m. trousers, breeches 70.
llawen (wrth) a. glad to see, welcoming towards 424, 434, 603; cpv. *llawenach* 201, 815; adv. *yn llawen* gladly, willingly 630.
llawer a. many 345; *ll. o* many of 492; *o lawer* by a great deal, much+cpv. 123, 246, 265.
llawn a. full 452, 587R. (Ir lán.)
llawn-aruawc a. fully-armed 345.
llawr m. floor, ground 10, 192, 285, **llowr** 669. (Ir lár.)
llawvorwyn f. (hand)maiden 685; pl. *llawuorynyon* 4, 582.
lle m. place 220, 240, 327; *noc yn lle* than anywhere 85W, *noc yn lle arall* than elsewhere 327; *lle ny* where . . . not 401; *o le arall* from elsewhere 447; *yn y lle* immediately 490, 507, 677.
llech f. slab, stone 148, 151, 167. (Ir leac.)
lleḃeist, see *llaḃ*.
llei cpv. a. less, smaller 108, 733.
llenn f. covering 11, 349. (Ir leann.)
lleon adv.; *o'r lleon* from here 303 note.
lles m. advantage, profit, good 102, 401. (Ir leas.)
llesteir (ar) m. hindrance, impediment (to) 93.
llestyr m. vessel, dish 81, 328, 695; pl. *llestri* 329.
lletty m. lodging(s) 9, 231, 572.
lleuassei, impft. 3 sg. dare 715, **llyfassei** ibid. R.
llew m. lion 433, 665, 670; pl. *-ot* 134. (L. leo.)
llewenyḃ m. welcome, hospitality 704, 791, joy 800. (Cf. llawen.)
llewni vn. fill 344. (Cf. llawn.)
lliein m. (table-)cloth 68, 324; pl. *llieinyeu* 81W.
llinyn m. (bow-)string; pl. *-eu* 46.
llit m. rage, fury 523.
llithraw vn. slip, fall, drop 753.
lliw m. colour, paint 319.
lliwaw vn. colour, paint 319.
llofft f. upstairs room 316, 317, **lloft** 316, 318. (ON lopt.)
lloneit m. the fill (of something) 23, 588.
llosgi vn. burn 350, 778; pres. 1 pl. *llosgwn* 762. (Ir loscadh.)
llu m. crowd, host 349, 353, 360; pl. *-oeḃ* 344. (Ir sluagh.)
lluḃedwisc f. travel-stained clothing 69, **lluḃeticwisc** ibid. R.
lluḃet m. weariness (with travelling) 553.
llun m. shape, form, figure, image 432.
lluyḃyaw vn. muster, mobilize (an army) 464.
llwdyn m. young beast 172, 187.
llwyt a. grey 663. (Ir liath.)
llwyth m. load, burden, as much as one can carry 111, 124, 125. (Ir lucht.)
llydan a. broad 71, 431. (Ir leathan.)

llygat m. eye 109.
llygru vn. violate 736.
llyma interj. behold, here is 539.
1. llyn m. pool 199, **llynn** lake 583. (Ir linn.)
2. llyn m. drink 84, 85, **llynn** 328. (Ir lionn.)
llyna interj. there is, that is 795.
llys f. court 5, 8, 91. (Ir lios.)
llywychedic a. shining, bright 40, 280.

mab m. son 2, 31, 728; pl. *meibon* 730, 735. (Ir mac.)
maccwyf m. squire, page 639, **mackwy** ibid. R.; pl. *mackwyeit* 642, 651.
mack-, subj. stem of vn. *meithryn* rear, nurse, cherish; impft. subj. 1 sg. *mackwn* 397; 3 sg. *mackei* 671.
madws m. (high) time 90, 725.
mae, see *bot*.
maeðu vn. beat, strike 278; impft. 3 sg. *maeðei* 357.
maen m. stone, jewel 301, 694, 773.
maes m. plain, field, open country 39, level ground 107; *y maes* outside 286.
mal conj. like, as 224; *mal y* as 248, 761, how 450, so that 115, 532; *mal na* so that . . . not 149.
mam f. mother 31.
manac, manag-af, -assei, -wn, manegeis, see *menegi*.
mantell f. mantle 52, 71, 431. (L. mantellum.)
march m. horse 65, 74, 118; pl. *meirch* 346, 526, 793, *meirych* 640.
marchawc m. knight 159, 185, person on horseback 162; pl. *marchogyon* 453.
marmor m. marble; as a. 168.
marw a. dead 337, 754; *a ffan uu varw y harglwyð* and when her lord died 605. (Ir marbh.)
mawr a. great, big, extensive 32, 39, 107, 123, 457. (Ir mór.)
mawreð m. 195 note.
með m. mead 15, 22, 24. (Ir miodh.)
meðgell f. mead-cellar 22. (með+cell, L. cella.)
medru vn. hit, hit upon; impft. 2 sg. *medrut* 401; pret. 3 sg. *medrawð* 282.
meðw a. drunk 792. (OIr medb.)
meðwl m. mind, thought; *ar ueðwl* as if to 420.
meðyant (ar) m. power, authority (over) 129, 138.
megys conj. like, as it were 145.
meibon, see *mab*.
meint m. size, bigness 259, 469, greatness 340, 739, amount, space (of time) 460. (Ir méid.)
meir(y)ch, see *march*.

VOCABULARY

melyn a. yellow, golden(-haired) 42, 43, 51; f. *melen* 291, 353; pl. *melynyon* 644.
melyngoch a. orange 11. (melyn+coch.)
menegi (y) vn. tell, declare, relate 7, 99, 102; pres. 1 sg. *managaf* 102, 410, 413; 3 sg. **menyc** 115; impft. 1 sg. *managwn* 99; pret. 1 sg. *manegeis* 94; 3 sg. *menegis* 119; plpft. 3 sg. *managassei* 166, 236; impv. 2 sg. *manac* 410.
merch f. daughter 517, 720; pl. *-et* 789.
methedic a., cpv. *methedigach* 214 note.
meu poss. pron. mine 550.
mevyl (y) m. shame (on) 401, 570, **mefyl** 416. (Ir meabhal.)
mi pers. pron. 1 sg. I, me 14, 27, 29.
mil f. thousand 113, 469. (L. milia.)
milgi m. hunting dog, mastiff 671.
milwr m. warrior 126, 417. (L. miles+gwr.)
milwryaeth f. valour, feat of arms 411, 444.
minneu disjunctive pron. 1 sg., I for my part 18, 25, 225, **minheu** 79, 96.
miui redupl. pron. 1 sg. 402, 765, **myvy** 645, **myui** 765.
moes f. custom 7.
moesswch (at) impv. 2 pl. (no vn.) give 541.
molyant m. praise, commendation 225. (Cf. Ir moladh.)
mor adv. so (degree) 223, 398, how (i.e. to what an extent) 598.
morwil m. walrus 47, **moruil** 49. See *ascwrn*.
morwyn f. maiden 59, 61, 290; pl. *morynnyon* 87, 245.
motrwy f. ring 300, **modrwy** 568.
mur m. wall 773, 776. (L. murus.)
mwg m. mane 176, 566. (I.e. mwng, Ir mong.)
mwy cpv. a. bigger 123, greater 170, as pron., more 27, 225; spv. *mwyhaf* 367 note, 690, 790.
mygen f. mane 208. (myngen.)
mynet vn. go 8, 21, 78; *mynet yn* become 608, 809; *mynet a* take, conduct 341; *mynet dwylaw mynwgyl (y)* embrace 542, 545; pres. 1 sg. *af* 381, 415, 630; 2 sg. *ey* 628; impft. 1 sg. *awn* 765; 3 sg. *ai* 608; pret. 1 sg. *euthum* 550R; 3 sg. *aeth* 193, 333, 510; 3 pl. *aethant* 256, 475; pres. subj. 1 sg. *elwyf* 308; 2 sg. *elych* 104; past subj. 3 sg. *elei* 817, 820; impv. 2 sg. *dos* 419, 589, 705; 2 pl. *ewch* 440, 645.
myngrych a. curly-maned 566. (mwng+crych.)
mynn prep. by (in oaths) 220, 766, **myn** 224.
mynnu vn. desire, want, intend, determine 178, 242, 741; pres. 1 sg. *mynnaf* 18; 2 sg. *mynny* 426; 3 sg. *myn* 540, 636; 1 pl. *mynnwn* 766; impft. 1 sg. *mynnwn* 141, 203, 252; 3 sg. *mynnei* 816; 2 pl. *mynnewch* 765; pret. 3 sg. *mynwys* 659, *mynnawd* 756.
mynwgyl m. neck 372; pl. *mynygleu eu traet* their insteps, ankles 44. (Ir muineál.)

mynych a. frequent; adv. often 221. (Ir minic.)
mynyð m. mountain 580, 729; pl. *-eð* 235, 575.
y mywn prep. in 67, 245, 647; adv. (motion) in 281, 651, (rest) inside 287.

1. na (asp.) conj. neither . . . nor 83, 181, 187; before vowels **nac** 344; with art. *na'r* 86.
2. na (len. asp.) neg. conj., that . . . not 83, 199, 692; before vowels **nat** 91 note, 111, 213; with obj. pron. 1 sg. *na'm* 13; 3 sg. m. *nas* 83, 212.
nachaf interj. behold 41, 76, 170.
Nadolic m. Christmas 63. (L. (dies) natalicius.)
na'm, see 2. *na*.
namyn prep. except, other than 58, 82, 216, but 464; *namyn vn mab* 31 note; *ny . . . namyn* only, nothing but 128.
nas, see 2. *na*.
nat neg. conj. 2. *na*+copula, that it is not 726, 801.
nawð m. protection, quarter 805. (Cf. OIr snádud.)
neb indef. pron. someone, anyone 204, 205; *y neb a* the one who, anyone who 8, 9; *neb ryw* any kind of 33, 325.
nef f. heaven, sky 152. (Ir neamh.)
neges f. errand, mission 426. (L. necesse.)
y neill a. the one; *ar y neill law y* on one side of 719; pron. 777.
neityaw vn. dart, leap; impft. 3 sg. *neityei* 666; pret. 3 sg. *neidyawð* 751.
nerth m. strength 774. (Ir neart.)
nerthu vn. strengthen, assist; pret. 3 sg. *nerthwys* 768.
nessaf (y) spv. a. nearest, next (to) 79. (OIr nessam.)
nessau (at, ar) vn. approach, draw near (to) 585, 667.
neu conj. (len.) or 8, 82, 96, **ne** 63.
neuað f. hall 8, 58, 750.
neur (len.) affirmative part. *neu*+perfective part. *ry*, 613.
newyð a. new 44; as verbal prefix, newly, freshly 52.
ni pers. pron. 1 pl. we, us 21, 92, 93; **ninneu** disjunctive pron. 1 pl., we for our part 21, 762, 794.
niuer m. company (of warriors), retinue, band of retainers 352, 475, **nifer** 469. (L. numerus.)
no conj. (asp.) than 27, 56, 62; before vowels **noc** 85, 170; with art. *no'r* 61; with poss. pron. 2 sg. *no'th* 102.
nos f. night 117, 201, 676, **noss** 201.
not m. mark (for shooting at) 49; pl. *nodeu* 49J.
ny neg. part. (len. asp.) not 32, 86; before vowels **nyt** 5, 81; as rel. 84, 108, 111; with obj. pron. 3 sg. *nys* 205, 386, 756; with perfective part. *ry*, **nyr** 154.
nyt neg. part. *ny*+copula, it is not 70, 111, 164.

1. o prep. of, from, expresses the agent with the vn.; (made) of 10, 12, (consisting) of 11, 22, (more) of 28, in respect of 33; with art. *o'r*

VOCABULARY

29, 36, 72; with poss. and obj. pron. 1 sg. *o'm* 635; 3 sg. m. *o'e* 75, 251, 438, *o'y* 98, 631, 648; f. *o'e* 360, 657; 3 pl. *oc eu* 313; with pers. pron. 1 sg. *ohonaf* 102, 401, 426; 3 sg. m. *ohonaw* 276, 326; f. *ohonei* 173; 1 pl. *ohonam* 402; 2 pl. *ohonawch* 445, 542; 3 pl. *onaḋunt* 42, 61, 519, *ohonunt* 42R.

2. o conj. if 161, 298, 416; before vowels **ot** 465; with neg. *ony* 93, 163, 413; with perfective part. *or* 465; with copula, *os* if it is 466, (= *o*) 162.

och interj. oh, alas 514; as n. f. sigh, groan 682.

odidawc a. strange, wonderful, remarkable 28, 328; eqv. *odidocket* 215; spv. *odidockaf* 29.

oḋis prep. below 282.

oḋyma adv. from here 294.

oḋyna adv. after that 20, from there 295 note.

oḋyno adv. from there 145, 287, 308.

o'e, see (1) 1. *o*, (2) 2. *y*.

oeḋ, -ut, -wn, -ynt, oes, see *bot*.

oet m. appointed time 695 note, 731.

offeren f. mass 64. (L. offerenda.)

ofyn m. fear 585. (MIr omun.)

ohon-af, -am, -awch, -ei, -unt, see 1. *o*.

ol m. track; *yn ol* after 152, 405, 491, *yn y ol* behind him 645, 743; *ar ol* behind, following 353, 491.

olew m. oil; *dodi olew ar* anoint, administer extreme unction to 332. (L. oleum.)

oll a. all, whole 230, 310, 346.

o'm, onaḋunt, see 1. *o*.

ony, see 2. *o*.

onyt, 2. *o*+neg. part.+copula, if it is not 444.

o'r a, 1. *o*+rel. pron. *yr*+2. *a*, of that which (etc.) 34, 172, 188.

orffreis f. border, fringe, orfrey 71 note, 431.

os, see 2. *o*.

o'y, see .1 *o*.

pa interrog. part. what 129, 185, 340; *pa ryw* what kind of 89, 142; *pa le* where 141; *pa beth* what 142.

paladyr m. shaft (of arrow or lance) 271, 509; pl. *peleidyr* 46, 48, 521.

palaf f. paw 752. (L. palma.)

palffrei m. palfrey 207, 212. (OFr, ME palefrei.)

pali m. a rich material, brocaded silk 11, 43, 52. (OFr paile.)

pallu (y) vn. fail; pret. 3 sg. *pallwys* 762.

paluawt f. stroke (of the paw, hand) 751. (Cf. palaf, dyrnawt.)

pan conj. (len.) when 54, 63, 87, **pann** 360; with infixed obj. pron. 3 sg. *pan y* 815; that 186 note.

panyw conj. *pan* 'that'+copula, that it is 236, 462, 533.
paraf, see *peri*.
parattoi vn. prepare, make ready 231.
parawt a. ready 209, 257, 675. (L. paratus.)
parc n. park, enclosed ground 580, 583 note.
parch m. respect, proper treatment 791.
pardwgyl m. hind bow of saddle, cantle 283.
parth m. part, side 38, 238; *parth a* in the direction of, towards, to 41, 58, 159. (L. partem.)
parwn, see *peri*.
Pasc m. Easter 64. (L. pascha.)
paun m. peacock 47, **pawin** ibid. R. (L. pauonem.)
pawb pron. each one, everyone 547. (Ir cách.)
pebyll mf. tent; pl. -*eu* 547. (L. papilio.)
pebyllyaw vn. pitch (a tent) 500; pret. 3 sg. *pebyllywys* 654.
pedeir, see *petwar*.
pedestyr m. person on foot 163. (L. pedester.)
pedrein f. crupper 174, 526.
pedwareḃ, see *petwar*.
pei conj. if 13, 698, neg. *pei na* 98, 397, *bei na* 746; as copula, if it were 530; *beyt uei* if she were 358.
peidyaw vn. cease 494; pret. 3 sg. *peidyawḃ* 178.
peis f. tunic 43, 52, 71. (L. pexa.)
pell (y) a. far, distant (from) 279; cpv. *pellach* 695.
pellennig m. traveller, one from a distance; pl. -*yon* 7.
pen(n) m. head, tip, top 145, 175, 277; pl. *penneu* 136, 356, *penheu* 47; *penn yr elin* elbow 12; *ymphen* on (top of) 122, at the end of, after 596; *am ben* upon 150; *ar penn* on 307. (Ir ceann.)
pengrych a. curly-haired 42, 51, **penngrych** 758; f. *penngrech* 290. (Cf. myngrych.)
pennffestin m. mail-cap 274, **penffestin** 508.
penngwch pwrqwin 274 note.
pennteulu m. captain of the royal bodyguard 818.
peri vn. cause, have (something done) 397, 399; pres. 1 sg. *paraf* 428; impft. 1 sg. *parwn* 398.
perueḃ m. centre, middle; *ym p.* in the middle of 10, 107, 349, *ympherueḃ* 146.
pessychu vn. cough 406.
peth m. thing 143, 221, 398; pl. -*eu* 28, 737.
petwar num. m. four 125; f. *pedeir* 59, 643, 785; ordinals, m. *petweryḃ* fourth 69; f. *pedwareḃ* 461.
pieu, def. vb. pres. 3 sg. owes 25, (who) owns 333, 605, 707; impft. 3 sg. *pieuoeḃ* 241, *pieweḃ* 581, *pioeḃ* ibid. R. (Cf. WG § 192, GCC §§ 83–84 (88–89).)
pleth f. fold; *p. y dwyclun* fork, crutch (of the body) 753. (L. plecto.)

plith m. midst; *o blith* from amidst, 3 pl. *oc eu p.* 313; *ym p.* among 562.
pob a. each, every 33, 42, **pop** 361, 477.
poeth a. cooked, hot 700. (Cog. L. coctus.)
pony (asp. len.) interrog. neg. part. 187; before vowels **ponyt** 219.
pori vn. graze 113, 136, 674.
porth m. gate(way) 280, 293, 646. (L. porta.)
porth vn. bear, weather (a storm) 176, **porthi** ibid. R., support, feed, entertain; pret. 3 sg. *porthes* 723; impers. *porthet* 202. (L. porto.)
porthant m. entertainment, feeding 249.
porthawr m. porter, gatekeeper 5, 6. (L. portarius.)
pren m. tree 146, 156, 167, **prenn** 262, 267. (Cf. Ir crann.)
prenuol f. case, coffer 374.
presseb m. manger, crib, stall 715. (L. praesepe.)
priawt a. wedded 606; mf. spouse 688R. (L. priuatus.)
priodas f. marriage 448.
profi vn. try out, attempt 419. (L. probo.)
prouant m. fodder 75J.
pryt m. time; *pryt nawn* afternoon (nones = 3 p.m.) 39, *p. n. hir* late in the afternoon 330 note; *pa bryt* when? 426; as conj. that, neg. *pryt na* 388, 389.
punt f. pound (money) 616. (OE pund.)
purðu a. pure black 160, 189, 498.
purgoch a. bright red 208.
purwyn a. pure white 665.
pwy interrog. pron. who? 94, 362, 616. (Ir cia.)
pwyth m. recompense, quid pro quo 653. (L. punctum.)
py interrog. a. what? which? 250, 332, 336, *py un* which (one)? 734, *py beth* what? 760; pron. 387, 459.
pyst pl. of *post* m. post, pillar; *p. kwyr* large wax candles 350. (L. postis.)

rac prep. because of, for 56, 199, 214; *rac bronn* before, 3 sg. m. 714R; *rac eu caffel* before they are taken, lest they be taken 635; with pers. pron. 1 sg. *ragof* before me 64, on my way 119; 3 sg. m. *racðaw* from, before him 162, on his way 234, 711, *ofyn r.* fear of him 585; f. *racði* on her way 315, 593.
racko demon. a. that yonder 211, 305, 365, **racco** 605, 607, 644.
ractal m. frontlet 42, 291.
ragof, see *rac*.
rannu vn. share, divide, distribute 700; impft. 3 sg. *rannei* 452. (Ir roinnim.)
redegawc a. swift-flowing 37.
rei indef. pron. pl. some 77, ones 80, 492, 529, *y rei goreu* the best (ones) 628.

reit m. need, necessity; *nyt r. ytti* you need not 164, 463.
roði (y) vn. give (to) 322, put 589; pres. 1 sg. *roðaf* 444, 633; 3 sg. *ryð* 131; impft. 1 sg. *robwn* 212; pret. 3 sg. *robes* 525, 531, 594; impv. 2 sg. *dyro* 808.
y rof, see *y rwng*.
role n. 67 note.
ruthyr m. rush; *mynet r. y wrth* hurry away from 595.
y rwng prep. between 286, **rwng** 722; with pers. pron. 1 sg. *y rof* 212, 394, 408; 3 sg. m. *y ryðaw* 648, 701, *y ryngtaw* ibid. R.
rwygaw vn. tear, rend 355, 776.
rwymaw vn. bind, tie up 804.
ry perfective part.; with vn. 276 note; = rel. *a* 598; converting pres. subj. into pft. 607.
ryð, see *roði*.
y ryðaw, see *y rwng*.
ryðhau vn. deliver, set free 465.
ryðit m. freedom, liberty 656.
rynnawð (y wrth) m. short distance (from), short time 51, 339, 688, **rynawð** 105, **rynhyawð** 596.
ryt f. ford 705.
ryweð a. remarkable, wonderful 199, **ryueð** 356, 763.
ryvic m. presumption, arrogance 32.
ryw m. kind, sort 89.

saeth f. arrow; pl. *-eu* 46. (L. sagitta.)
saethu vn. shoot (at) 49, 240, 472.
sarff f. serpent, snake 664, 666, **ssarf** 668; pl. *seirff* 134. (L. serpens.)
sef, copula+pron. 3 sg. m., this is what ... 1, 240, 289, **ys ef** 444.
seith num. seven; *seith ugein* seven score 616.
ser pl. stars 133; sg. *seren*.
seric m. silk 353. (L. sericum.)
seuyll vn. stand 133, 241, 473.
sodleu pl. heels 284; sg. *sawdyl*. (Ir sál.)
swch f. point, lower sharp end of a shield 175. (Ir soc.)
swrcot m. surcoat 71, 431. (OFr sourcot.)
sychu vn. dry 376, wipe 669R. (Cf. L. siccus.)
syndal m. sendal, a rich material 335, 353. (OFr cendal.)
synwyr m. sense 392. (L. sentire.)

tal m. forehead 110, 508, upper end 144.
talu vn. pay, repay 25; impv. 2 sg. *tal* 26, 28.
talym m. a (considerable) period of time 227.
tan m. fire 320, 370, 530.
taraw vn. strike 131, 668; pret. 3 sg. *trewis* 273, 752.
taryan f. shield 175. (OE targe.)

tat m. father 31.
tauawt m. tongue 221.
tawḃ m. tallow, fat, dripping 199.
tebic a. probable, likely 60, 88.
tebygu vn. suppose, think likely; pres. 2 sg. *tebygy* 151; impft. 1 sg. *tybygwn* 32, *tebygwn* 391; 3 sg. *tebygei* 347; past subj. 1 sg. *tebyccwn* 98.
tec a. fair, beautiful; eqv. n. *tecket* beauty 246; cpv. *tegach* 60; spv. *teckaf* 19, 61, 364, *teccaf* 36, 580.
tei, see *ty*.
teimlyaw vn. touch, handle, feel 586.
teir, see *tri*.
telediw a. fine, handsome, perfect 316, 637, 678; cpv. *telediwach* 721; spv. *telediwaf* 785.
temyl n. 11 note.
teulu m. household, retinue, warband 230, 415, 511. (Ir teaghlach.)
ti pers. pron. 2 sg. thou, thee 101, 151, 185; redupl. **tidi** 297, 534, 746, **tydi** 306, 368, 770; disjunctive **titheu** 186, 306, 403.
tir m. land, country 604. (Ir tír.)
tlysseu pl. jewels 657, 813; sg. *tlws*.
toḃi vn. melt; pret. 1 sg. *tobeis* 199. (Cf. tawḃ.)
torri vn. cut, break 271; pres. 3 sg. *tyr* 508; pret. 3 sg. *torres* 283, 525.
toruen f. tuft; pl. *toruenneu* 620.
tra conj. while 14, as long as 164, 302, 781.
trachefyn, tra'm kefyn, see *drachefyn*.
traet, see *troet*.
trannoeth, see *drannoeth*.
traws a. oppressive, tyrannical; see *Du Traws*.
trech cpv. a. stronger, more powerful 439.
tref f. town 429.
treiglyaw vn. visit 688.
trenhyḃ adv. the day after tomorrow 696.
treulaw vn. consume 615; pret. impers. *treulwyt* 555.
trewis, see *taraw*.
tri num. m. three 121; f. *teir* 454, 460, 469; ordinals, m. *trydyḃ* 522; *trydeḃ* 68, *trydet* 662, 682.
trigyaw (ar) vn. settle, decide (on), stay 816; pret. 3 sg. *trigywys* 562, 818; impers. *trigywyt* 467.
trimis m. period of three months, quarter 555, 559, 563.
trist a. melancholy, sad 456, 727; eqv. *kyndristet* 718, *kyn tristet* 787. (L. tristis.)
tristau vn. grow sad 571.
tristyt m. sadness, grief, gloom 384, 724, **tristit** 385, 727, 788; *kymryt t.* be downcast, saddened 100. (L. tristitia.)

tro m. turn; *ar dro* wandering about 576.
troell f. rowel (of a spur); pl. *-eu* 284.
troet m. foot 109; du. *deutroet* 722; pl. *traet* 44, 54, 292.
troi vn. turn; pret. 3 sg. *troes* 532.
truan a. pitiable, sad 608, 733, 797.
trwy prep. through 193, 273, 289; with pers. pron. 3 sg. m. *trwybaw* 105, 283, *trwybaw oll* all over him 577.
trychant num. three hundred 820.
trydeb, trydyb, see *tri*.
tu m. side 106, 720; *o bop tu y* on each side of 290; *tu draechefyn* back, backwards 406.
tuchan m. panting 158, 183.
tubet f. cover (of a cushion) 12; pl. *tubedeu* 72.
twel m. towel 322, 371; pl. *tweleu* 77, *tyweleu* ibid. R. (OFr toaille.)
twrwf m. noise, tumult 151, 152, **twryf** 170, 265, 491. (L. turbo.)
twyllwr m. deceiver 569, 691.
twym a. warm, hot 373.
twymaw vn. heat 371.
ty m. house, household 465, 468, 607; pl. *tei* 290.
tybygwn, see *tebygu*.
tynnu vn. pull 72, 600, 648, take out 374, draw (a sword) 527.
tyr, see *torri*.
tyryeu pl. towers, turrets 707; sg. *twr*. (lOE, OFr tur.)
tyuu vn. grow; pret. 3 sg. *tyuawb* 577.
tywyll a. dark 530.

uch cpv. a. louder 359; pos. *uchel*.
uchel a. loud 406. (Ir uasal.)
ucher m. evening, nightfall 519. (Cog. L. uesper.)
vchot adv. (up) yonder 104, 144.
ubunt, see *2. y*.
ugeint num. twenty; *pedeir ar ugeint* twenty-four, — *hugeint* ibid. R., 59, 787, *seith ugein* 616.
vn num. & pron. one, a single 31, 42, 87; with art. and neg. none at all 5, neither one 519.
vnben(n) lord 427, 436; as a form of address, sir 92, 769.
unbennes f. lady 293.
vndyn m. one man, as pron. anyone 351, cf. note 34.
vnwlat (a) a. belonging to the same country (as) 34 note.
utkyrnn pl. horns, trumpets 348; sg. *utcorn*.

val conj. as (if) 585; *val y* as, so that 137, 173, 629, *ual y* 236; neg. *ual na* 287. (Len. of *mal*.)
y velly adv. thus 176, **uelly** 289, 454, **velly** 549.
vi, see *fi*.

VOCABULARY 95

vy (nas.) poss. part. 1 sg., my 14, 32, 65; before labials **vym** 176, before dentals **vyn** 175, **uyn** 728, 808, before velars **vyg** 204, 220, 686.

y uynyð adv. up 103, **y vynyð** 207, 342, 502. (Cf. mynyð.)

weithon adv. now 25, 93, 336. (i.e. y weith hon 'this time', OIr in fecht sa.)

wely di interj. behold 653. (i.e. a wely di 'dost thou see?'.)

wrth prep. (**vrth** 603) beside, by 4, 59, at 64, in response to 132, attached to 149, 168, to 408; with pers. pron. 1 sg. *wrthyf* 87, 98, 128; 2 sg. *wrthyt* 115; 3 sg. f. *wrthi* 387, 424, 631; 3 pl. *wrthunt* 434. **Y wrth** prep. about, concerning 216, 256, from 309; with pers. pron. 2 sg. *y wrthyt* 550; 3 sg. m. *y wrthaw* 595; 3 pl. *y wrthunt* 51.

wtwart m. woodward, forester 112R. (lOE wuduweard.)

wy pers. pron. 3 pl. they, them 303; **wynt** 345, 482, 578; disjunctive **wynteu** 769. (Cf. hwy, hwynt, hwynteu.)

wyf, wyt, see *bot*.

wyneb m. face 532, boldness, effrontery 389 note. (Cf. OIr enech.)

1. **y** poss. part. 3 sg. m. (len.) his 2, 12, 23; f. (asp.) her 314, 354, 358.
2. **y** prep. (len.) to, for (purpose, indirect obj., motion) 7, 18, 39; with pers. pron. 1 sg. *y mi* 56, 123, 133, *im* 33, 410, 728, *ym* 90, 166; 2 sg. *y ti* 115, *itt* 298, 426, 438, *itti* 19, 296, 382, *itty* 400, *ytti* 60, 83, 98, *yt* 99, 106, 549; 3 sg. m. *iðaw* 9, 57, 79; f. *iði* 363, 401, 422; 1 pl. *yn* 82, *in* 727, *ynni* 227, 770; 3 pl. *uðunt* 8, 18, 48; with art. *y'r* 8, 21, 41; with poss. or obj. pron. 1 sg. *y'm* 186, 403, 552; 2 sg. *y'th* 303, 698; 3 sg. m. *y* 231, 312, *y'w* 572; f. *y* 145; 3 sg. m. *o'e* 9, 311; f. *o'e* 448, 736, 759; 3 pl. *y eu* 137, 476, 547.
3. **y** (= 2. *y*+1. *y*), see 2. *y*.
4. **y** indirect rel. part. 13, 39, before vowels and *h*- **yð** 180, 193, 313; with obj. pers. pron. 1 sg. *y'm* 202, 504; 3 sg. f. *y* 366; 3 pl. *y* 240.
5. **y** (len.) (= 3. *yn*, forming pres. participle) 180 note.
6. **y** art. the 7, 24, 32, before vowels **yr** 5, 10, 18.

yd, yð, ytt, preverb to some forms of *bot*: 1, 10, 242, 551.

yg, ym, see 1. *yn*.

ym, see 2. *y*.

y'm, see (1) 2. *y*, (2) 4. *y*, (3) 1. *yn*.

yma adv. here 103, 381.

ymaðoydi vn. wound each other, fight 803.

ymadrawð m. speech, saying, utterance 223, 632.

ymbrawf (a) vn. contend (with) 743.

ymchoelut vn. turn, return 174, 509, **ymhoelu** 570W, **ymhoelut** 646, 649.

ymdan-af, -aw, -ei, -nunt, see *am*.

ymbangos vn. show oneself, appear 602.
ymdeith adv. away (motion) 193, 231, 548, **ymeith** 404.
ymdeni, see *am*.
ymbiban vn. talk, converse 14, 88; m. conversation, discourse 18, 20, 25; pres. 1 pl. *ymbibanwn* 94; impft. 3 sg. *ymbibanei* 91; 1 pl. *ymbibanem* 92.
ymbibanbyn m. conversationalist; pl. *-bynnyon* 92.
ymbibanwr m. conversationalist, raconteur 27.
ymbihauarchu (a) vn. fight boldly 803.
ymbiot (a) vn. overthrow, ? unhorse each other 767.
ymedewis pret. 3 sg. of *ymadaw (a)* vn. leave, quit 783.
ymffust vn. fight, lay on 528.
ymgaffel (a) vn. succeed (in); impft. 3 sg. *ymgaffei* 278.
ymgaru vn. show affection to each other 544.
ymgeissaw (a) vn. attack each other, contend with 251.
ymgubyaw vn. hide (oneself) 595.
ymgyfogi vn. smite each other, fight 272.
ymgyrchu vn. attack each other 190, 518, 524.
ymgyweiraw vn. equip, arm oneself 34, **ymgyweiryaw** 468.
ymlab (a) vn. fight 744, 746; impft. 3 sg. *ymlabei* 745; pret. 3 sg. *ymlabawb* 782.
ymlit vn. pursue 278.
ymlithraw vn. drag oneself, crawl 599.
ymolchi vn. wash (oneself) 76, 229, 322.
ymsang m. press, crush (of a crowd) 544, **ymsag** 546.
ymwan (a) vn. joust 271, 499, 505; m. jousting, encounter 500.
ymwelet (a) vn. visit 423, 428.
ymyl m. edge, border 344; *yn y.* beside 262, 646R. (Ir *imeall*.)
1. **yn** prep. (nas.) in 32, 39, 45, before labials **ym** 10, 49, 596, before velars **yg** 1, 110; with pers. pron. 1 sg. *ynof* 100; 3 sg. m. *ynbaw* 36, 321, 361; f. *ynbi* 125, 198, 259; 3 pl. *ynbunt* 77; with poss. part. 1 sg. *y'm* 188, 462, 691; 2 sg. *y'th* 156; 3 sg. m. *yn y* 2.
2. **yn** (len.), introducing indef. complement 40, 60, 74.
3. **yn,** with vn. forming analytic tenses 14, 80, and pres. participle 4, 44, 49; with obj. pron. 2 sg. *y'th* 305.
4. **yn** (len.), with a. forming adv. 20, 75, 170.
5. **yn,** see 2. *y*.
yna adv. then 39, 73, 87.
ynb-aw, -i, -unt, see *1. yn*.
ynneu, see *inheu*.
ynni, see 2. *y*.
yno adv. there 6, 58, 84.
ynof, see *1. yn*.
ynteu disjunctive pron. 3 sg. m. 112, 114, 128.
yny, see *hyny*.

VOCABULARY

1. yr, art. the, before vowels 1, 5, 10, *h-* 61, and sometimes consonantal *i-* 387, 394, 405.
2. yr prep. for, on account of 173, 570, (in exchange) for 212, 655; since (time) *yr hynny hyt hebiw* from that day to this 551.
y'r, see 2. *y*.
ys pres. copula, is 684, 770; *ys gwneuthum* 390 note.
ysgarlat m. kind of material 335. (OFr escarlate.)
ysgwyð f. shoulder 307, 314, 322.
ysgyfalhau vn. be empty, be on holiday 429 note.
ysgynnu, see *eskynnu*.
ysnoden f. lace, ribbon 53 note. (OE snód.)
ysp pl. guests 6; sg. *osp*. (L. hospes.)
yspardun m. spur; pl. *-eu* 284.
yspeilaw vn. despoil, strip; pret. 3 sg. *yspeilwys* 196. (L. spolio.)
yspeilty m. robber's den 808.
yspeilwr m. despoiler, robber 808.
yspytty m. hospital, i.e. hostel for pilgrims etc. 810. (L. hospitem, hospitium+ty.)
yspyttywr m. hospitaller 809.
yssic a. bruised, sore, worn away 356.
yssu vn. devour 681, 730.
yssyð, see *bot*.
ystarn f. harness 75.
ystarnu vn. harness, equip 209.
ystauell f. chamber 2, 9, 244, stable 211 note. (L. stabellum.)
ysteneit f. jugful 15, 22. (OE stǽna.)
ystlys f. side 664; *gan y*. beside 37, 237, 583.
ystondard f. pennon, small flag 160, standard 644. (OFr estandard.)
ystrat m. vale, valley 145. (Ir srath.)
ystret n. row 290 note. (Ir sreath.)
ystyllen f. board, plank, panel 319.
ystyr mf. meaning, explanation, cause 341, 788; 476 note. (L. historia.)
yswein m. groom, ostler; pl. *ysgweineit* 75W note, *ysweineit* ibid. R. (ON sveinn.)
yt, see 2. *y*.
y'th, see (1) 2. *y*, (2) 1. *yn*, (3) 3. *yn*.
ytti, see 2. *y*.
yuet vn. drink 24. (Cf. Ir ibhe.)
yw, see *bot*.
y'w, see 2. *y*.

PROPER NAMES

Arthur 1, 5, 10. (L. Artorius.)
Kei uab Kyner 3, 16, 21.
Kenuerchyn descendants of Kynuarch, grandfather of Owein 820 note.
Kynon uab Clydno 3, 17, 26.
y Du Traws 782, 800, 805. (Cf. du, traws.)
Glewlwyt Gauaeluawr G. of the mighty grasp 5.
Gwalchmei 455, 512, 531.
Gwenhwyuar wife of Arthur 3, -*war* 62, -*far* 222.
Lunet 386, 420, 685.
Owein uab Uryen 2, 26, 219.

Kaer Llion ar Wysc Caerlleon-upon-Usk 1, 565. (L. Castra Legionum.)
Prydein Britain 75W, **Ynys Prydein** 62, 213, 559.
Rangyw (yr Angyw) Anjou 517.

PRINTED IN GREAT BRITAIN
AT THE UNIVERSITY PRESS, OXFORD
BY VIVIAN RIDLER
PRINTER TO THE UNIVERSITY

£1.05